Now hey there people won't you lend an ear,

Cos I've a story to tell and I'm telling it here,

I was born in a town in the great UK,

From a baby to a boy to a man today,

And I'm a musical man and I'm a man of verse,

But I got a little problem and it's getting worse,

My life was so well planned,

Survivin' and a jivin' in a funk band,

But rapping it's my bread and butter,

But it's hard to rap when you're born with a stutter

from 'Stutter Rap' by Morris Minor and The Majors

Also by Tony Hawks

Round Ireland With A Fridge

Playing The Moldorans At Tennis

A NOTE TO THE READER

An adapted version of the chapters chronicling my adventures in the Sudan can also be found in *The Weekenders* (Ebury Press, £7.99), an anthology of Sudan-inspired travel writing by myself, Irvine Welsh, Alex Garland, Bill Deedes, Victoria Glendinning, Andrew O'Hagan and Giles Foden. It won the WH Smith award for Travel Book of the Year. All proceeds from its sales go to Operation Lifeline Sudan.

www.tony-hawks.com

ONE HIT WONDERLAND

TONY HAWKS

ONE HIT WONDERLAND

EBURY
PRESS

First published in Great Britain in 2002

Ebury Press
Random House, 20 Vauxhall Bridge Road, London SW1V 2SA

Random House Australia (Pty) Limited
20 Alfred Street, Milsons Point, Sydney, New South Wales 2061, Australia

Random House New Zealand Limited
18 Poland Road, Glenfield, Auckland 10, New Zealand

Random House South Africa (Pty) Limited
Endulini, 5A Jubilee Road, Parktown 2193, South Africa

Random House UK Limited Reg. No. 954009
www.randomhouse.co.uk
A CIP catalogue record for this book is available from the British Library

ISBN 0 09 188208 7

Typeset by seagulls
Cover design by PUSH, London

Cover photo Getty Images
All photography © Tony Hawks unless otherwise credited

Printed and bound in UK by Mackays of Chatham plc, Chatham, Kent

Papers used by Ebury Press are natural, recyclable products
made from wood grown in sustainable forests.

CONTENTS

ACKNOWLEDGEMENTS

Much to my surprise I wasn't able to complete this book without the help of others. So, regretfully, it falls upon me to offer thanks to the following: Mark King, Hugo, Jason and Jason, Nigel and Liesa, James Harman, James Hodgkinson, Paul Cole, Paul Crockford, Robert and Sophie at PFD, Matt Bjerreggard, Kate and Vlad, Tony and Christian at the Kashmir, Sarah, Claire and all at Ebury, Brad, Steve and Robin, Jane for sorting things, Jake for good advice and crossing out bad jokes, Jakko for support and musicianship, and finally Willie, for all of the above, and for liking me enough to just keep on helping – long after it would have been fair to tell me to piss off. Oh, and everyone else who's in the book.

PROLOGUE

Music was my first love, and it will be my last
John Miles, 1976

The 12.42 from Brighton pulled in at London's Victoria station
and off stepped a raw 22-year-old hopeful, a guitar slung over his
shoulder. He was green, hungry, with empty pockets but a bag
full of dreams. Music was his first love, but now it was to be his
life; and this city, a noisy metropolis overflowing with people and
possibilities, was where he was going to fulfil his ambitions.
Nothing else mattered.

I don't actually know who that young man was, because I was
on the next train up – the 1.18. However, all of what could be
said of him was true of me too. I just had a bigger bag, that's all.

I was ready for my new career. Over the years I'd practised
endlessly at piano and guitar, collaborated in numerous
unpromising school bands, and progressed with the art of songwriting to the point where people sometimes actually asked to
hear my creations again. I was going to make it in the music
business, and the subject wasn't up for discussion. Never mind
that I didn't really understand how the music business worked,
or indeed what 'making it' actually meant – I wasn't going to let
minor details like that stand in my way.

And so, arriving in the big city, armed with a hugely impressive repertoire of songs encompassing the entire range of musical
styles from Elton John to Billy Joel, I quickly set about securing
gainful employment. By night I played piano and sang in some of

1

the capital's less prestigious pubs and wine bars, and by day I slept off hangovers and opened rejection letters from record companies and music publishers.

The months began to drag by, and it wasn't too long before it became apparent that I was destined for a new career. In The Hollybush, the Hampstead pub which benefited from my crooning on Monday nights, I noted that I was beginning to get far more of a positive response from the audience when I fooled around *between* the songs, rather than when I'd actually just finished singing one.

'When are you playing here again?' I began to be asked.

'Next Monday.'

'In that case we'll see you again then. You're funny.'

Was that what they said to Ray Charles after a sell-out gig? Did Elton get requests for the one about the two nuns in the bath? Sadly I guessed they did not.

A year later I was a comedian.

At least that was what it said in my résumé.

NAME: **Tony Hawks**
OCCUPATION: **Comedian**

Where did it all go wrong?

FADE IN TOP OF THE POPS

'Tony, you must get people making bets with you all the time.'

This was what I kept hearing, and given my recent history of accepting wagers you would certainly expect this to be the case. However, what actually happens most of the time is that people come up to me and say, 'You must get people making bets with you all the time.'

For the most part, the bets that *have* emerged have been entirely influenced by the fact that I once hitch-hiked round Ireland with a *fridge*. Consequently I have been urged to make journeys to distant parts of the world lugging miscellaneous pieces of furniture or domestic appliances. One potential bet did differ from these others, but it bore too much resemblance to my second wager, in which I'd attempted to beat the entire Moldovan national football team at tennis, one by one. I received the challenge when I made the mistake of allowing myself to share a few drinks in the pub with my friend Arthur.

'I bet you, Tony,' he croaked, while coughing cigarette smoke into the already smoky atmoshere, 'That you can't sleep with the entire Azerbaijani netball team.'

As my initial laugh subsided, I was struck by a rather depressing thought. Had I become a strange kind of plaything for other people? Was I the mug who just went off and did whatever was asked of him? And if I was, then what was I trying to prove?

In the days that followed I began to wonder whether I should take on another bet at all. It was true that my life had been greatly enriched by the experiences of my first two eccentric

3

quests, but it was also the case that both of these had been born of genuine arguments and had not simply been concocted because I was a man with a reputation for taking on silly bets. These more recent offers of wagers had been devised by people with half an eye on mischief, half an eye on stretching me to the limits and half an eye on having their name mentioned in a book (and yes, they *were* all people with one and a half eyes).

Maybe I just had to accept it. The 'ludicrous bets' part of my life was over. This might not be such a bad thing anyway; it could be a sign that I was more mature now, and that I'd finally acquired enough inner peace not to have to keep proving myself.

That was what I thought, anyway, as I walked up the path to Jakko's house, bottle of wine tucked underneath my arm. I was a little nervous about the evening ahead, mainly because I was single, and when you're single and you're invited to a dinner party there can be mischief afoot. Quite often it isn't 'Hey, let's invite Tony, it would be nice to see him again' but more 'Hey, let's invite Tony, he'd be perfect for Sally, wouldn't he?'

As I waited on the doorstep, I reminded myself that Jakko and his wife Amanda had no track record on the eager match-making front and so the evening ahead was likely to be little more than a relaxed and pleasant get-together.

And that was exactly how it began. Jakko had assembled an agreeable gathering who were all happy to guzzle the results of Amanda's unquestionable culinary skills. All the guests had connections with the music business, no doubt because Jakko was himself a versatile musician who composed, produced and for a while had been the guitarist with Level 42. At the table there was Simon, a slightly eccentric bass player who I'd met on many occasions and who had a tendency to indulge in elongated anecdotes; Joni and Mark, a jolly couple who dabbled in the management side of the business; and Victoria, a singer-songwriter whose looks definitely would have made her someone I wouldn't have minded being paired up with, had those been the ulterior motives for the dinner party after all.

I took it as a good sign that rather late in the evening Victoria showed enough interest in me to ask the habitual dinner party question.

'So Jakko, how do you know Tony?' she offered with a cheeky smile.

'Ah, now therein lies a story,' he replied.

'What do you mean?'

'Well I was the producer,' he continued with mock grandeur, 'of Tony's smash hit record.'

'What?' asked an incredulous Victoria.

'Tony had a hit record,' said Jakko, more matter-of-factly this time, 'and I produced it.'

Victoria spun round to look at me, her face beaming with excitement .

'Is this *true* Tony?' she asked.

'Yes. I used to have a group called Morris Minor and The Majors and we had a Top Five smash with a song called "Stutter Rap".'*

'Never!'

'Really!'

'I don't believe you.'

Victoria looked among the other guests for evidence that I'd been winding her up, but she was greeted with reluctant nods which confirmed my story.

'I'm afraid, Victoria,' said Simon, rather drily, 'that Tony penned a rather low grade rap spoof of the Beastie Boys, and lots of unsophisticated teenagers wasted their pocket money on it.'

'It got to Number Four in the charts,' I offered boastfully, thinking that this somehow justified the song's indisputable naffness.

'Number Four! Wow!' squeaked Victoria. 'That's a big hit.'

'Yes, Tony still lives off the royalties,' said Simon, engaging me with a playful smile. 'Isn't that right?'

I sighed, finding myself the victim of my own honesty. The last time we'd all got together round at Jakko's I'd revealed that my last PRS royalty statement** was the princely sum of 5p. Understandably this had been the source of much amusement,

* *To hear 'Stutter Rap' or any of the other songs in One Hit Wonderland – go to www.onehitwonderland.com*

** *The PRS is the Performing Right Society collects royalties for public performances for songwriters.*

and led to sarcastic discussions about how I should best spend my retirement.

'Well, the payments to me have diminished a little over the years,' I said, hoping that the exact sum wouldn't have to be mentioned, and that I might still retain some credibility with Victoria.

'Yes, and let's not forget the rather apposite review which the *Melody Maker* gave it,' interjected Jakko, with customary cynicism, but pleasingly leading the subject away from the 5p royalty statement. 'It was a four-word review. It went "Stutter Rap – utter crap!"'

'I don't know why you always bring that up,' I protested, suddenly feeling somewhat under attack from all sides. 'You produced the record, after all.'

'Yes, but if you remember, Tony, I was so embarrassed by it that I used a pseudonym.'

'And what was that?' asked Joni, lured into the discussion for the first time.

'Grandmaster Jellytot,' said Jakko with a broad smile, and much to everyone's amusement.

Behind all the sarcasm, I was pretty sure that Jakko was secretly rather proud of his involvement with 'Stutter Rap'. I knew from past conversations with him that he'd come to view its success as one in the eye for the music business, a business that he'd somehow come to loathe over the last decade or so. For him, as for so many of his colleagues, he'd come to see how the commercial side of the industry cared little for nurturing the musical integrity of the artist, and only about one thing – profit. Consequently whenever Jakko spoke about the 'music business', his words were laden with bitterness. Sometimes when I heard him moaning, I wondered if he'd forgotten to be thankful for the natural musical talent he'd been given; the kind of talent most people would give their eye teeth for.

'The thing about that *Melody Maker* review,' I said, defensively, 'is that we weren't a band who were hip or cool, and they resented the fact that we were shifting lots of copies. It sold well over 200,000, you know.'

'So what happened after that?' asked Victoria.

That was a very good question.

~

What *had* happened? Why had our little musical trio ended up in the dubious company of the other wastrels and misfits listed under the generic term 'One Hit Wonder'?

I like to think it was because we only really had a hit by accident. I'd invited Paul and Phil, two mates of mine, to join the band Morris Minor and The Majors, whose main aim was to perform an act on London's alternative cabaret circuit and earn a few bob while we all waited for something better to come along. In the event, we found that we actually *became* that better thing. Having been invited to appear on Channel 4's *Saturday Live*, we chose to perform my absurd song 'Stutter Rap', and would you believe it, the next morning Virgin were on to us wanting to release it as a single. The rest, as they say, is history, although admittedly it's history which tends to be overlooked by most teachers. For some reason 'Stutter Rap' hasn't yet made it on to the national curriculum.

One of the biggest thrills of being involved in this ephemeral runaway success – apart from the power-lunch meetings at record companies, the limousines, the interviews and the new-found attention – was that I got to achieve an ambition that I'd held as a teenager. I got to appear on *Top of the Pops*. As a kid I had been totally seduced by the tacky cheapness of it all. I didn't even mind that most of the people who performed on the show never sang. Miming seemed totally acceptable to me because it meant that the acts would sound exactly like the record. The brazen fraudulence didn't bother me. Pop stars were glamorous, pop music was fun and the DJs who fronted it were ... well, embarrassing. However much you wanted to believe otherwise, the Radio 1 disc jockeys who hosted proceedings were too old, too out of touch, and too transparently vain. There was a sadness about them too. Never mind that they would outlast most of the bands and artists that they were introducing, you got the strong feeling that they would have given anything to have been one of those acts. But they weren't. They were the people who introduced the entertainment. That's all. These guys were big celebrities, but there was nothing worth celebrating about them. And somehow, they knew it.

Peter Powell was the DJ who introduced us. His enthusiasm seemed refreshingly genuine and I liked him for that.

'Ladies and gentlemen,' he bellowed above the adolescent cacophany, 'I don't know much about these guys – but I can tell you that they have a very funny record on their hands. Please give a big *Top of the Pops* welcome to Morris Minor and The Majors!'

As Camera 1 carved a swathe through the impressionable teenagers on the studio floor, I readied myself for the opening line of the song. Girls screamed as the lights came up on us. Yes, they screamed. Never mind that we had made ourselves look deliberately uncool with heavy creases down the front of our jeans, daft hats and pencilled-on moustaches – we were pop stars now and pop stars were sexy. Suddenly I was the star I'd dreamed of being in my teenage slumber. Just like David Bowie, John Lennon, Elton John, Dusty Springfield, The Pretenders, The Stones, The Who and the rest, I was on *Top of the Pops*. And it felt damn good.

I was living my dream.

The trouble was that it was a dream which only lasted three minutes and forty seconds. Rather naively, we still thought we were pop stars when the performance was over and we were chaperoned back to our dressing room. Never mind, we could soon be partying with the other pop stars on the show – bands like Wet Wet Wet and The Stranglers. Shortly we'd be flirting with the bevvy of beautiful hangers-on who would almost certainly be among their entourage.

'What happens now?' I asked Sarah, the girl from the BBC who'd been charged with looking after us.

'How do you mean?' she replied with a puzzled expression.

'Well, is there some kind of party?'

'No, that's it I'm afraid.'

'But surely there's somewhere to have a drink?'

'Well, the trouble is we've closed up the Green Room because all the other bands have gone.'

'Gone? It's only 8.30, how could they have gone?'

'Wet Wet Wet had to dash off to fly back to Germany to continue their European tour – and all the others had pressing commitments too.'

'Oh.'

'You can have a drink in the BBC Club bar I suppose, but it's a bit shit in there.'

'I see. Right. Thanks.'

~

Our arrival in the BBC Club bar doubled the attendance of the place, and confirmed just how accurate Sarah's description of it had been. We sat down to three pints of flat bitter not far from two middle-aged, beer-gutted, nerdy engineer types. Across a few yards of stained carpet sat a man who we thought we recognised as the bloke who did the weather for the local news programme. One had to assume from the way he was gloomily peering into his half of lager, that a vicious cold front was about to move in from the east. The three of us, the three pop stars, quietly sipped our beers wondering why we were celebrating the biggest night of our lives in the company of two fat blokes and a depressed weatherman. What had happened to the groupies? Where was the excitement and the glamour?

'Well, what shall we do?' asked one of my fellow pop stars, Paul, as he slugged on the last dregs of his pint.

'Well, I think I'm going to get an early night,' said the third pop star, Phil, as he deposited his empty glass on the table.

'You what?' I replied, genuinely astonished.

'I know it sounds a bit naff but I'm not feeling that great and I've got an early start in the morning.'

'But Phil, it's quarter to nine!'

'I know. But nothing is happening and I haven't got the energy to force it.'

'I feel a bit shitty actually,' added Paul apologetically. 'I might turn in too.'

'What?'

'Sorry mate, but this place is depressing.'

'But we could go out somewhere and wallow in the glory – we've just been on *Top of the Pops*.'

'Yes, but no-one's going to know that,' remarked Phil. 'It doesn't get broadcast till tomorrow night.'

'Yeah,' said Paul, 'and if we go up to girls and tell them that we're going to be on *Top of the Pops* tomorrow night then they're just not going to believe us.'

'So that's it then is it?' I asked in disbelief.

The boys nodded sheepishly. It was.

I was home by 9.30. Foolishly I'd set a whole night aside for the night when I lived out my teenage dreams, when as it turned out, a couple of hours would have sufficed. Clearly I should have had other things arranged. I rang a few friends to see if there was anything happening but everyone was out, so I grabbed a can of beer from the fridge and took myself off to bed. It was at this point that I realised that the rock star life wasn't for me. I just wouldn't be able to take the pace.

Morris Minor and The Majors did bring out a follow-up record which was another spoof, called 'This is the Chorus'. It made fun of the formulaic pap which was being churned out at the time by the Stock, Aitken and Waterman production line. What we had failed to realise was that most of the kids who had bought 'Stutter Rap' were also heavily into Kylie Minogue, Rick Astley and all the rest from the S.A.W. stable, so effectively we were biting the hand that fed us. Purely on the strength of a strong video, we made some extremely lowly number in the charts, and that was pretty much that. This time round, when the publicity girl from the record company called, it became clear that we weren't being treated exactly as we had been when we were a Top Five act.

'Tony, can you do an interview at 3 p.m. tomorrow on Greater London Radio?'

'Yeah sure, what time will you send the car?'

'Err, well, we're not sending a car. We thought you could make your own way there.'

The bubble had well and truly burst.

'That bubble well and truly burst, didn't it Tony?' echoed Jakko nearly fifteen years later, as we all made a start on what was probably the fifth bottle of white wine.

'What does it feel like to be a One Hit Wonder?' asked Simon, almost childlike.

'I'm not a One Hit Wonder,' I protested, 'I haven't finished my life yet, so I could still have another hit.'

'OK, why don't you try and do it then?' asked Victoria.

There was silence at the table. Victoria waited patiently for a response to her question. Jakko, who was now in mischievous mood, provided an answer.

''Cos he's too old now.'

'I'm not too old,' I objected, indignant.

'You bloody are! Kids aren't going to buy anything with your ageing mug on the cover.'

'Well, maybe I could write a hit for someone else,' I said, filling the gap which I'd allowed in the vain hope that someone would spring to my defence over the age thing.

'That's even harder,' said Mark, making his first contribution to the rather pointless debate. 'As someone involved in management I can tell you that trying to get someone cover one of your songs is one of the most difficult things to do in the whole of the music business. I suspect that your musical career, sparkling though it once was, Tony, is sadly now over.'

'Well, I don't think that's necessarily the case,' I protested stubbornly, suddenly being fuelled by exaggerated and alcohol-induced self belief. 'I'm sure I could have a hit if I set my mind to it.'

'The trouble is, Tony,' said Victoria, who with every sip of my wine was approaching the status of 'completely irresistible Victoria', 'millions of people are trying to have hits. It's not like all your other achievements. No-one else was trying to hitch-hike round Ireland with a fridge and no-one else was trying to beat the entire Moldovan national football team at tennis. In the music world the competition is just too intense.'

I looked at Victoria, slightly drunk as I was, and I thought I saw an opportunity. Maybe I could create something between us right now which could bond us, set us apart from the others at the table.

'So, Victoria, are you saying that I wouldn't be able to do it?' I asked, hoping that gentle confrontation might lead to intimacy. 'And if you are, would you be prepared to make a bet with me?'

Victoria smiled, and thought for a moment. For the first time in the evening we were looking deep into each other's eyes. It felt good.

'All right,' she said finally, 'I bet that you can't have a Top Twenty hit – anywhere in the world, either as a writer or a performer, within two years.'

Wow. I was impressed. A neat little bet, very tidily presented. It seemed that Victoria had a sharp brain to accompany her more obvious attributes.

'How much?' I asked.

'Oh just a sportsman's bet. Let's not cheapen this with cash. Honour is enough.'

Honour, funnily enough, was one of the last things on my mind right now.

'OK, you're on,' I said as I leant across the table to shake her hand.

Victoria and I lingered with the handshake and continued to look into each other's eyes. I hoped that this might mark the beginning of something special.

As it happened, it did.

PART I
BIRD'S EGG

They told me you were trouble, I heard so many things

About how you'd leave me on the ground — how I'd never clip your wings

But sure enough when winter came, you headed off for warmer shores

Thinking that the fun would all be yours

Chorus

You broke my heart like a bird's egg but now the yolk's on you

You never thought when you took off that I'd find someone new

Cos when you quit the lovenest, you forgot that I fly too

You broke my heart like a bird's egg but now the yolk's on you

When your cuter sister came round to comfort me

I thought all she would offer would be words of sympathy

But I guess that she saw different, she said she's longed to take your place

Well I bet that's news to wipe that smile right off your face

Chorus

Did you know, when you chose to desert me

Did you know, just how much you'd hurt me?

Now sometimes when I look into her eyes

It's like I still have you.

Chorus

Fade out

CHAPTER 1 TIGER FEET AND CUPS OF TEA

'You don't have to do it,' said Victoria, from the end of the phone-line. 'It was only a bit of a fun. Drunken high spirits and all that.'

'No, I want to,' I said, keen to move the conversation on to a discussion about how we might go for a drink together soon. 'And by my reckoning, the terms of the bet should allow me enough time.'

'Well, one way or another, we'll know by the time I get back.'

'Get *back*?'

'Yes, I'm moving to New York for a couple of years so I can work with some of the songwriters over there.'

'Oh,' I said, hoping that my tone of voice hadn't revealed the deadening thud of disappointment which my heart had just felt. 'And when do you leave?'

'Thursday.'

'Oh. I see.'

'Good luck with the bet though.'

'Yes. Thanks.'

Curses.

As a teenager, like most of my peers, I had always pretty much hated country music. As far as I was concerned, it was sung by old people wearing silly hats who churned out tunes which all sounded the same, with lyrics that made you feel nauseous. I had this picture of it being the kind of music that was enjoyed by people who'd been bullied at school or – and I'm not sure how I ended up with such a specific category – by those who walked with severe limps as a result of injuries sustained in the workplace. Myself, I eschewed this musical genre because I was hip, and as a hip person I listened to Mud, Sweet and Suzi Quatro like all the other hip people at my school. I was happy with my musical tastes and I didn't need anyone to come along and start meddling with them.

Consequently I was extremely concerned one day when I found myself inadvertently singing along with 'Blue Bayou' by Linda Rondstadt and then, only moments later, turning up the radio when Kenny Rogers started crooning about Ruby not taking her love to town. More worryingly still was that I was forced to admit to myself that I actively *liked* the song 'Sundown' by Gordon Lightfoot. What was happening to me? Had I gone soft? Of course at school I kept this information close to my chest whenever playground badinage turned to the subject of one's favourite songs of the day, and I would simply walk away if ever the conversation descended into a routine rubbishing of country music (although I did tend to stick around for discussions about the pros and cons of Dolly Parton, mainly because I had noticed that these very rarely focused on her melodic range or the timbre of her voice).

Only now do I understand what was happening to me all those years ago. I was beginning to appreciate lyrics. Somehow the pop songs of the day were failing to interest me on enough levels. I was becoming drawn to songs which could communicate an idea or arouse an emotion within me. Mud's classic 'Tiger Feet' was fine to jump around to excitedly, but it did little to stimulate any deeper thoughts.

> *That's neat, that's neat, that's neat, that's neat,*
> *I really love those Tiger Feet*

What exactly *were* 'Tiger Feet'? And why was the singer so keen on them? Trust me on this, a detailed study of the lyrics provides very few answers to these salient questions.

Country & Western music I discovered, however, offered a boldness in the lyrical department which defied belief. Kenny Rogers shamelessly sang about both Lucille and Ruby, two women who were leaving him, one despite two hungry children and a crop in the field, and the other because his legs (and presumably another valuable part of his anatomy) had been rendered inoperative by the Vietnam war. The contrast with Mud's song couldn't have been greater, unless of course Tiger Feet is actually a term to describe the injured feet of a war veteran, but somehow I doubt it.

Another reason why I was drawn to country music was because it didn't appear to take itself too seriously, unless of course its fans were simply too daft to recognise the comic nature of some of the songs its writers had produced over the years. Proof of this was contained in an email which a friend sent me, listing the following country titles which, believe it or not, were actually written and recorded:

'Drop Kick Me, Jesus, Through The Goalposts Of Life'
'I Fell In A Pile Of You And Got Love All Over Me'
'I Don't Know Whether To Kill Myself Or Go Bowling'

Subtle they may not be in their imagery, but almost every aspect of life is covered in these masterpieces – religion, love and death. I'm particularly fond of the doleful 'I Don't Know Whether To Kill Myself Or Go Bowling', a song which is not afraid to confront this everyday social dilemma. But the country music writers didn't leave it there. The list goes on:

'I Wanna Whip Your Cow'
'I'd Rather Have A Bottle In Front Of Me
Than A Frontal Lobotomy'
'If My Nose Were Full of Nickels, I'd Blow It All On You'

None of life's stones is left unturned by these intrepid lyricists. In these three titles we are forced to consider the vital issues of money, drink and animal flagellation. Some of us may be disturbed by the raw honesty of 'I Wanna Whip Your Cow', but isn't it a feeling that all of us have felt at some point or another? How much better to have the subject explored through music than for us to do what we do day after day when we see someone else with a cow – lapse into denial and in spite of our natural urges, pretend that we don't want to whip it. There are yet further contributions to our understanding of life:

'My Head Hurts, My Feet Stink, And I Don't Love Jesus'
'She Got The Ring And I Got The Finger'
'You Can't Have Your Kate And Edith Too'

The quality just doesn't dip.

'You Can't Roller Skate In A Buffalo Herd'
'Pardon Me, I've Got Someone To Kill'

These are two of my particular favourites. 'Pardon Me, I've Got Someone To Kill' serves as a gentle reminder that manners are always important whatever the situation. It's also nice to see a song in there which tackles what we humans have done to our environment. In the plaintive 'You Can't Roller Skate In A Buffalo Herd', the writers draw our attention to America's dwindling buffalo stocks and the sad repercussions for those of us who made it our business to roller skate among them. A song which works on so many levels, being variously melancholic, didactic, edifying and enlightening, while all the time remaining fundamentally not very good.

Having read through the email which contained these song titles, I began to wonder if the country music scene would be one in which my particular brand of song could flourish, albeit with a few minor modifications. If I was really going to have a hit, then perhaps Country & Western could give it to me. There seemed to be room for wit within a lyric, but with the whole song communicating some kind of message. These country bods had no time for the ambiguous, esoteric, or sometimes facile lyrics of the pop world. And what's more there seemed to be more than an even chance that you could get a release even if your creation was unusual or eccentric. Given that I already had an idea for just such a song, this was most propitious.

I'd come up with the title a couple of years ago while idly wandering around a park when I should have been trying to write an article for a newspaper about how young stars are exploited and used by a cynical entertainment industry. Like most writers I claim that going for a bit of a walk can stimulate the imagination and facilitate the creative process. This can be true, but more often not, it has a more useful purpose in acting as a buffer to the unsavoury task of actually sitting down and starting work. The brain asks the question 'Walk in the park or work?' and the body answers by slipping on some outdoor shoes and heading for the door.

As I strolled along the park's meandering tarmac path, deep in thought about how useful it would be if I were deep in thought about the subject on which I was later hoping to write, my attention was drawn to a yellow and white blob on the ground before me. A tiny bird's egg had fallen from a tree above and smashed on the path. For a moment, the sight of the fractured shell and the splattered yolk made me feel a little sad. Here before me was a perfect analogy for how the hopes and dreams of talented youth are smashed by those who cynically hold the media's reins of power. If only I had made that observation then, how much easier my morning's work would have been. Instead I came up with a song title.

'You Broke My Heart Like A Bird's Egg
But Now The Yolk's On You'

It was, I thought, a work of genius. As I walked home I ran the title around in my head and I managed to convince myself that all it needed was a bog standard country melody and a few more words and it was a cast-iron hit. This, if nothing else, was proof of how good walking in the park is for stimulating the imagination. At the time, however, it had got no further than that. The title had been logged in an old notebook, but the song had never been written. Now, with my mind on the task of having a hit record, doing something about the 'Bird's Egg' lyric became something of a priority.

Jane was the perfect person to call on for advice. I'd met her through the producer of all my hits to date, Jakko, when she'd been working as a music publisher. After years in the music business she'd recently decided that she wanted to work with people who were more mature, and so she'd left to bring up two small children. When I called her up and told her about my plans to make 'Bird's Egg' a hit, she made what I considered to be an unusual suggestion.

'Why don't you try collaborating with another songwriter?' she mooted.

I'd never really considered this before, having always written songs on my own up to this point.

'It would feel too weird,' I said, with resistance.

'You'd enjoy the process,' said Jane, assuredly. 'You really would. I'm sure of it. You should start off with Steve – you'd get along swimmingly.'

'But how can I start writing with someone I've never met before?'

'You'll be fine. Writers do it all the time these days. Steve's been working out in Nashville where they collaborate on a daily basis with people that they've never met before in their lives.'

'Really?'

'Yes, why don't you give it a go?'

'I don't know. Anyway, what makes you think he'll want to do it?'

'I'll impress on him what a great songwriter you are.'

'How?'

'I'm not sure yet, Tony, but rest assured I shan't be mentioning "Stutter Rap".'

On the morning Steve was due to arrive, I began to have serious misgivings about this whole thing. What were we actually going to do? I didn't know what music he liked and I had absolutely no idea what kind of a song he wanted to have a go at writing. All I knew about Steve were the things that Jane had told me – that he was a professional songwriter, that I'd like him, that he was used to collaborating with new people, and that he'd written songs for Boyzone, Belinda Carlisle and Natalie Imbruglia. This all sounded a bit too impressive, and now that the man was about to arrive at my door I became worried that all I was going to be able to provide for him was an embarrassing waste of time.

I sat waiting on my settee, restlessly fidgeting. This was worse than a blind date. At least on a blind date you know that if it turns out to be a non-starter, there are only a couple of hours that you have to endure together, and you can always numb your senses with alcohol. There was no such option for us. It was ten o'clock in the morning and we'd committed ourselves to a day of work together. And what would happen if neither of us felt in the mood? What about the muse? Was it possible just to be creative with a total stranger at the drop of a hat? I allowed myself to begin to get precious about how my artistic integrity was being compromised by this whole process.

When the doorbell rang, for a terrible moment I actually considered not answering the door. Oh yes, it was a spectacularly cowardly option but it did suddenly have enormous appeal. After all, I could just call Steve later and explain what had happened.

'So sorry, Steve, something urgent came up and I had to dash out ... maybe we could arrange another time ... yes, how about August 2010?'

Taking a deep breath, I opened the door to a man with blond hair swept back into a pony tail. He had a guitar in a soft case slung over his shoulder.

'Hi,' he said, with as much assurance as one syllable could afford.

'Hi,' I replied keenly, at slightly too high a volume, 'you must be Steve.'

Goodness, he must have been impressed by my powers of deduction.

'Yes. Hi Tony.'

We shook hands and I began to relax. He seemed a nice guy and I didn't foresee any problems in us getting along just fine. I invited him in and immediately put the kettle on, a simple act which we British do to set guests at ease in even the most awkward of situations – it's almost as if the gentle purring of the kettle soothes any jangly nerves and eases the path to social intercourse.

As it transpired, being at ease was not a problem for me and Steve, and instead of knuckling down and writing a song, we chatted and exchanged stories while drinking as many cups of tea as it was possible for us to do without endangering our lives. I learned that Steve was an Englishman who lived an extraordinarily peripatetic lifestyle, dividing his time equally between Los Angeles, Nashville and London – writing songs in each city with a variety of different writers. I had no idea what had been going through his head when he had agreed to work for a day with a comedian and author who had attained a certain notoriety for taking on wacky bets, but here he was, and it was great to see him – and wouldn't he like another cup of tea? The moment of truth, however, couldn't be postponed any longer. Steve finally broached the subject.

'Any ideas for a song, then?' he asked.

'Er ... well ... there was one ...'

'Fire away,' he said. Then, clearly noticing me tense up, he continued, 'Relax, it's not important, it just might be a starting point for something.'

'Well, I thought of doing something which might work in Nashville.'

The thought of going to Nashville and plying my musical and lyrical wares had been at the back of my mind for some time. After all, it was the home of Country & Western music, and I reckoned that was as good a way to have a hit as any other.

'Yeh. So what's the idea?' asked Steve.

'Er ... well, I had this line,' I mumbled without confidence. 'I'm not sure about it but I thought it might work.'

'Go on.'

I hesitated. Had I known this man long enough to suggest the 'bird's egg' line? Maybe I should offer up instead the other, safer, and rather more bland title about love which I'd also prepared for this moment. I took a deep breath, and then a decision.

'How about this? ... "You broke my heart like a bird's egg but now the yolk's on you".'

Steve immediately began to chuckle. Initially I wasn't sure if he was laughing because the line had amused him, or because I'd had the audacity to suggest it as plausible for inclusion in a song.

'That's funny,' he averred, 'and as far as I'm concerned it's a song that has to be written.'

The rest of the day was devoted to that cause. Our time was largely divided between pacing up and down the garden in search of rhyming couplets, strumming guitars in the living room in search of the appropriate melody, and drinking cups of tea. Things really began to take shape at around midday when we arrived at a chorus which pleased us both. We sang it together.

You broke my heart like a bird's egg but now the yolk's on you
You never thought when you took off that I'd find someone new
When you quit the love nest — you forgot that I fly too
You broke my heart like a bird's egg, but now the yolk's on you

'I like that,' said Steve, 'it's got something.'

'I think so too,' I said with a genuine smile. 'We should celebrate with a cup of tea.'

'Good idea.'

After tea, we felt it was time for a lengthy break for lunch, and it wasn't until that was successfully completed that we felt able to begin work on the verses. Pleasingly these followed without too much of a struggle and a rough version of the song was completed before the day was out.

'Do you think it would sell in Nashville?' I asked, as Steve began to put his guitar away, having completed another hard day at the office.

'I don't know. Why, what were you planning on doing exactly?'

'I was wondering if I could go there and try to get someone famous to record it.'

Steve's expression changed when he saw that I was clearly serious.

'Well, it might be worth a try,' he said. 'But you'll need a demo of it. Where are you going to do that?'

'I reckon my mate Willie will do it,' I said confidently. 'Another cup of tea?'

'Ooh – yes please!'

I'd met Willie when I'd organised a little musical jam session at my house with some friends, and friends of friends. Over the course of that evening Willie had proved to be an invaluable addition to proceedings, seemingly knowing the words and music to every song which had ever been written. He led us and held us together as we meandered and stumbled from one half-remembered song to another. The night was a triumph and we'd all agreed that we should do it again. Six months and numerous jam sessions later I felt I could safely say that he'd become a friend in his own right. Unfortunately for him, this newly acquired status meant that the task of making the 'Bird's Egg' demo had fallen to him.

Like most professional musicians nowadays, Willie had built a studio at his house. The adjoining garage no longer provided warmth and succour for beaten up, overworked motor cars, but instead it hosted a confusing array of computers and machines which flashed little coloured lights and generally communicated the message 'keep away!' to technophobes like me. Willie was there, ready and waiting at the controls, when my two mates, Brad and Nigel, turned up to play bass and drums, respectively. I picked up my guitar and started singing them the song and soon they were playing along and a nice little groove was developing.

Willie soon announced that we weren't far off the point when we could go for a take and he readied himself for the moment when he'd cue us in and press 'play' and 'record' at the same time (or has it got more sophisticated than that now?). Whatever the worries of the day had been for each of us, they mattered little now. We were lost in a world of verses, choruses, chords, rhythm and beer. We were artists in the midst of creating a three minute canvas of sound. Music was doing its job and bringing joy.

'You've all done me proud,' I said, at the end of the evening as we listened back to our night's work. 'It sounds great.'

The boys nodded proudly and beamed like kids.

'You know what?' I said.

'What?'

'I think this is so good, we should take it to Nashville.'

There was a brief silence, and the boys looked up at me.

'What do you mean by *we* should take it to Nashville?' enquired Willie.

I looked around me and didn't see oodles of enthusiasm for the idea. What was the problem? Was I the only romantic dreamer here?

I sighed.

'OK lads, I'll send you a postcard.'

CHAPTER 2 **CRAZY**

My bags were packed and sitting in the hallway. The cab would be here any minute. I sipped my tea and took a moment to ponder what the coming weeks might bring. I had serious misgivings about whether this was the right place to start. On the one hand it felt right to begin my quest in a city which was famous for music, and Nashville was certainly that, but would I be welcome there? Nashville was the holy city of Country. Its lyricists wrote about drink, troubled marriages, bibles and broken hearts. What could I possibly have to offer? I lived in Wimbledon where you only saw a stetson if a Texan turned up to watch the tennis, and where most of the cowboys you came across were the ones who put in sub-quality loft conversions. Nashville was the home of a music which had originated in the Appalachian mountains generations earlier and which had grown into the country sound we know today. I had never been a part of that culture, and had little understanding of what it really meant to its people. I was surely a rank outsider. And only fools bet on them.

'Enjoy your flight,' said the cabbie as he dumped my bags at the airport set-down area and voraciously pocketed my cash.

'I'll try to,' I replied.

'Just do what I do, and watch all the movies. The time passes quicker.'

Not for the first time, I ignored the advice of a cab driver, and on the flight I tuned into the audio channels from the airline's extensive entertainment options. Since I was embarking on a journey in search of a hit record, I figured that I may as well use my time by listening to as many hits as I could before the plane touched down. I started on the pop and rock channel. Bon Jovi was doing his stuff, bellowing about being 'halfway there' in the song 'Living on a Prayer.'

I was puzzled by the whole concept of this song. I couldn't understand why he was so excited by the prospect of being *halfway* there. Surely it would have been better to have waited till he'd got the whole way there before he started shouting about it. I really felt that the levels of enthusiasm he was exhibiting in his vocal performance were not apposite for someone who had only completed 50 per cent of the journey. At this rate he'd be a bit puffed by the time he was three-quarters of the way there, and completely knackered at the point of arrival.

I switched channels on my headset, hoping to find a song which would not activate the picky, pedantic side of my brain. I failed hopelessly because the first song I happened upon on the 'easy listening' channel, was 'Stars' by Simply Red, in which Mick Hucknall was singing about how he intended to fall from the stars straight into his lover's arms, seemingly without a moments consideration for the dangers involved in such an act. Falling into people's arms is a risky business at the best of times, but doing it when your tumble commenced somewhere quite as high up as the stars is just foolhardy.

This would make a great opening track for a compilation album called 'Songs that hurt', the opening track of which would be 'It's Raining Men'.

I took off my headphones and devoted my time wholeheartedly to considering what might lie ahead for me in Nashville. Most of me felt pretty good about things. My optimism, which has always teetered on the very edge of self-delusion, allowed me to believe that something quite special was about to happen. My songwriting skills, which in my view had long been a well-kept secret, were about to emerge and become recognised. This trip had all the potential to mark a turning point in my career. However, the more practical voice inside me, which always had to sit patiently through these periods of reverie before it got its chance to be heard, was reminding me that I was entering one of the most competitive arenas in the world. Rather than being heralded as a fresh new writer, I was far more likely to hear a string of different euphemisms for 'Get lost and stop wasting our time'.

I looked out of the window and saw that the Atlantic had been crossed. Below me was American soil. The land of opportunity. The place where they said 'zucchini' instead of 'courgettes', 'pants' instead of 'trousers', and where President Clinton called it 'getting close to someone emotionally', when everyone else called it a 'blow job'.

I wondered how I was going to enjoy America, and whether this trip would prompt some shift in my current opinion of the place; that in spite of all its good points, it remained a land where hundreds of different nationalities had converged, only to become homogenized into one vast culture which embraced very little outside the pursuit of wealth. Admittedly, dabbling with a cast of characters drawn from the music business was unlikely to change this much, since there was little chance it would bring me into contact with America's most gentle, enlightened and spiritually developed individuals. But you never know. Just before I'd left Britain, a friend had alerted me to something which Hunter S Thompson had written about the world into which I was about to immerse myself:

'The music business is a cruel and shallow money trench, a long plastic hallway where thieves and pimps run free, and good men die like dogs. There's also a negative side.'

So nothing to worry about there then – I'd be just fine, provided I could avoid the positive and negative sides.

Steve and Robin looked pleased to see me as they waited by the sliding door of the customs hall at Nashville airport.

'Welcome to Music City USA,' said Robin, echoing the message that was emblazoned on a huge banner above our heads.

I have to confess at this stage that I wasn't starting my quest on the bottom rung of the show-business ladder. I had carefully planned my trip so it would coincide with Steve being in Nashville, and I had every intention of exploiting his network of contacts in order to 'make it'. I'd figured I needed a few short cuts since I was only investing a short period of my life in a task to which many have devoted decades, and even then without success. Steve's girlfriend, Robin, didn't fall into this category.

Having embarked on a career in songwriting on the advice of a New York waiter who'd seen some lyrics she'd dashed off on a napkin, she'd recently co-written a massive Billboard Number One hit for Faith Hill called 'This Kiss'. At the same time that this song was charting, she'd been sitting at Number Two in the country charts with another one she'd co-written – 'Out Of My Bones' by Randy Travis. Not a bad week, all things considered.

'Are you ready to eat?' asked Steve.

'Why, do you have something planned?'

I was a little alarmed to learn that Steve and Robin had arranged for us to go straight to dinner with another songwriter friend called Holly. Holly, I soon discovered, had just written two big country hits and was, in Robin's words, 'really hot right now'. We were also being joined by Whitney, who was one of Nashville's top song-pluggers. I was excited by this, but by the same token it had all come a little early for me. I would have preferred not to have had to turn on the charm immediately after a nine-hour flight when my body clock was telling me it was two o'clock in the morning. I knew that these people could be important to me and I was fully aware that Robin and Steve had set this whole thing up precisely for that reason. But in my experience, losing your train of thought while intermittently stifling yawns never makes that much of an impression, and that was all I felt good for.

As it happened I needn't have worried unduly. After a short drive through Nashville, which struck me as being little more than a rather ordinary American city, we arrived at a rather ordinary American diner. Here, the assembled company weren't able to pay me much attention, largely due to the overwhelming and relentless nature of Holly's monologues about her career and emotional life. All that was required of me was the occasional approving nod when she glanced my way in mid-oration. I wondered, as I listened to her self-obsessed ramblings, if the thought had entered her slowly unravelling mind that I was an Englishman who had just arrived in her country and that it might be polite to take a moment to ask how my journey had been.

'I just don't think I'm ready for a relationship right now,' declared Holly at one point, oblivious to the world around her.

On behalf of all men everywhere I felt a strong wave of relief.

I was fading fast as Steve drove me to the Writers' Boarding House in the leafy suburb of Sylvan Park.

'You'll like it at Buddy and Carol's, they're great,' said Steve as he dropped me outside the pleasant-looking white house. 'They'll look after you, they're both songwriters too.'

I'd been expecting some kind of hotel, but the Writers' Boarding House was, in reality, simply Buddy and Carols' house – the loft of which they rented to transient writers. Inside I was greeted warmly by my new landlords.

'Would you like a bourbon for a nightcap?' asked the pretty, gentle-voiced Carol.

'Yes please,' I replied, ignoring the fact that according to my body clock it would be something closer to a breakfast-cap.

'You have a large room upstairs with an en suite bathroom, Tony,' said the laid-back Buddy who just *looked* like a songwriter. 'If there's anything you need – just holler.'

'I will. I'm good at hollering.'

'I'm sure you're going to have a great time here,' said Carol.

'Me too.'

'All the British people who've stayed in the Writers' Boarding House have had a fulfilling time here in Nashville,' added Buddy, almost in a whisper.

'It's a good omen,' I said, before knocking back my whisky and heading off to bed to dream of success.

I woke up before I found out whether I'd won the award or not. Most frustrating. I tried to go back to sleep and allow the dream to carry on where it had left off, but of course this was impossible. Seconds earlier I'd been nominated for the Best Newcomer award at the annual Country Music Awards – sitting proudly in the audience, adorned in top-of-the-range cowboy boots and hat, and flanked by a sycophantic collection of hangers-on from the record company, all of whom I stood to make very rich. However, now that my body had made the unconscious decision of switching from the unconscious to the conscious, I was lying in a bed in a boarding house, wondering why I was shivering.

Opening the bathroom window provided the answer. Outside, it was bloody freezing. I had not been expecting this. Nashville,

Tennessee was supposed to be hot. Oh dear. This new development was set to expose serious deficiencies in my packing.

'You can't go out like that,' declared a concerned Carol half an hour later, as she intercepted me by the front door. 'It's *really* cold out there. It's unseasonably cold for October. Most unusual. Here, borrow this coat. It's a little old, it used to belong to my father, but take it.'

'Thanks.'

I put it on. It was a huge old-fashioned great coat which weighed heavy on my shoulders and stirred mixed feelings within me. I was reassured by its undoubted warming qualities but was less enthused by the way it left me resembling a wanted sex offender. I was too polite to hand it back to Carol and so I resigned myself to the fact that I'd just have to scare people all morning.

As directed by Buddy I wandered two blocks to a local coffee shop for breakfast. 'America' jumped out at me. The wide streets, the porches dotted with hollowed-out pumpkins in preparation for Hallowe'en, the postboxes at the end of long drives, and the capacious Buicks and Chevrolets whirring past.

A lady walking a dog approached me but crossed the street rather than pass by. You could see her point of view. It wasn't just the fact that I was adorned in a flasher's overcoat; to this lady I was disconcerting in another way too. I was *walking*. I remembered that I'd been warned that this could happen in America, for I was transgressing an unwritten rule; the rule that stated that unless you were out with the dog, then walking was something which was only done by the criminally insane. The common thinking seemed to be that if God had meant us to propel ourselves from A to B without resorting to external machinery then he wouldn't have given us wheels, five-speed gearboxes and stomachs which took premium unleaded. (I shudder to think where the nozzle would have gone when refilling at the garage. 'Shall I fill 'er up, sir?' 'Yes, but I wonder if you could be a little gentler than you were last time ...')

Nashville, it has to be said, is not an attractive place. Like many US towns it relies on the motor car, and every establishment, be it a hairdressers, a solicitors, a cake shop or a bank, needs to provide parking facilities; and let's be honest here, car parks just aren't pleasing on the eye. There were no town squares or market places. Just roads, roads, big blocks, small blocks and car parks. It didn't really feel like a town of creativity and action, but these are things which aren't always visible to the naked eye. I would need to look beneath the surface.

The coffee shop was closed. How could this be? Wasn't I in a country which more or less prided itself on being able to provide round the clock coffee? Disappointed, I started to wander back to Buddy and Carol's when I noticed, and then followed, a sign directing me to a local church. Here I would find the soul of America. Maybe all the people who served the coffee were here, giving joyous thanks to the great coffee provider in the sky. On a whim, I decided to go into the church to see if America's reputation for 'quality of service' was justified. As I sidled into the rear pew of the small, unimpressive '70s building, I was to be disappointed again. There was no enraptured praising here, and only fifteen or so of Nashville's inhabitants had chosen this as their place of worship this Sunday.

The sermon had already begun and was being conducted by the Reverend Lovejoy from *The Simpsons*. In fact as I looked around me I began to feel like I had somehow walked into an entire episode of the TV show. Each member of the congregation had the requisite levels of absurdity and grotesqueness to qualify as one of the cartoon's myriad characters. The minister hesitated momentarily as he acknowledged me, the new arrival to his flock, presumably a little surprised to see a fledgling face, and one which didn't belong in this particular cartoon. He coughed unhealthily and then proceeded with an incomprehensible reading from Tychicus Col. 4. 1–9 which he rendered even less accessible by employing a monotone delivery and generally giving a flawless demonstration of 'uncharismatic'. He made quite a picture as he stood there in his pulpit, adorned in a brown suit, brown shirt and brown tie, painfully unaware of what an unappealing clothes selection he'd made. To compound his unattractiveness, he'd combed long strands of greasy hair across the top of his shiny head, in a vain and completely unsuccessful attempt to delude his congregation into believing that there before them was a man with a healthy head of hair. Yes, he made quite a picture, but not one you'd buy an expensive frame for.

Finally, the moment came for the Reverend Lovejoy to follow his abstruse and unfathomable reading with the abstruse and unfathomable lesson which was to be learnt from it. I'd already learnt mine; never to listen to this man speak publicly again.

'The Lord knows when you are sinning,' he asserted, with a hint of enthusiasm which was slightly alarming, 'the Lord knows when your thoughts are impure and the Lord knows when you have given in to temptation.'

For a few moments I grappled with a huge desire to stand up and shout, 'Look mate, are you also aware that the Lord knows you're bald? If so, then why don't you dispense with that ridiculous haircut?'

But that wouldn't have been the right thing to do. I realised that leaving the church was a better option and so I shuffled out, abandoning the dubious cast of characters to continue with the quiet, monotonous enrichment of their lives without my unwanted cynicism. By the door I quickly took a moment to sign the guest register:

Name	Address	Remarks
Tony Hawks	England	Popped in but found it rather dull

I had to. The Lord would have known if I'd lied.

Despite its bleak name, the 'Loveless Cafe' was much more like it. Following a short drive into Nashville's easily accessible countryside, Steve, Robin and I took brunch and discussed my plans. The place was bustling and busy, and we were seated at a table above which were framed photo after framed photo of gleaming singers, all seemingly eager to endorse the food in this establishment. It seems that even outside Nashville, you were embraced by the elongated arms of the country music scene. As she tucked into the big scones called 'biscuits', for which this diner was famed, Robin was more inquisitive than the company had allowed her to be the previous evening.

'So what exactly are you hoping to achieve here in Nashville?' she asked politely.

'I'm going to play the "Bird's Egg" song to as many important people as I can and I'm going to search for a singer who
might be interested in recording it.'

'Well, good luck,' said Robin with a little laugh. 'You gotta
try these things.'

I was delighted by Robin's response. From it, I took her to
be something of a kindred spirit who, like me, believed that we
only learn and grow by trying new experiences. *So what* if you fell
on your face? That was just part of the process. Simply follow the
advice of Dorothy Field's inspirational lyric – from a song written half a century earlier – pick yourself up, dust yourself off and
start all over again.

Fear of failure is something we learn as grown-ups. If kids had
it, then the toddler wouldn't risk falling over by trying to walk,
and as a result adults would still be crawling from a to b – which
is something we only really do when we're pissed, or trying to
escape from prisoner of war camps.

'Maybe Bama could help you,' suggested Robin.

'Who's Bama?' I replied.

'He's someone we know who works in radio who has got a
lot of contacts. I think you guys should meet each other.'

'If you could set that up, it'd be great,' I offered enthusiastically.

'On another more practical note,' said Steve, who had just
completed chewing an impressively large mouthful which he'd
taken quite some time earlier, 'how are you going to manage for
transport? I mean I'm happy to give you lifts, but after today I'm
going to be busy writing with different people at different times,
all over town.'

'Well, I've decided,' I said proudly, 'that if I can manage
without hiring a car, I will. I want to take a stand against the
motor car.'

'Very noble, but I'm not sure that this is the place to do it,'
advised Steve. 'The public transport system in Nashville is abysmal.'

'So, I'll do a lot of walking.'

'You're crazy,' said Robin.

'Yes,' I said with what felt like a broad, and somehow
British, smile.

To my mind, 'crazy' wasn't necessarily a pejorative term. I
took it to mean that you weren't dull.

I was in a heavy sweat, my clothes uncomfortably sticking to my back. Yes, it was cold, but I'd been walking and walking and walking, and my body was beginning to protest. I was making the journey from my lodgings towards the centre of town, and it was now becoming clear to me that I'd made a significant misjudgement with regard to the scale on my map. The distances that needed covering were much greater than I'd calculated, and it was now becoming painfully clear to me that walking everywhere was going to mean I would always arrive in a state of exhaustion.

My intention had been to do a little Nashville solo sightseeing, but I was dog-tired by the time I finally trudged into the legendary area known as Music Row, the hub of the music industry in Nashville. I don't think it was the fatigue which caused me to be enormously disappointed, more the fact that there really just isn't anything to see. Just a few blocks of buildings which house record companies and music publishers. Even the legendary RCA recording studios where Elvis recorded was simply an unimpressive one-storey building with no windows and an unexciting door with a small notice commemorating the King's one-time presence there. Hardly worth the one and half hour walk, which alas now needed to be repeated in order to get home.

'My God you look wiped out!' said Carol, as I arrived back at the guest house.

'Yes, I am a little tired,' I lied, 'I've just walked into town and back.'

'Why, you're crazy!'

This time I was less enamoured of the description. My aching muscles made it feel far more like fact than playful banter. I *was* crazy. Walking just wasn't an option, and tomorrow I would have to sort out another mode of transport. The only up-side of my exhaustion was that I slept soundly that night with no interruption. It may be slightly eccentric, but I can strongly recommend walking to the point of exhaustion as a first-rate cure for jetlag.

In the morning I elected to listen to some of the local radio stations, to hear what my Nashville songwriting competitors had come up with, but alas, as I whizzed around the dial with my tuning knob, all I could hear was DJ babble. I couldn't believe it. I was in Nashville and yet not one record was being spun.

'Here comes Bob with the latest travel news ... now Bob,

what *is* that shirt you're wearing? Is it any wonder that you can't find yourself a woman? Say Bob, what do you make of that situation out there in the Middle East?'

'Wow, that's a tough one, Perry. I guess those guys are pretty uptight out there. Maybe it's all that sun. So what exactly *is* it you don't like about the shirt?'

My hand reached out and retuned the radio before the irritatingly jovial Perry could offer us his lengthy critique of Bob's chemise. Still, at least I now had a better understanding of the Middle East crisis. Seconds later my radio was tuned to another station, the morning crew of which were offering similar fare.

'Did anyone see *Ally McBeal* last night? Now Calista Flockhart – is she too thin or *what*?'

The 'off' switch suddenly seemed irresistible and after making use of it, I was rewarded with silence, beautiful silence, which remained unbroken until I broke it myself, downstairs in the kitchen.

'Do you know if anyone hires out bikes in this town?' I asked Buddy as he poured himself a coffee.

'Maybe. You could call a couple of the bicycle shops and ask, but if that doesn't work then Carol's got an old one in the basement. I'm sure she wouldn't mind you borrowing that.'

A few phone calls later I had established that America's entrepreneurs had not adopted bicycle hire as their favourite method of generating wealth, and as a direct result I found myself lifting a very old bicycle out of Carol's cellar. It looked like it had last been ridden when Elvis was still doing his stuff in the recording studios up the road.

'Maybe that's not such a good idea,' offered Buddy as he looked on in wonder when the machine and I finally surfaced from below stairs.

'Oh she'll be just swell as soon as we get us some air in her tyres,' I replied, adopting what I thought to be authentic vernacular.

A few minutes later Buddy was looking distinctly worried as I wobbled around in the street on the first test drive.

'Are you going to be alright on that thing?' he enquired with genuine concern.

'I haven't done this for years,' I said, displaying all the confidence of a child whose father had just released his supportive, balancing hands for the first time.

'Are you sure you know what you're doing?' asked Buddy with something of a furrowed brow.

'Yes, it's all coming back to me. You don't forget this. It's just like riding a bike.'

The test drive was a success. It was a ladies' bike which only operated in one gear, but the brakes functioned effectively and it was just about big enough to accommodate my lanky frame. What's more, I liked it. It was a charming old thing which had to be admired for having survived so long in a society that generally favoured discarding things just as soon as a new model came on the market. I felt ready to use it to ride to my first appointment in Nashville – lunch with Bama. All I needed to do was stop and pick up a padlock at the bicycle shop which was conveniently situated en route, and so I mounted the relic of a bicycle, satchel over my shoulder like a kid on his first day at school.

'You're crazy,' said Buddy, again.

Oh well, better than being dull.

CHAPTER 3 SECRET COMBINATION

The man in the bike shop had a healthy physique and a neat moustache, but no sense of humour.

'Would you happen to have a padlock for my bike?' I asked as I wheeled it through the doorway and presented it to him. 'You may not have anything that fits it. As you can see, it's the very latest model on the market.'

'Would you like one that opens with a key or a combination, sir?' he returned, without even a hint of a smile.

'Er … combination please. If I have a key I'll only lose it.'

'You know with keys, the trick is to put them in the same place every time. People only lose keys because they're so random about where they choose to—'

'Combination please,' I quickly reiterated before he could fully demonstrate his sober disposition with a long discourse on how best not to lose things.

'Very well, sir, combination it is.'

Ten minutes later I was putting its effectiveness to the test as I attached the bike to a post outside a large bookshop which had caught my eye. I was in danger of arriving a little early for my lunch appointment and I figured there was time for a quick nose around, specifically for *Round Ireland with a Fridge* which had just been published in the States. When I returned to the bike, having found one copy of my book and moved it to a more prominent location in the bookshop (something I'm told that authors do all the time), I began the process of releasing the bike by tapping in the four digits I had chosen. 1485 – an easy number to remember because that was the year that Henry VII ascended to the British throne after defeating and killing the Yorkist king Richard III at the Battle of Bosworth.*

Having entered the magical number there was no response from the lock. A little perplexed, but not yet panicking, I reshuffled the numbers and then realigned the four which were supposed to provide release. 1485. Still nothing. This was not good. I immediately began to do what all non-practical people do in this situation and simply repeat the same action continuously in the hope that by magic it will somehow produce a different result. (This is triggered by exactly the same part of the brain which instructs us to keep checking the same place over and over again when we're searching for something.) I continued reshuffling and realigning the numbers for a further five minutes until my temper, as well as the cause, was in danger of being lost. The bike, in the meantime, remained doggedly padlocked to its post.

I tried a new tack. I stepped back to survey the scene from a few yards away, the theory being that from there I could analyse the situation with a more focused overview of my predicament. I took a deep breath and calmed myself as best I could. After a couple of minutes, hard-thinking I came up with an idea – that I should approach the bike, reshuffle the numbers and then realign them. I did so. 1485. Of course, nothing. I cursed my luck for having purchased a combination lock which didn't release, from a humourless bastard who would be mildly amused by the pickle which I was now undoubtedly in.

I took a moment to consider the phone call I would have to make to Carol. It did not enthuse me greatly.

'Hi Carol … You know the bike I just borrowed off you? … yes, the one that used to be safely stored down in your basement … yes, well it's still safe, it's just in another part of Nashville that's all. No-one's going to take it anywhere because it's been secured to a post outside a bookshop. If you get a pen I'll give you exact directions on how to find the post in question, just so you know where to go if ever you want to see it.'

Naturally enough I chose to stall the making of this call, thinking that one to the humourless man in the bike shop would be a better place to start. Maybe he could provide a practical

* *Come on, you knew that, surely.*

solution, after all he'd sold me the faulty equipment in the first place and he was to blame for my plight. However, when I called 'Information' from the callbox to try and get the number, the polite lady on the other end of the line was unable to help.

'I'm sorry, sir, but we really need a name or an address before we can help at all.'

'But it's a bike shop. How many bike shops can there be in Nashville?'

'I really don't know sir.'

'But don't you call yourself "Information"?'

'We do sir, but we need a name or an address.'

'So you want information from *me*. That's funny because I called wanting information from you – what with you being called "Information" and everything.'

'I'm sorry sir, but we really cannot provide a number purely from knowing the nature of what a store sells.'

I probably wrangled for a further minute before conceding to myself that I was simply deflecting my current padlock frustration on to this poor woman. I managed a begrudging but nonetheless magnanimous apology, and hung up. Then, as I stood powerless before the phone, I looked up and saw the answer to my problems. From this distance I could see that the post was only about six feet high. I figured that I was tall enough and strong enough to lift the bike over the post, thus liberating it from its inanimate captor.

I returned to the street where I waited for a suitable lull in passing pedestrians before commencing operations. I was naturally concerned that my actions would attract attention, especially given that I was adorned in a 1950s great coat which made me resemble a degenerate street urchin. When the coast was clear and I eventually began lifting, I found it to be harder than I'd imagined, the bike proving to be extremely prone to tipping in unexpected directions and getting tangled up with items of clothing. I was dealing with a mode of transport designed more for horizontal rather than vertical movement. Take it from me, bikes – especially old American ones – are rubbish at going upwards. Just as I had the bike precariously balanced at head height and I was poised like a weightlifter to make that final exertion for the big result, a car pulled up by the kerb in front of me.

I froze.

Returning the bike to ground level would have seemed like an admission that I was involved in a blatant act of larceny. To have continued lifting the bike skywards would have been to have carried out that very act right there in front of this car driver. Far better that the middle-aged man now emerging from this car believed me to be involved in the very deliberate act of lifting this bike to head height for a legitimate reason, and one which needn't concern him. He looked at me and I nodded back congenially, as anyone might who was involved in the ordinary daily activity of bike-lifting.

'Is everything OK?' he asked, a little wrong-footed by the scene before him.

'Fine thanks,' I replied, still with bike held aloft. 'Just fine.'

Of course, I could have told the man the truth – that everything was not fine and that, for complicated reasons, I was involved in the act of stealing my own bike, or to be more precise, that of my landlady. But somehow all this information seemed a lot for the driver to assimilate, and I felt confident that evasiveness was the correct course of action. The man continued looking at me and I had no option but to carry on resolutely smiling back at him. I was unsure how long I could hold the position I was in, such was the weight of the bike, but after a further uncomfortable few seconds, the man capitulated and headed off towards the bookshop, seemingly satisfied that if I was a burglar then at least I was one who was at ease with himself and who enjoyed his work.

The man gone, I heroically hoisted the bike to freedom, and began cycling back up the road to give the moustachioed humourless conman in the bike shop a piece of my mind.

'Do you realise that this combination lock has a major flaw?' I asked him as he emerged from the back room and approached the counter.

'Do you have a problem sir?'

'Yes I do. This combination lock doesn't release.'

'I see. Let me just take a look at that.'

'Yes, I think you'd better.'

'What are your four numbers?'

'1485.'

My dour-faced friend crouched down beside the bike and lined up the four numbers.

'There you are you see,' I said. 'It doesn't relea...'

I looked down in horror as the combination lock released before my very eyes.

'Did you press the button at the side after lining up the numbers?' he asked, already knowing the answer, much in the manner of a schoolteacher dealing with a miscreant pupil.

The button at the side? How could there be a button at the side? Why had I not seen the button at the side?

'Did you not see the button at the side?' he asked, even allowing himself a smug smile. His first one for more than five years, I bet. The bastard.

'Er ... no. There's a button at the side is there?'

'Yup. And if you don't press it, the combination lock stays put.'

'Yes.'

'But now, because I've pressed the button, it has released.'

'Yes.'

I needed to get out of this place, and fast.

'Thanks for your help,' I mumbled disingenuously, grabbing the bike and legging it out of the shop.

A glance at my watch now told me that I was running late for my lunch appointment, and that I would have to take the short cut through the university campus to get to Music Row. It was difficult to know why I was of such interest to the gently ambling, book-laden students as I pedalled my antique two-wheeler through their territory, but I drew stare after inquisitive stare. It could have been that I resembled an avuncular and dearly loved professor who had won everyone's hearts with his eccentric ways, but it was probably far more likely that I was a dead ringer for the man on the '*wanted*' poster in the students' union bar. I suddenly became extremely self-conscious and felt a need to get back out into the real world as soon as possible, so I began pedalling quicker, trying to ignore the fact that this just made me look a more desperate figure.

When I finally arrived outside the restaurant, ten minutes late and flushed from frantic pedalling, I rehearsed my opening line in my head.

'Hello, Bama, I'm not normally this purple.'

~

Inside the restaurant I discovered that Bama wasn't there yet. God, I hate it when that happens. You break your neck to get somewhere only to discover that you could have just taken your time. Of course, watching this happen to other people pleases me greatly. When I'm travelling on the London Underground there's nothing I like more than watching someone sprint on to a tube train only to find that it doesn't leave for another ten minutes. I don't mind being late for my appointment if I've had the enjoyment of looking at someone trying to conceal their embarrassment as the sweat slowly trickles down their forehead and the train stays firmly rooted in the station with its doors thrown wide open for anyone to mosey on board.

However when it happens to me, then that is another matter.

I ordered a beer and sat at the bar waiting for Bama to arrive. I was less than a couple of sips in when a short, slightly tubby young man in T-shirt, jeans and sneakers walked into the restaurant.

'Hi, I'm Bama,' he announced confidently to the maître d'. 'Is Tony here?'

The maître d' shrugged in a slightly grumpy manner which suggested that he rather resented Bama's over-familiarity but then added a half-hearted point in my direction, recognising me as a possible Tony.

'Hi Tony,' said Bama, realigning himself in my direction. 'I'm Bama. How ya doing?'

'I'm fine,' I said, shaking his hand. 'Pleased to meet you.'

We were shown to a table where we began to discuss my reasons for being in Nashville. Bama's reaction was extremely positive.

'I'd like to help you, Tony,' he said. 'I used to work full time for a radio station but now I'm just doing some freelancing. At the moment I'm making a programme in which I interview songwriters about the story behind their songs, but that isn't too time-consuming so I've got a little spare time right now.'

'How do you think you could help?' I asked.

'Well, I know a lot of people in this town. I could introduce you to them and we could play them your track.'

Before I could tell Bama how brilliant an idea this was, we were interrupted by an eager waiter who offered us menus and described the day's specials in far too much detail.

'The *tooners arssum*,' added the waiter, once he had concluded a lengthy list of the day's available dishes.

'I beg your pardon?'

'The *tooners arssum*,' he repeated.

Still none the wiser, I looked to Bama for elucidation.

'He's trying to tell you that the *tooner* is *arssum*,' explained Bama.

'I'm sorry,' I whimpered, 'I still don't follow.'

'He's talking about the *tooner*,' said Bama. 'Don't you know *tooner*, the fish?'

'Oh I see – he means that *the tuna is awesome.*'

'That's correct, sir,' intervened the waiter. 'The *tooners arssum.*'

'I see,' I said, quickly assimilating this new information.

I wasn't sure that I wanted an awesome tuna. An every day regular kind of tuna would do me just fine. And anyway, how did they know it was awesome? Surely any tuna which was truly awesome wouldn't allow itself to get caught.

'I'll have the pasta please,' I said, handing back the menu.

The waiter looked hurt. Too bad. He'd have to shift his *arssum tooner* elsewhere. I can be a hard bastard at times.

Over lunch I discovered that Bama was passionate about singers, songwriting and the music business in general. His knowledge of it seemed to be encyclopaedic. He told me how his dream was to make a radio show for the BBC, broadcast live from Nashville, and somehow I think that he'd got the impression from Robin and Steve that I could help make this happen. Rather naughtily, I didn't let on to Bama that this probably wasn't the case, realising that his enthusiasm could be potentially quite useful to me. I wasn't particularly proud of this behaviour but I figured it was excusable given that I had a lot to achieve in a short amount of time, in a business which was known to be as tough as they come.

'Hey Tony,' said Bama. 'Why don't we make a start on this just as soon as we finish lunch? Do you have the CD of your song with you?'

'I do.'

'Then we'll take it over the road and I'll play it to Eric.'

'Eric being ...?'

'He's Byron's son and he works at Song Garden Music Publishing. His Dad Byron Gallomore writes and produces for Tim McGraw. Tim's really hot right now. Actually I know he's looking for material for his album at the moment. Who knows, your song might even interest him.'

'Does Tim do songs of a slightly quirky nature?'

'Not really. Why, is that how you'd describe your song?'

'Kind of, yes.'

'Well, let's just see. I need to see Eric about something anyway, so I'll just slip the playing of your track into things when it seems appropriate.'

After lunch it only took us a couple of minutes to complete the two block journey from restaurant to Song Garden Music, and we made our way into the reception area of the compact modern building.

'Are you sure this is OK?' I asked.

'Sure,' replied Bama. 'Eric's cool.'

Bama approached the young and pleasant-faced receptionist.

'Hi, how ya doing?' he said. 'I'm Bama. Is Eric here?'

'Er, I'm sorry, who did you say you were again?'

Bama turned to me and gave me a little smile as if to intimate that this girl must be new here otherwise she'd sure as hell know who he was.

'I'm Bama, a friend of Eric's,' he said, returning his attention to her.

'OK, take a seat and I'll see if he's free. What's it concerning?'

'Oh nothing. Just stuff. Eric and I are friends.'

Two minutes later a young, quite cool-looking guy appeared in reception and Bama immediately jumped to his feet.

'Eric, how ya doing. It's me, Bama. This is Tony Hawks, an author from England, he's writing about Nashville. It's good to see you man, how are you?'

We paused for handshakes and Eric greeted us warmly. The poor guy had clearly been caught a little off-guard by Bama's sudden arrival and enthusiastic manner. By the time we were moving into Eric's office, Bama had begun cheerful banter about the current form of some baseball team, and I had begun to form some theories as to how Bama operated. It was clear that Eric and Bama weren't friends at all. In fact I got the distinct feeling that they had met only once before and that Eric had no recollection of that occasion. What was impressive, however, was that Bama had remembered every detail from that last meeting, right the way down to Eric's girlfriend's name and his favourite baseball team.

'Tony's got a song on a CD,' Bama suddenly announced, quite out of the blue. 'Do you want to hear it?'

Eric stiffened noticeably.

It was as if he recognised that all the preceding cheery, chummy banter had been leading to this moment, and that he was now in an awkward spot.

'Er,' hesitated Eric, 'it's just that I listened to a lot of tracks this morning—'

'Come on,' said Bama, thrusting the CD into Eric's hands. 'It's only three minutes long. Have a listen. It's great!'

I don't know why Bama was wasting his time making radio programmes. The man was clearly a born salesman. Not only had he wheedled his way into the office of a top executive but now he was enthusing about a product which he'd never even heard.

I started to become extremely uneasy as Eric turned and pushed the CD into the mouth of the extravagant hi-fi system which towered behind his plush leather chair. I felt powerless. Had I been giving a performance then at least I would have been able to channel my nervous energy into that. Instead I would just have to sit and listen and try not to stare at Eric and will him to like it.

Eric nodded approvingly as he listened to Willie's impressive bottleneck guitar intro. I nodded back to let him know that I approved of his approving nod. Bama nodded too. I'm not sure why, probably just peer pressure. The vocals began and Eric tilted his head, almost as if this aided the listening process. The verse passed without any more approving nods but I felt strongly that he was pleasantly surprised by what he was hearing. I began to feel good about things. Could it just be that the first person who heard the song was going to fall in love with it?

Then the big moment. The chorus.

'You broke my heart like a bird's egg but now the yolk's on you ...'

I looked up at Eric at the conclusion of the line and was delighted to see his face light up with a big smile. This, I had to

allow myself to concede, was looking very good indeed. Maybe
we had got lucky. However, at the end of the chorus Eric suddenly spun around in his big chair and hit the stop button. Then
he pressed eject, retrieved the CD, spun back around again and
handed it to me.

'That's funny,' he said. 'That's definitely funny but it's not for
me. It's not what I'm looking for.'

'Don't you want to hear the rest of it?' I asked, still reeling
from the brutal speed of the rejection.

'No need,' said Eric. 'I know what we're looking for with
Tim's album and that's not it.'

'But—'

'Thanks for your time anyway Eric,' intervened Bama,
before I had chance to suggest that there were more people
than Tim McGraw in the world. 'And we'll talk baseball over a
beer some time.'

'I'm kinda busy but if there's time ...' said Eric, demonstrating a huge lack of enthusiasm for the idea.

We made our way rather soberly out of Eric's office, and back
in the reception area Bama gave me his explanation of events.

'Tony, that's just the way it is in this business. They don't
have time to listen to things all the way through. It eats into the
amount of time they have for lunch and sitting on their asses
staring out the window.'

'How about you? Did *you* like the song?'

'Well, I liked the way it started. Maybe we could listen to it
at EMI,' he declared boldly.

'Oh dear,' I said, still rather shaken by the last experience.
'We're not going to just burst in on someone again, are we?'

'It's OK, I'm interviewing a guy called Dennis who co-wrote
the Number One song "I Need You" for Leanne Rimes. While
we're waiting for him in the conference room we'll play it all the
way through.'

We made our way across the two blocks to EMI's offices,
Bama commenting on what an advantage Nashville offered in
this regard.

'Everyone is within just a few blocks of each other here,' he
remarked. 'If we were in LA now we'd have to jump in the car
and drive for at least half an hour.'

Soon we were climbing the steps of the modern building and pushing open the big wooden door to the EMI conference room where we were greeted by a luxurious interior – and Dennis.

'Oh hi Bama,' he said. 'I'm early, I hope that's OK.'

Dennis was a well-groomed man with an open, friendly face. He greeted us both and happily sat nodding his head while Bama told him all about my reasons for being in Nashville. He even agreed to listen to the 'Bird's Egg' song, even though I got the feeling he'd fitted this interview into a fairly tight schedule and was anxious to get it over with.

'That's a lot of fun,' he said, having listened studiously to it throughout, and having shown no real emotion. 'Why don't you pitch it to the Dixie Chicks? If you get someone cool to do it, then it will be cool.'

I liked Dennis's logic, and it made sense. For years in my youth Abba were considered to be uncool but when a few hip bands started doing cover versions of their songs then they were fashionable all of a sudden. But how were we going to get this track to the Dixie Chicks?

'You'll have to leave that one with me,' said Bama, as I said goodbye to him on the steps of the EMI building. 'I'll meet you here at 12.00 tomorrow and we'll do some more work getting the song to people.'

'Thanks for this, it's a real help.'

'That's cool. It's fun. I know a lotta people in this town and it's groovy catching up with them,' said Bama, without a hint of irony.

'See you tomorrow, and thanks.'

When I got back to the Writers' Boarding House, Carol and Buddy laughed heartily when I recounted the fiasco of the bike and the padlock, and they were impressed that I'd managed to get my song listened to by some senior figures in the industry.

'It's much tougher to do that than it used to be,' said Carol gently, as she sipped on her herbal tea. 'The trouble is, Tony, this town has changed so much over the last ten years. It's getting like LA.'

'The scene in Austin, Texas, is a little more laid back,' said Buddy who, if he'd been any more laid back himself, would have fallen off his chair.

'In what way has it changed?' I asked.

'Well, all the money men have moved in,' explained a slightly melancholic Carol. 'Most of the big record companies have a major part of their operations here now.'

'And now they're finding it tough 'cos the boom is over,' added Buddy. 'Sales in country music are way down. Not long ago they accounted for 40 per cent of the US market – now they're down to 7 per cent.'

'The worst thing is that every record company is playing safe,' lamented Carol. 'Years ago there was room for someone with innovative and crazy ideas. I fear not now.'

'Really?' I said, looking and feeling a little hurt.

'Really.'

Of course, by the time I'd turned in for the night, I'd managed to convince myself that Carol had got it all wrong. I wasn't going to subscribe to a negative outlook like that. Tomorrow was another day, and I was going to continue my search for someone with the imagination to hear what I could hear.

A hit.

A lovely hit, all about broken hearts and bird's eggs.

CHAPTER 4 GOD DOESN'T MIND 'SILLY'

The local coffee shop was somewhat lacking in character and could have been a coffee shop anywhere in the Western world, had it not been for the zealous and professional affability of the staff.

'Enjoy your breakfast,' said the nice young man, as he handed me the tray.

'I will,' I replied, before adding, 'and I'll have a nice day too,' thinking it clever to get in there first.

I sat down at my table and devoured both my breakfast and the local paper, the *Nashville Scene*. It seemed that there was a lot going on in this town, and not just for music lovers. I noticed an advertisement at the bottom of one of the pages asking for players for the Nashville Beach Volleyball club. Beach volleyball? Hang on, don't you need beaches to have beach volleyball? And don't you need coastline to have beaches? Maybe the whole thing was just a scam to get the women playing volleyball in swimsuits instead of normal kit. The listings also showed that you could go line dancing every night of the week if you so desired, provided your temperament could take that much excitement. I dipped back into my past and began to recall an old girlfriend of mine who for a while had believed that when people referred to line dancing they were actually saying *lion* dancing. On one occasion when she was invited to go to a Country & Western club and try it, she refused, claiming that it was too dangerous. (It was difficult to work out how I'd not managed to make that relationship work.)

By the time I'd made significant inroads into my coffee I had begun reading the entire section which was devoted to listing the different venues which had Songwriters' and Open Mic Nights. I decided that I ought to make a live performance of my song at some point during my trip, since that might be the only real way to discover what really *worked* about it. The question was, where would I do this? The list before me was so extensive. A look at the map suggested that there was only one place tonight which was going to be within cycling distance – and even that was going to be something of a schlep.

The venue was rather worryingly called The 23rd Psalm Cafe and tonight, even more disconcertingly, was billed as being *Rock 4 Jesus Christ Nite*. 'New singer-songwriters welcome' the advert read. I was certainly 'new' and I liked the idea of being 'welcome', but surely any songs that were performed would need to have a connection to God or something spiritual, and the 'Bird's Egg' song was hardly that. Still, I thought, it would be good to try and lose my musical virginity in this town, and I toyed with altering the lyrics to 'Bird's Egg' making it the devil who 'the yolk was on', rather than a former lover. Perhaps the hero of the song could embrace the Lord ahead of the Prince of Darkness. But then I thought that it might actually be easier to write something new. I mean, one of those happy clappy 'we all love God' songs couldn't be hard to knock off? Surely? All you had to do was go on and on about how God had infiltrated every part of your body and that how, as a direct result of that, you no longer felt the need to inject heroin or beat up loved ones as often as you had done previously.

Spurred on by a combination of excitement and strong coffee, I took out my napkin and began to scribble some words. They flowed from me, and soon a beautiful, sensitive lyric was written.

Oh I've got the Lord in my armpit,
And I've got holy water on the knee,
He's there between my toes and he gets right up my nose,
I guess it's just his way of loving me.

Yes, I've got the Lord in my armpit,
He's a headache that really doesn't hurt,
I can feel his ripples in my pious pointy nipples,
And if you're lucky you can see them through my shirt.

Cos he's here, he's there, he's omnipresent everywhere,
He's a busy bee that Lord of mine, I don't know how he finds the time,
He's filled himself right up inside of me
(It's been over a week, I don't like to take a leak)

Yes I've got the Lord in my armpit,
And you can hear him loud and clear in my cough,
He's the wax in my ear that means I cannot hear,
Whenever people tell me to sod off.

He's there in a clenching of my buttocks,
And you can have him where you like if you don't sin,
The Lord could be your nanny in every nook and cranny,
So open up your bowels and let him in.

Exhausted by the effort, I stopped and looked at my work. I rather liked it, but I had a strong feeling that I might upset people if I ever sang it out loud, so I folded up the piece of paper and stuffed it in my back pocket, promising myself that it would stay there until I got back to England. Sometimes, I reflected, it's best to understand that you're going to be a misunderstood artist before you create any misunderstanding.

The religious theme to the day continued when I found myself with fifteen minutes to kill after having cycled into town to meet Bama for another song-pitching session. As I reached the bottom of Broadway (yes, Nashville has one too), my eyes were drawn to a huge supermarket which was set back from the main road. I noted with some interest that it was called LIFEWAY – the Christian Store. It seems that in America *everything* can be bought and sold – even God. I padlocked my bike to an adjacent parking meter (I was assuming that not everyone in the vicinity had embraced the commandment 'Thou shalt not steal') and I made my way inside.

It seemed to be a perfectly normal store which sold books, CDs, cards and T-shirts. It even had a sign up saying 'Shoplifters will be prosecuted', which seemed particularly un-Christian. Surely the sign should have read 'Shoplifters will be preached to, prayed for, and then forgiven'.

The book section had a huge stash of titles which were presumably designed to enlighten and edify but which, I'm afraid, brought out the devil in me. The cynical, scornful, sniggering devil, who, in spite of my best efforts, I'd never fully vanquished. However, given the titles of these books, I think even the most faint-hearted of Christians would have forgiven me. Each one provoked a different reaction.

The Ways of God (smirk)
He Chose the Nails (broad smile)
Building a Contagious Church (titter)
What God Does When Women Pray (audible chuckle)
The God Chasers (loud cackle)
Bad Girls of the Bible – and What We Can Learn from Them (guffaw)
Really Bad Girls of the Bible [sequel to *Bad Girls of the Bible*] (roar of laughter)

Once I'd regained my composure I became infused with a sense of mischief, and I made my way over to a middle-aged lady who was seated at one of the tills.

'Hello, this is a Christian store, isn't it?' I enquired politely.

'It most certainly is, sir,' came the even more courteous reply.

'In that case, could you tell me how much the Christians are?'

'I beg your pardon?'

'Do you sell Christians?'

'Well, no sir, we don't,' she said, slowly allowing a smile to develop. 'But we like to talk about them.'

She seemed a nice lady and I suddenly felt a little ashamed of my rather infantile behaviour.

'Of course,' I said, as meekly as I could. 'I'm sorry – I was just being silly.'

'God doesn't mind silly,' she said with a joyous beam. 'Have a good day.'

Exactly, I thought, what a wise lady. 'God doesn't mind silly.' Perhaps I should write a book of my own for this very store – called *God Likes a Laugh*. I wouldn't be looking to make a lot of money from it – just hoping to outsell *He Chose the Nails*, that's all.

'This is a very religious town, isn't it?' I said to Bama as I met him outside Sony Records.

'It's the buckle of the bible belt.'

'What do you mean?'

'Ingram Publishing used to publish the bibles for all around the world. When people think of this town then they think of music but Nashville is actually a city founded on healthcare, insurance and bible manufacturing. Music Row is relatively tiny in terms of the people it employs.'

'And how many churches are there here?'

'Well over a hundred.'

'Wow! And are you religious?'

'Well, I go to church on Sunday, but I don't pay my tithe.'

'You don't pay your what?'

'Tithe.' I was clearly none the wiser and Bama could see that some sort of explanation was needed. 'Do you want the long answer or the short answer?'

'Well,' I said, looking at my watch, 'we've still got five minutes before our first appointment, so why don't you give me the long one?'

'OK,' said Bama, visibly drawing breath. 'The "tithe" is basically a tax, and a tithe originally meant a tenth. In Leviticus, chapter 27, verse 30 it says: "A tithe of everything from the land, whether grain from the soil or fruit from the trees belongs to the Lord; it is holy to the Lord." And so the contemporary application of this is for a Christian to give 10 per cent of his income to his church. Many people probably don't reach the 10 per cent mark, but that doesn't mean that they aren't still giving thousands to their church annually. But each person has to make their own decision.'

'And you've made yours.'

'Well, I'm kinda broke most of the time. What about you?'

'Well, I've already got an agent who takes 10 per cent of what I earn. I'm not sure that I need another one.'

'Ten per cent for an agent in the sky isn't much.'

'Well, that's true. And I suppose He'd be good at being in the right place at the right time – what with being omnipresent and all that.'

Bama proceeded to take me on another mini-tour of the Nashville scene. Moving from office to office I met with 'wannabe' songwriters, successful producers, record company executives, song pluggers, singers, musicians and a host of pretty, polite receptionists. Most of these encounters involved little more than an exchange of hellos, a few pleasantries and a 'see you around', but one or two went a stage further. One such was an encounter with Anthony Smith, whom we bumped into in the corridor of a small complex of offices above a retail shoe outlet.

'Why don't you guys come into my office for a coffee?' he said, genially. 'Or tea for you, Tony, I know you English like your tea.'

'Coffee will be fine,' I said, trying to show that not all Englishmen are totally reliant on an afternoon hit of tea.

We made our way into Anthony's office which had an impressive array of framed discs adorning the walls. One said 'Congratulations to Anthony Smith for co-writing the Number One smash hit "What About Now?" by Lonestar'. The office was as impeccable as Anthony's appearance. This didn't make him particularly different to most of the characters I'd met so far – Nashville seemed to be a clean-living, almost fastidious kind of a place – but what did set him apart from the rest was that he was black.

'I came over here from Birmingham, Alabama – and after working in LA,' he explained as he reclined in his luxurious leather chair. 'I'd been writing with Donna Summer, and when she decided to come and live here I decided to give it a go too. There are a lot of fabulous musicians and writers and it's a real nice vibe living here.'

'Have you experienced any prejudice? This is the South, after all, and country music is very "white" music.'

'I don't find it hard. People think that it would be, but that really isn't the case. There are one or two racist individuals but they're not a problem because I don't want to work with them and they don't want to work with me.'

'Tony's got a great song you just gotta hear,' chimed in Bama, changing the subject completely.

My agent was doing his stuff again. On the one hand I was a little irritated that Bama was interrupting a natural conversation by suddenly making Anthony sit through my song – but then on the other hand, I was here to sell this song and it wasn't going to get sold if no-one heard it.

As the first few bars of the song began, Anthony nodded approvingly.

'I like it,' he said, looking at me without really making proper eye contact.

However, that was the only positive reaction for the entire three minutes forty seconds that it took for the masterpiece to run its course. At its conclusion he stood up, removed the CD from the player and turned to me.

'What was that lyric?' he asked. 'You broke my heart like a *what?*'

'Like a bird's egg.'

'Oh, I see.'

Not only had Anthony been unable to identify correctly what I'd been singing about, but even when it had been explained to him, it failed to raise even the faintest of smiles.

'What do you think?' asked Bama.

'I think it's a good recording and I like the tune. But I don't think that lyric will work in this town.'

'Really?' I said, rather dejectedly.

'I just don't think that people here will find that funny.'

Anthony certainly didn't. In fact the playing of the song seemed to precipitate the conclusion of our little impromptu meeting and we were soon shaking hands and wishing each other luck. I tried hard not to show that I was really rather hurt. To throw him off the trail I smiled excessively, in a manner which I now imagine may have looked a touch scary.

'Anthony,' I asked as we got to the door, 'what do you enjoy most about Nashville?'

'Well, I always tell people that it's two things.'

'And what are they?'

'Leaving and coming back.'

This was a remark which was either laden with significance, or totally meaningless. I don't know why, but I gave Anthony the benefit of the doubt. But right now, the thought of leaving this place seemed a much more exciting proposition than ever bothering to come back. But that could all change very quickly.

Especially since there was a very exciting party invitation waiting for me back at the Writers' Boarding House.

~

Annie, seemingly like a lot of Steve and Robin's friends, had co-written a lot of big hits, including the monster 'This Kiss' with Robin. Her party, therefore, was going to be in a substantial house just out of town and would be attended by the elite of Nashville's songwriting community. A great opportunity for me, or so I was told, to meet important people and to 'network'.

Annie's home reflected her successful career. It was set back from the road, nestled among leafy, well-tended gardens. Given that it was built on one storey, its size manifested itself in width. It really was an exceptionally wide house. When Steve, Robin and I were greeted and ushered inside by a uniformed member of the catering team, most of the other guests were already mingling in the capacious living room. The next ten minutes were a manic merry-go-round of introductions, at the end of which I was starting to feel dizzy. I met a lot of people, but I didn't get a chance to have a meaningful exchange with any of them, and something about the atmosphere in the room told me that this was unlikely to happen.

I may have imagined it, but there seemed to be some kind of status thing going on. If people knew who you were and what you'd achieved, then you were that much more worth an investment of time. This may have been a birthday party but it hadn't escaped my attention that business was the number one topic of conversation. 'So and so' is recording this track, 'so and so' has just got a track on the new Garth Brooks album, and so on, and so on, and so on. All of this was understandable enough I suppose because at parties that's what people do – talk about things that they have in common with each other – but for me it just seemed a little too energised, too important, and too ... well, too much. I wanted to call out 'relax already, none of this really *matters*', but it would have been rude, especially since I was drinking other people's drink, eating other people's food, and didn't really have a concise and persuasive argument to offer in terms of what *did* actually matter.

After about an hour or so of small talk in which I was very much under the wing of Steve and Robin, I took the brave decision of breaking out on my own and soon I found myself in the garden, not far from a slightly eccentric-looking woman who was standing by the floodlit fish pond. I wandered over.

'Hello,' I said.

'Hi,' she replied, genially enough.

I hesitated. I was unsure of what to say next. I didn't want to ask if she was a songwriter because if she was, which was almost certainly the case, then that would have meant that the music business would probably become the topic of our conversation, and I'd had enough of that inside the house. Even though I had specifically come to this town to make inroads in the music business, just now it was the last thing I wanted to talk about.

'This is a very wide house,' I said, eventually.

The woman looked up at me, surprised. Her face seemed to light up.

'Yes,' she said. 'Too wide in my view.'

'It's a lovely house, but there's wide and there's too wide, and this is nudging towards being the latter.'

It was an odd beginning to a conversation, but its very oddness seemed to be what pleased us both.

'What do you think of the fish?' she asked, gesturing with her head towards the surface of the water.

'They are colourful and mostly about the right width,' I replied. 'Beyond that I have no real view.'

'You're weird,' she said, smiling.

'Thank you very much.'

'Not at all. Better to be weird than boring.'

Our unlikely but nonetheless pleasing conversation continued for some fifteen minutes during which time we managed to acquire very little information about each other, other than the fact that we preferred talking nonsense to business. This lady's name, career and marital status all remained a mystery.

'I have to go now,' she suddenly said, glancing at her watch.

'What? Go home? Already? It's only ten o'clock.'

'Not home. I have to go back to work. Inside.'

'I don't follow.'

'I'm in charge of the food. We have to clear it all away now that everyone has finished eating. It'll take us about an hour, but if you're still around then we could carry on our little chat.'

'Yeah. OK. You got yourself a date. 11.00 p.m., back here, by the pond.'

'Bye.'

'Bye. Don't drop any plates.'

'I won't, I'm a professional.'

I returned to the stagnant sanity of the party. My status hadn't appeared to have changed much and I remained some-one that no one was especially interested in. I suppose I'd hoped that being from England with a 'cute' accent, I might have made more of an impression, but the fact remained that I was at a party where the guests were well travelled and regularly came into contact with English writers, producers and artists, so I was nothing special. My reason for being in Nashville didn't make me a particularly attractive proposition for social engagement either, given that I was essentially a 'wannabe' songwriter – and one, for that matter, who was on the very bottom rung of the ladder. (For some reason, a decade earlier 'Stutter Rap' had made no inroads in the country mar-ket, it seemed.) In songwriting terms I shouldn't really have been here at all. So, with my ego unpampered, I did what most British people do in this situation, and began to make more regular visits to the fridge (which was also very wide, by the way) for beer, lovely beer.

'You seem like you may be starting to get a little drunk,' said my unusual lady friend some time later, after I'd greeted her at the fishpond.

'It's something I do well. I'm not one who believes in hiding his light under a bushel.'

'At the risk of being a little conventional, can I ask you what you're doing here at this party?'

I gave my new-found chum the full story, doing my best not to slur. After I'd finished my explanation, she began to laugh.

'So let's get this straight,' she said. 'You gotta have a hit record to win a bet and you're at a party with a living room full of successful songwriters, producers and publishers. But you make an appointment to have a conversation by the fishpond with the lady who's doing the catering?'

'Is that not the best way to make it to the top?'

'Not that I'm aware of.'

'But I don't like it in there,' I said, gesturing towards the house. 'There's a distinct absence of joy about the place. But I like you. You're nice.'

'Thank you. I think so too. But even so, it's not like I'm going to be of any use to you.'

'That's exactly it!' I said excitedly.

'What is?'

'That's exactly what I don't like about parties like these – they're full of people hoping they'll meet someone who'll be of use to them.'

'Welcome to Nashville, sweetie.'

'I see. Thank you.'

'Hey, wait a minute. Does that mean you are saying I'm of no use to you?'

'It's precisely *because* you are of no use to me that you have become useful to me. You are providing a perfect antidote to the usefulness of the others.'

'You're weird.'

'Thank you.'

I became thoughtful and looked into the fishpond, which now seemed to have twice as many fish in it.

'Hey, tell me honestly now,' I said, attempting deep and meaningful, 'do you think it's possible that those people inside the house have somehow missed the point?'

She thought for a moment and then looked up, with a new and earnest expression.

'No,' she said firmly, 'I think that the point has missed them.'

A profound thought. Certainly after eight bottles of beer.

'I have to go now, my friend,' said my mystery pondside pal rather suddenly, almost as if her recent emission of wisdom had drained her. 'I think it's good that we don't know each other's names. Somehow it makes our time together more special.'

'It's been really nice meeting you.'

'You're a nice guy. I wish you luck.' Then through a broad beam she added, 'To do what you're trying to do you're gonna need luck by the barrel-load.'

When I finally went back inside, after a solitary period of reflection by the pond, the majority of guests had gone. The five or six who remained were draped across sofas listening intently to some music. No-one was talking. Then I noticed Steve, who was hovering on the edge of proceedings, not quite in or out of the room.

'What's going on?' I enquired, after I'd moved across to join him.

'They're listening to some demos of Annie's new songs.'

'Really?'

Steve nodded.

'But it's her birthday party,' I protested. 'She should be dancing and having a good time – not thinking about work.'

'That's why she's successful,' he said, with a shrug and a wry smile.

It seemed I had a lot to learn.

CHAPTER 5 LET'S GO BOWLING

For the next few days I was back on the treadmill. As before Bama would pick me up and drive me to various meetings with a host of different people from the business. His selling skills meant that I was generally portrayed as being far more important than I actually was, and consequently I got to meet many people of a higher status than might have been expected from a first visit to this town. I had lunch with one of radio's top morning DJs Gerry House, and I was a special guest at a record company showcase for a new artist. (For one slightly dull hour I watched a man in a stetson sounding exactly like every other male country singer I'd heard since I'd got into town.) I also met with a reporter from *Country Music Weekly*.

'How would you describe the current country music scene?' I asked him, after Bama had introduced me.

'I can give it to you in one word,' he replied. 'Turmoil.'

'Why?'

'Because nobody really knows what the music is supposed to *be* any more.'

'What do you mean?'

'Just listen to the song "Murder On Music Row", then you'll know what I'm talking about.'

Bama later explained that 'Murder On Music Row' had been a track recorded by George Strait which had never been released as a single but had caused huge controversy when it had been nominated for Country Music Association Song of the Year. Later that night I listened to a copy of it back at my digs. It soon became clear that it was a song lamenting the changes which had come about in the last five years since country had started to reach out to a much wider audience.

> *For the steel guitar no longer cries and fiddles barely play*
> *But drums and rock'n'roll guitars are mixed up in your face*

Other lines included:

> *Old Hank wouldn't have a chance on today's radio*

A reference to Hank Williams, generally regarded as being the single most important figure in country music history. And:

> *The mighty dollar and the lust for worldwide fame*
> *Slowly killed tradition and for that someone should hang.*

It seemed that the writers of this song felt rather strongly about the subject. While I could understand their frustration at the potential loss of their beloved art form to the commercial hybrid sound of 'New Country', it did seem rather harsh to suggest that the punishment for 'mixing drums and rock'n'roll guitars up in your face' should be death by hanging. Or is that me just being a wet liberal? I began to wonder what particular form of execution they would favour for me, should 'Bird's Egg' ever become a million seller. But alas, that didn't seem to be a matter for too much concern just now.

Just as the sun went down over Nashville I straddled my bike once again and began the now familiar cycle into town, this time with the added burden of a guitar, which was slung over my shoulder. Tonight I was determined to perform my song to a live audience, and I'd been told about the Sixties-sounding 'Pub of Love' which was supposed to be a cool place to get up and strum your stuff. I was a little nervous when I set off but all worries about the performance were soon displaced by the greater levels of concern which resulted from the task of cycling an old bike whilst carrying a guitar. I wobbled and wavered but to my credit I didn't fall off, and I was soon pulling into the street of my final destination. So far, so good. I tried not to think about getting home, because it was almost certain that the ordeal of singing my song to a Nashville audience would demand subsequent and substantial beer consumption, and that wouldn't necessarily contribute to a safe return leg.

When I arrived at the 'Pub of Love' I realised that my previous concerns were of no matter whatsoever because the pub bore all the hallmarks of an establishment which had closed down some weeks earlier. The door was boarded up and the windows were covered with fly posters, mostly advertising gigs in rival venues which had probably contributed to putting this place out of business. The irony was not lost on me. I sighed, not just because I'd cycled all that way for no reason with the added burden of a guitar, but because I suspected that the 'Pub of Love' might have lost out to the burgeoning new chain of bars that might be called 'Pub of Dollars' and which would care little about promoting live music.

I consulted my map only to learn that the other venues which had 'open mic nights' that evening were well beyond my cycling range. Shit, why had I been so stubborn about the car thing? Not having a motorised vehicle really was proving to be a severe hindrance. At this rate there was a real danger that I could return to London without giving even one 'live' airing to my song.

A brief sightseeing tour was quickly slotted into the schedule to replace the 'Pub of Love' experience, and I headed downtown to the part of Nashville which attracts the coach loads of out-of-towners. In this area, bar after bar offered a live band, most of which seemed to be pretty damn good. Unsurprising I suppose, given that Nashville is a town with no shortage of tip-top musicians. Down on the banks of the Cumberland river I saw a huge paddle steamer, and for a moment I imagined I experienced a part of Mark Twain's South, until I noticed the oversized tourists waddling over to it from the nearby coaches. I cycled up a couple of blocks and peered in through the window at the Wildhorse Saloon. On the distant stage, across a huge auditorium, I could just make out an obese punter being hauled up from the audience and urged to sing by a slick MC with glamorous assistant in tow. The audience tittered and cackled. It didn't look like quality entertainment to me, so I remounted my bike and resumed my tour of the area. However, just as I set off I was approached by a policeman who was at least fifteen years younger than me.

'What are you doing sir?' he asked, authoritatively.

It has struck me that policemen are like teachers in this regard – they ask questions to which they already know the answer.

'I'm cycling my bike,' I said timidly, but with unerring accuracy.

'On the sidewalk?' he said, with eyebrows raised.

'Yes, on the sidewalk. Is that not allowed?'

'No sir, it is not.'

I wondered for a moment what punishment might befall me as a result of my cruel and thoughtless behaviour.

'Sorry,' I said, as pathetically as could, hoping that this would be the required level of contrition.

'OK, sir, I'm gonna let you go on your way with only a warning,' he said, in the tired manner of someone who'd said these words a hundred times before. 'But I don't wanna find you cycling on the sidewalk again.'

I felt a little ashamed to be guilty of an offence normally the preserve of fourteen year olds, but that feeling was tempered by a small glow of pride – that at least I was prepared to rebel against the system, albeit in a way unlikely to make any front-page headlines.

What the incident did do though was make me deeply concerned that my trip was losing its way. I had come to Nashville on a mission and, after all the meetings and opportunities I'd had, here I was being told off by a policeman for cycling on the pavement. Wasn't there a case to suggest that I was underachieving just a little?

I stopped at the next callbox and lifted the receiver with a great sense of purpose.

'Steve?' I said, when the call had been answered.

'Yes.'

'It's Tony here. You know that recording session you've booked in the studio for tomorrow – how many songs are you going to record?'

'Four. Why?'

'Well, could you make it five, and include "Sex'n' Trucks'n'Rock'n'Roll"? I'll help pay for the studio time and musicians.'

'Well ... there might be time I suppose.'

'Please!'

'Oh OK, I'll see what I can do,' he said, a little surprised by the urgency of my tone. 'Tony, you seem a little desperate suddenly.'

'I've just had an incident with a policeman which has focused the mind somewhat.'

'My God, are you OK?'

'Yes. Just about. I'll explain when I see you. Bye.'

'Bye ... er ... yes ... bye.'

'Sex'n'Trucks'n'Rock'n'Roll' was a second song that Steve and I had written together after our initial effort with 'Bird's Egg'. Steve actually preferred it, thinking that because it was less jokey and without a bloody great pun in the chorus, it was actually a more viable proposition to find a Nashville artist who might record it. I'd always maintained that 'Bird's Egg' had that something special, but maybe, just maybe, I'd have to concede that I'd been wrong all along. Perhaps recording the song at this session, which Steve had originally booked just to produce demos of songs which he'd written with other co-writers, might furnish it with the magical quality which would make it a hit. And having a hit was what really mattered, after all.

During the long cycle home, long stretches of which were tiresomely uphill, I kept an eye out for a suitable place to dine, but every restaurant I passed seemed too formal and too full of couples, and I just didn't fancy dining alone in any of them. In the end, it was the banal takeaway food outlet Checkers which got my vote, and I made an impulse purchase of a veggie burger and fries and sat down on a wall to consume this gastronomic delight. Behind me I heard a man humming, and I turned around to see a scruffy black guy studying Checkers' exciting menu. Then he started singing the words 'Why do I have to be poor? When am I gonna be rich?' – to no recognisable tune. He saw me and I smiled at him, which may have been a mistake on my part, given that it caused him to come over and ask for money.

'You got a spare dollar man?' he enquired, unthreateningly.

'Yes I do as a matter of fact,' I replied, feeling and sounding extraordinarily English.

I handed him a dollar bill, I suppose because I'd been touched by his plaintive musical refrain.

'Hey man, that's cool. Thanks, man. You're a cool dude – what's your name?'

'My name is Tony.'

'My name is Cleve,' he said, extending a dirty hand for me to shake. 'I'm hungry. Real hungry. I've had a cool evening though man. I've had two Budweisers and a doobie – and that's me done. That's all I need, man. I'm high and I'm happy.'

Without waiting for an invitation, Cleve sat down on the wall beside me and thus provided me with a totally new experience, because I'd never before eaten dinner alongside anyone who referred to a joint as a doobie.

'One doobie and I'm done man, that's all I need,' repeated Cleve, seemingly expecting some kind of response.

'One doobie, splendid, well done,' I said, sounding like Prince bloody Charles.

'I don't do crack. Man, that's bad.'

'Again – well done.'

'What do you mean, man?'

'Well done for sticking to the doobies.'

'I like you man. Wait a minute I got something for you,' he said as he began reaching around in his pocket.

I became a little nervous.

'Here you are man,' he said, brandishing a scrap of paper. 'Here's my card. Give me a call some time. Let's go bowling.'

This was all rather sudden. Generally speaking I like to know someone a little better before I make any serious commitment to an evening of bowling.

'This is where I used to work,' said Cleve, producing another battered card from his pocket.

High though Cleve may have been, it was difficult to work out which part of his brain had conceived the idea of passing on the card of his former place of employment.

'You can keep it,' he said, nodding towards the card.

'Thanks.'

Excellent. If I got bored in the morning I could phone the number on the card and have someone tell me that Cleve didn't work there any more. That would be fun.

'I got some other stuff to show you,' said Cleve, rummaging in his pocket again, seemingly genuine in his belief that he was producing material of use to me.

'See this?' he said, now producing a crumpled photo of a woman. 'This used to be my lady.'

'I see.'

'In fact, she used to be my wife.'

Oh dear. I had to do something fast before my dinner guest either became maudlin, or spent the next twenty minutes providing me with more evidence which backed up something which was already abundantly clear – that Cleve's life used to be much better than it was now.

'Cleve,' I said, seizing the initiative and rising to my feet, 'I have to go now – but I have your number and I'll give you a call some time and we'll go bowling.'

'You do that. You call man. We'll go bowling.'

'Goodbye,' I said with a wave, as I began walking towards my bicycle. 'Speak to you soon.'

'Bye man.'

As I pedalled my way back home through the darkness, which could have been harbouring a hundred other Cleves, I imagined a conversation which could take place in the morning.

'How'd it go last night, Tony?'

'Oh, it went OK, Steve. Thanks for asking.'

'Make any contacts?'

'One. This guy gave me his card.'

'Will you follow it up?'

'We'll see.'

In truth though, it could be argued that Cleve had been as useful to me as anyone I'd yet met in Nashville.

I woke up excited. I was about to do what I'd heard countless pop stars talk about doing in interviews. Today I was going 'into the studio'. True, I'd spent hours in studios of late, but they'd all been cramped appendages to residential property. Today I was going to a commercial recording studio, where staff would greet you, offer you coffee, go and fetch lunch and generally treat you like you were important. Of course, you were paying handsomely for the privilege of being pampered in this way but it still felt exciting. Especially in Nashville. Today I was going 'into the studio' in Nashville, USA. I lay on my bed, fully awake and yet somehow still able to dream.

'And now ladies and gentlemen, Song of the Year goes to two guys who aren't from this town, nor are they from this country.

They are two British guys who came to Nashville with little more than a head full of ideas and big hearts. They've reminded us that Country can be fun. Let's hear it for Tony Hawks and Steve Booker, writers of *Country Music Weekly*'s Song of The Year "Sex'n'Trucks'n'Rock'n'Roll".'

I rose proudly, but instead of moving to the stage, I headed for the bathroom and embarked on routine morning ablutions. I could still hear the applause though. It continued right through the washing of the face and well into the brushing of the teeth. Thankfully it had died away by the time I found myself in a seated position. Even my well-honed imagination couldn't win the battle against reality and sustain this glorious illusion through the unglamorous exertions of this next undertaking.

It was a beautiful, crisp, bright, autumnal morning. It felt great to be on my bike. On my bike and on my way 'into the studio'. I returned each motorist's suspicious look with a life-affirming smile. Yes, I was a man on a ladies' bicycle in a tramp's grey overcoat, but what they didn't know from behind the wheels of their oversized, gas-guzzling motor cars, was that I was on the way to the studio.

I arrived at eleven, only to discover that the studio was in fact a dull-looking brick building with no windows, and resembling a small industrial unit. There was nothing about the exterior which gave a clue as to the magic which lay within. I rang the buzzer and soon the door was opened and I was greeted by an enthusiastic teenager with long hair tied into a pony tail, which I presume is compulsory in places like these, even though it ceased to be fashionable decades earlier.

'Who are you working with?' he asked.

'Steve Booker.'

'The British guy?'

'Yes, that's him.'

'Are you British too?'

'I am, yes.'

'I thought so. I like the way you guys speak. It's through here. Can I get you a coffee?'

'Yes thanks. White, one sugar.'

I was led into the main control room where I could see the back of a man who was seated before a huge recording console.

Massive speakers towered in front of him, and lights flashed and flickered on the displays of a vast array of bewildering machinery. Advances in technology over the last twenty years have enabled miniaturisation of all this gadgetry, and recording studios can now be crammed into bedrooms, but here, as in America itself, 'big' was celebrated and 'big' meant better.

The man before me spun round in his chair.

'Hi, I'm Herb, your engineer,' he said, proffering his hand for greeting. 'I guess you must be Tony.'

'That's me, how's it all going?'

'Just fine. As luck would have it, we're just moving on to your song.'

Herb gestured to his left and I turned to see that beyond a large glass division, there was a huge live room with musicians set up and waiting for instructions from the control room. In the middle of the floor, with screens and partitions all around him, sat the drummer, headphones on, and waving his sticks to get the attention of the other musicians who were cocooned in their own little partitioned booths. I felt another rush of excitement. Hey, Nashville musicians in a Nashville studio, and about to play my song too.

Herb pushed down a button on the recording desk and spoke through a microphone.

'OK, you guys,' he said, 'ready to go for a rehearsal?'

'We're ready Herb,' came the voice of the drummer, through the towering speakers. 'A one, a two, a one, two, three, four ...'

And that was it. The band were off. An eight bar intro with a wailing guitar, backed by a driving drum beat and pumping bass. I could hear an organ too, and then Steve's guide vocal kicked in. I never could have imagined the song could sound so good, so quickly, and seemingly with so little effort. It was magical. Just moments ago it hadn't existed for me in this form and yet now I was hearing what felt like the definitive article. A country song, played by country musicians.

Steve sang well, although the plan was to replace his vocal later in the day when a session singer would add an authentic country vocal.

'Hey, that's a cool lyric,' said Herb, as he reached to full-stretch and moved some faders on the enormous desk.

You could tell that Herb was an engineer in Nashville, by the mere fact that he listened to the words. Normally the lyrics would be the last concern of a studio engineer, who in my experience could work for eight hours on a song and then still not have a clue what it was about. Our song told the story of a singing star who had become jaded by years of touring and adoration, and longed for the simple life.

On stage with my guitar I guess people think my life is pretty cool
But in my bid to be a star I wasted all that stuff I learned in school
I could have been a doctor I could have got ahead
I could have been a big noise down on Wall St but all I've got
instead ... is ...

Chorus
Sex'n'trucks'n'rock'n'roll, that's all that's out there on the road
Screaming girls and sell out shows — My God it's a heavy load
It's a hell of a life trying to get through it
But I guess someone's gotta do it
All that fun can take its toll
Sex'n'trucks'n'rock'roll

I looked through into the live room and saw the musicians with headphones on, eyes focused on the musical notation in front of them, feet tapping, and deep in concentration. Piano, bass, drums, electric guitar, acoustic guitar and pedal steel guitar merging to create one full sound. I caught Steve's eye and he winked at me. What a thrill to hear our work becoming a song, and without the usual procedure involving computers, synthesizers or drum machines. Right now 'Sex'n'Trucks'n'Rock'n'Roll' existed because human beings were playing it.

When the musicians had finished running the song, Herb communicated with the musicians through the microphone on the recording desk, and they exchanged a few thoughts on the performance which had just passed.

'I think we can go for one now,' said the drummer, after he'd successfully officiated on a couple of points which had been raised by the guitarist and the bass player.

'What do you think, Tony?' asked Herb, turning to me in the control room.

'Er ... yup ... sounds good to me. I think they should go for one.'

'Are you happy with the general sound?'

'Yes, it's terrific,' I gushed.

'I've put the guitars at ten to two. Is that OK?'

Oh dear. I realised what had happened here. Herb was assuming that I was some kind of big shot songwriter or music producer, and that I understood this kind of technical speak. As far as Herb was concerned, I'd travelled all the way from the UK to oversee this project and that wasn't something you did unless you knew what you were doing. Except in this case. In this case that logic didn't apply. I didn't have a clue.

'Yup, that sounds fine,' I said, trying to sound knowledgeable and authoritative.

Evidently I did a fine job, because Herb had more to ask.

'Shall I put the Lexicon on the steel?'

'Good idea.'

'I'm gonna put slapback on Steve's vocal, just to see if that's the sound you'll eventually want to go for.'

'Yes, why not.'

'And shall I split the guitars?'

Now hang on, surely splitting the guitars was going too far. Wouldn't it be just plain irresponsible, certainly without the permission of the guitars' owners?

'OK Herb. Split the guitars. And let's go for a take!'

God, I was good. This record producing was a whole lot easier than I'd imagined it to be.

Five minutes later the track was announced by Herb as being 'in the can', and everyone moved on to the next song. No cups of tea, no joking around, no messing. No opportunity for me to listen back to it over and over again. This was work, and I was around professionals.

'Happy, Tony?' asked Herb.

'Very happy,' I replied, my boyish grin surely revealing that I wasn't the experienced producer that Herb had taken me for.

At the end of the session, Steve's song plugger Whitney arrived and listened to all the recordings. She seemed happy with most of what had been done, but I noticed that Steve waited till last before playing her our track.

'Hey, that's cool,' she said, as the end refrain faded. 'It's much better than I thought it was going to be. When you told me about it I thought that the idea sucked.'

'It's a triumph, Whitney,' I said, with my tongue half in my cheek. 'You get someone to cover it and it'll be a huge smash.'

'Maybe,' she said, thoughtfully. 'But you'll have to take the sex out.'

'What do you mean?'

'Well, you can't have a Country song with the word "sex" in it. No radio station will play it.'

'But this is the twenty-first century.'

'Doesn't make any difference.'

'So what shall we do?' asked Steve.

'Just change that word for something else,' said Whitney.

'But that's the whole point of the song,' said Steve. 'We can't just change it to another word of one syllable. The whole meaning would change.'

'He's right,' I said in support. '"Eggs'n'Trucks'n'Rock'n' Roll" just wouldn't be the same.'

'How about this,' chimed in Herb. '"Sixpacks, Trucks'n' Rock'n'Roll"?'

This was a pretty good suggestion I thought, but Steve was having none of it. He seemed to be a little upset that any change was required at all, but a decision needed to be taken before the session singer arrived to sing the song. And he was due in ten minutes.

'What about "Chicks'n'Trucks'n'Rock'n'Roll"?' suggested Whitney.

The thoughtful silence that greeted it said it all. No-one really liked it but it was the best we were going to come up with.

'OK, we'll go with that,' said Steve, unenthusiastically.

Whitney looked at me and I nodded. I couldn't bring myself to embellish my reluctant approval with sound.

'Phone call for you, Tony,' said Herb, holding up the phone's receiver and releasing us all from a slightly tense atmosphere that had developed.

'Who can this be?' I asked 'Nobody knows I'm here.'

'It's Billy Block,' said Herb.

'*The* Billy Block?' enquired Whitney.

'Sounded like him,' said Herb.

Whitney looked at me in amazement.

'How *do* you do it? You're in Nashville less than a week and you've got Billy Block phoning you.'

'Who's Billy Block?' I asked.

I didn't know it yet, but he was the man who was going to provide me with an evening that I was going to remember for a very long time.

CHAPTER 6 THE GUITAR PULL

I'd forgotten, but I had met Billy Block before. After lunch at the Sunset Grill with the breakfast show presenter Gerry House, Billy had been introduced and we'd shared the briefest of conversations. Billy, I now recalled, wrote and presented a popular Country Music TV show called *Western Beat*. Apparently he'd been at the recording studio earlier that morning on business, and he'd heard that Steve and I were coming in for our session, so he thought he'd ring on the off chance that I might be interested in the evening's events.

'Do you want to come to a guitar pull tonight?' he'd asked on the phone.

A guitar pull? What was this man talking about? I didn't need to pull a guitar. Did I?

'Er, I'm not sure,' I'd replied politely. 'What happens at a guitar pull?'

'Everyone brings a guitar and sits in a circle, and everybody sings one song each. They're some really special people coming – you'd be a fool to miss it.'

Not wishing to appear a fool, I'd told Billy that he could count on me being there, and now, just as we'd arranged, he was picking me up at seven o'clock sharp.

'Tony, this is my wife Jill, and this is our friend Carter,' said Billy as I climbed into his people carrier.

'Hi,' I said. 'Thanks for bringing me along. I've never been to a guitar pull before.'

'Oh they're great, you'll love it,' said Jill, and Carter smiled warmly.

These seemed like nice people.

'Where are we going exactly?'

'It's around a half hour drive up to Robert's house,' answered Billy. 'It's in the heart of the Tennessee countryside. You'll like it.'

Robert, I learned in the course of the journey, liked hosting guitar pulls. He lived in a big house and surrounded himself with exquisite antiques, but no one was entirely sure what the source of his money had been.

Robert greeted us heartily after we'd parked and walked up the long drive which led to the house.

'Come in and get yourselves some food and a drink,' he announced, in his rather cultured, Ivy League accent, 'and let me show you where you can leave your guitars.'

He led us through an immaculate house filled with beautiful wooden antiques, and into a room which was already jammed full of guitar cases, even though half the guitar-playing guests hadn't arrived as yet.

'Have a good time, Tony,' said Robert, gesturing towards the kitchen. 'Get yourself a drink and some food. Billy knows pretty much everyone who's coming, and I'm sure he'll make you feel at home. He's a great host.'

And Billy most certainly was. Every five minutes I was introduced to another impressive-sounding character from the Nashville music scene. I got the feeling that I was probably meeting huge country stars, but luckily I was able to behave with relative normality, being blissfully unaware of who was who in this city. In my experience, knowing too much about the person to whom you're talking when they know damn all about you, makes for awkward and stilted conversation. A few years earlier I'd been introduced to Paul McCartney after the opening night screening of *Wayne's World II* in London. I remember, I'd struggled to turn it into a lively or memorable exchange. His fame had barred the normal conversational routes to me. I could hardly kick things off with:

'So what do you do?'

Neither could I pay him polite compliments:

'I enjoyed The Beatles very much, they were a good group, well done.'

What actually happened was that Paul took the initiative,

probably being quite au fait with such social situations, and we'd ended up having a short chat about the movie *Spinal Tap*, until he made his excuses and moved politely along. The interesting point is that I remember every single detail of that meeting whereas I would be extremely surprised if Paul McCartney had any recollection of it having taken place at all. I guess this is what happens when ordinary people meet the Queen. The monarch must encounter so many countless oiks like you and me, that she is hardly likely to remember the conversation which had taken place, whereas the likelihood is that we would be able to recall its every last detail.

'God that's fantastic – you met the Queen!' people would say in response to our proud boasts. 'What did she say to you?'

'She said that she was very happy to be in our town and she said that it was a beautiful day and that she hoped that there would be many more like it this summer.'

'Wow.'

I like to think that every now and then the Queen is tempted to abuse her position and to mess things up for us by being deliberately weird.

'God that's fantastic – you met the Queen! What did she say to you?'

'She said that she thought all wood should be painted green and that it ought to be illegal to suck on mint humbugs in built-up areas.'

'Err ... wow. How lovely.'

In present company, however, not being in awe of who was before me didn't really make conversation flow any easier. These people lived in and around Music City USA and that was precisely what they enjoyed talking about. My lack of knowledge in this area was being hopelessly exposed. With each introduction, Billy offered a short curriculum vitae of the new person I was meeting, the details of which went sailing over my head. It must have just looked plain rude when I failed to make any reference to their glittering careers.

Things weren't any less challenging when I finally met someone of whose work I was vaguely aware.

'This is Raul,' said Billy as we stood in the yard to the rear of the kitchen, enjoying an al fresco beer. 'He's in The Mavericks.'

Aha! This was great. I knew The Mavericks, I'd greatly enjoyed their hit song 'Dance The Night Away' and the way they'd brought the use of brass sections and a Latin influence into the country genre. What's more I even recognised this Raul guy. And yet I was still stuck.

'Hi,' said Raul.

'Hi,' I replied.

Pause.

The onus seemed to be on me to come up with a passable opening gambit, but all I could think of was 'Are you busy at the moment?' or 'Nice evening, isn't it?'

Neither was impressive. I had to come up with something better, and there was an awkward pause while I thought hard.

'Nice evening, isn't it?' I said, almost blurting out the words in order to fill the now elongated silence.

'Yuh,' replied a lacklustre Raul at low volume, affording it the amount of effort it deserved.

There was another pause, until Billy turned back to us, having just chatted freely with a woman behind him.

'That's a beautiful old Mercedes I saw you pull up in, Raul,' he said with a confident smile. 'What year is it?'

My, Billy was good. If only I'd thought of that. Not only did he know these guys' careers inside out, but he knew what they enjoyed talking about.

'Do you know, Billy, I don't know its exact age,' replied Raul. 'Its history's a little confused but I think it's early seventies.'

'What do you think, Tony?' asked Billy, generously trying to bring me in on things.

It would have been social suicide to have said what I'd really thought – that it was a nice shiny old car with an engine up one end and a boot up the other. Far better to bluff.

'Definitely early seventies,' I offered authoritatively, and in a tone of voice which suggested that I had more to say on the matter.

Except that I had nothing more to add. I was already at full stretch on cars. So instead I hovered around hoping that I could contribute something to the discourse wherever it next veered.

'I'm working with K.T. Oslin right now,' said Raul proudly.

'Wow, that's amazing,' replied Billy.

They both looked at me, presumably to see if I wanted in on this. I didn't.

It was all too much.

'Excuse me, but I'm just heading off to the loo,' I said.

Raul grinned, no doubt because of my quaint use of the word 'loo', then he re-immersed himself in 'music biz' talk with Billy.

On the way to the loo, john, men's room, lav or bog – depending on your cultural heritage – I cursed myself for not being better at these kind of parties. This was where you made new contacts and found new and influential people with whom you might be able to collaborate. For the second time on my trip I was in the company of Nashville's songwriting elite and for the second time I was letting myself down badly. The trouble was that I was just no use at making small talk. I guess that back in England I'd have been able to fall back on football in emergencies like these. Oh, for the ease of a London party where 'Chelsea are having a bit of a rough run at the moment' will do you for a good five minutes, even if it only leads to a discussion about how much someone can't stand the wretched game.

The good news was that there was a queue outside the toilets. Somehow this made the prospect of conversation far less daunting because all of us were there for a reason and it really didn't matter that much whether we got on with each other or not. I soon began chatting with an utterly charming fellow in glasses who resembled a university lecturer, and who had just returned from a trip to England. He was so nice I didn't even mind that his name was Randy. His demeanour made me wonder if he was a little like me, a songwriter with ambition, but who hadn't yet cracked the scene. He seemed far more gentle than all the other characters I'd met to date. Maybe he didn't have the hardness and determination to make it in this business.

'Well, I'm next,' he said, as the toilet door opened before him. 'I guess this is where our conversation ends.'

'Yes.'

It would have been rude to have followed him in.

'A "guitar pull",' said Eric, 'is an old Nashville expression for tonight's proceedings.'

The large circle of chairs which filled the capacious living room was now filled by writers and musicians of diverse age and appearance. I counted twenty-five of us, all with guitars in our laps or resting against our legs like devoted offspring. Me, I was wedged between a large, rotund man brandishing a fiddle, and Eric, a jovial chap who had travelled up from Washington, DC especially for this event.

'In the old days,' continued Eric, 'the players would have been seated in a circle like we are, but there would only have been one guitar between everyone, and it would have been passed to each player in turn.'

'But why guitar *pull*?' I enquired like an eager student.

'Because the guitar got pulled from one player to the other.'

Given the present seating arrangements, a guitar would be all I'd allow to have pulled by those seated either side of me.

Our brief conversation was interrupted by Robert who was now standing in the middle of the room, clearing his throat.

'Let's kick things off with a little prayer,' he said.

What followed said a lot about the pious and God-loving nature of this town. Everyone in the room closed their eyes (except me of course – my eyes obviously needed to be open to have made such an observation) and Robert thanked the Lord for the food we had eaten and for the miracle of the music which we were about to give and receive. Then everyone in the room said amen to that. Including me.

I found it hard to imagine an evening like this beginning in such a way at a party involving the London or New York music biz, where drink and drugs were more likely to be the gods of the night. I looked around me and saw how relaxed everybody was, and I felt that this was not a big 'I'm a born again Christian' thing, but more of a polite thank you for all the joys of this world. I felt rather cheered by the gentle warmth of it all. Here was a room full of people who had just been charged with love's spirit instead of that from a whisky bottle. I presumed it most unlikely that there would be a fight at tonight's guitar pull. Unless somebody pulled the wrong thing, and I happened to be on the other end of it.

'So who's going to go first?' asked Robert, looking around the circle of songwriters for likely candidates.

I pitied whoever it was who would have to fulfil this role, for they would have to perform the dual function of breaking the ice and setting the standard. Nobody's body language suggested that they were putting themselves forward.

'Well,' said Robert, with the air of someone who had reached a decision, 'I think that since Eric has come all the way from Washington, he should go first.'

'How do you work *that* out?' protested an indignant Eric.

'I thought that the one who has travelled the furthest should show us the way.'

'But I haven't travelled the furthest,' offered Eric confidently. 'Tony here has come all the way from London.'

'Oh yes, sorry Eric, I forgot about Tony,' said Robert, spinning around to face me. 'Maybe you'd like to sing us something to get the ball rolling.'

Everyone in the room was now looking at me.

'Really?' I squeaked, almost mouselike.

'Absolutely, pick up your guitar and do your worst.'

I wasn't worried about doing my worst. My concern was that I would do my best, and that would be the worst they heard all evening.

'Err ... I'm not really ready,' I whined, hoping that someone else would feel sorry for me and be the guinea pig for the night's musical experiments.

'That's OK, take your time,' said Robert, becoming more and more like a teacher who wasn't going to let a pupil off the hook. 'We're not going anywhere.'

I picked up my guitar and quickly fiddled with the tuning nobs, giving myself a final moment to prepare for the next agonising three minutes. I found momentary consolation in the viewpoint that although going first was far from ideal, at least it meant that I wasn't following anyone brilliant. (A problem which would also be spared for the person going after me.)

'I come from England,' I began nervously, thinking that mentioning this might get people on my side. 'And we're not renowned for our country music. But I'd like to offer you my interpretation of that genre,' I added, a little pompously.

The room fell silent and all eyes focused on me. I felt suddenly terrified. Wasn't I just going to make a fool of myself? Surely I didn't belong in this company? I'd felt pretty confident during the drive up and I'd decided that I would sing 'Bird's

Egg' if the opportunity arose, but now as I looked at the circle of guitarists, all major talents poised to perform their own work, I suddenly felt a little ashamed of it. Yes, I liked the tune, and the lyric tickled me, but when all was said and done it was simply a piece of frothy nonsense.

I formed my left hand into the shape of the opening chord and placed it on the strings.

I took a deep breath, told myself that 'frothy nonsense' was what I did best, and then, like an anxious skier perched on the edge of an almost sheer drop, I launched myself off.

Like most things that we worry about, it wasn't as hard as I imagined it might be. Once I'd started singing I began to relax, and I looked up and saw friendly faces and I remembered that these people had been praying only moments before. They were not a hostile crowd. They wanted me to do well. I decided to sing my little heart out.

To my delight the end of the first chorus was greeted with laughs, and appreciative comments like 'Yeh!' and 'Way to go!' I moved into the second verse, suddenly riding on a wave of the room's good will and my own adrenalin. I looked down at my hand as it strummed the guitar and then I cheated a glance at the faces of my audience.

Big smiles.

I was beginning to enjoy myself. For the second chorus I felt confident enough to bounce my leg up and down – it must have made an odd sight, the Brit indulging in a kind of conservative flamboyance – before launching into my favourite melodic part of the song, the middle eight.

Appreciative nods. By the time I was halfway through the last chorus I was having so much fun that I was tempted to throw in a 'Yeehah', but thankfully wisdom prevailed. I hit the last chord and delivered the last line of the song, even attempting a kind of yodel on the last note.

Whoops and hollers.

'Hey I like this English country stuff!' someone called out.

Wow! I felt excited, relieved, and happy, but also I was glowing with pride. I'd done it. I'd gone first. The guy from England who wasn't a professional musician had kicked things off, and he hadn't done a bad job.

'OK Eric,' said Robert. 'You're next. You can't put it off any longer.'

As Eric began playing I wanted to get to my feet and say 'Not yet!' I wasn't ready to listen to *other* people's contributions. After a week of trying I'd finally got to sing my song, and not just to any two bit audience, but to a selection of country music's crème de la crème. What's more it had gone down pretty damn well. I couldn't just turn from performer into audience member in a matter of seconds. There was too much adrenalin flowing through my body. To borrow some of the vernacular no doubt used by those around me – I was *wired*, I was *buzzin'*, I was on a *natural high, man*.

All I remember of the next four singers was that the songs were good and so was their singing. The ones who followed also maintained this high standard, but I had calmed down to such an extent that I was now able to devote some attention to the content of the songs and recognise the skilled craftsmanship of the songwriting. Their performances could all be summed up in three words.

Better than mine.

About half an hour into proceedings it was Randy's turn. He'd been seated at an electric piano just outside the circle. I wondered if it was considered poor form to accompany yourself on a piano at a guitar pull. Maybe that's why the circle of chairs had excluded him. Randy began a rather timid introduction to his song, his voice barely audible at first. I began to feel worried for him. Perhaps he wasn't really up to this.

'I'd like to play a song,' he said in hushed tones, 'which I hawked around Nashville for four years or so. Everybody told me that no one would record it because it didn't have a chorus.' He nervously tinkled a few notes on the piano. 'So I tried to write a chorus but every one I came up with kept meandering on and on. I could have sworn I wrote one which lasted for two weeks. In the end I decided that the song was OK as it was and I just kept believing in it. Anyway, here it is.'

As he played the first few notes I felt a sympathetic knot in my stomach for him. However, as the melody of his musical intro- duction emerged, a few people in the room began to applaud gen- tly. Then I began to recognise something about what he was playing. It was familiar but I couldn't identify it. That melody, now what *was* it? This was like being in the music round of the pub quiz. Then it came to me, and it was all I could do to stop myself from blurting it out. It was 'You Needed Me', which had been a massive hit around the world for Anne Murray in the late '70s.

As Randy launched into the first line of the song, the applause of recognition grew and he managed a little smile. He had duped most of us into believing he was a novitiate songwriter when in reality he was something of a heavyweight. I couldn't help thinking this had been a conscious and mischievous deception on his part. However, the song, the performance, the sheer emotion of it all was stunning. I felt a tingle at the back of the neck. Randy was a true master at this.

The applause on completion of the song was overwhelming. I looked around at the other writers and I saw no trace of professional jealousy on their faces.

'It *still* needs a chorus!' joked Raul, who happened to be the unfortunate one who was due to go next. 'Just my luck to follow someone who's been inaugurated into the Country Music Hall of Fame.'

Raul was more than up to it though, and he gave a rousing performance, as did those who followed. 'George' sang a moving love song (later Billy told me that this had been George Ducas, who he described as being a 'happening guy'), and soon it was the turn of 'Tom', who sang a 12-bar blues which many of the other players elected to jam along with, with guitars which had sat idle on laps for most of the evening. Tom sang his heart out:

> I'm a good driver baby, climb on in,
> Well, the ride of your life is about to begin.

A man called Ollie produced a fiddle from nowhere and added yet more colour to the musical canvas. This ability to share in the work of others is definitely a bonus for musicians, and one which is sadly unavailable to comedians. If a stand-up comedian is performing a piece of material and other comics start joining in, then it's considered poor form. The comedian is a solitary creature. No backing band to share a joke with between gags. Just the performer, the microphone and the audience. It's really rather brutal. Really quite harsh. No wonder I was enjoying tonight's atmosphere so much.

What struck me the most was how genuinely moving most of the songs were. Each performer had only been allowed to perform one song and so invariably they had chosen one which meant a lot to them. They sang words which came from the heart and were set to music which, if not always the most original, was imbued with an intregrity of spirit. It may not have been 'soul' music, but it definitely had soul. I began to wish that I'd had the courage to have chosen a different song to perform myself. Perhaps I should have been brave enough to have put some raw emotion on show. I'd gone for frothy nonsense, just as I always do when I'm in 'performance' mode. I'd used comedy as a defence mechanism. Maybe next time I'd sing the song which leaves me with a tear in my eye.

Maybe next time.

'Thanks for a very special evening,' I said to Billy as he dropped me back at the Writers' Boarding House. 'It was really kind of you to think of me.'

'Don't mention it,' he replied with a twinkle in his eye. 'I told you only a fool misses Robert's guitar pulls.'

Of course the biggest problem with the guitar pull, like all good things, had been that it had come to an end. One by one the song-writers had climbed into their cars and driven back to the harsh reality of Music City, USA, where they now had to feed themselves and their families by selling their art instead of simply sharing it. Bills would have to be paid, and records needed to be sold, or they'd be reduced to busking with their guitars on street corners.

The rest of my stay in Nashville was something of an anti-climax. I think I'd lost heart really. Bama called me a couple of times and suggested trying to arrange more meetings but I told him not to worry. I mean how much fun was it going to be? I just didn't want to suffer any more music business types sitting down in judgement of my 'art'.

I began to realise that to make things happen in this town you had to put the time in. You needed to do what everyone else was doing and work with new people every day and come up with song after song after song. The thinking seemed to be that if you wrote fifty songs the law of averages meant that one of them had to be good. Certainly, in a world as competitive as this it was highly unlikely that anything mediocre was going to make the grade, so you needed to put in the hours in order to come up with that 'special' song. Then, of course, you needed that magic ingredient in the form of a healthy tranche of good fortune.

I ran these ideas past Steve as we shared a meal together at the Texas Longhorn on my last night.

'It seems that I've pretty much taken on a bet that requires me to write a great song and then be very lucky,' I conjectured between mouthfuls.

'Well, from my experience of you, you'll certainly be all right in one of those departments.'

I knew what he meant. Unfortunately.

'Nashville doesn't seem like the best place to be though,' I asserted.

'You can have your hit anywhere in the world, right?'

'Right.'

'Well, I bet it's a God-sake damn easier somewhere where you don't make yourself a small fortune if you succeed.'

'You think I should try a smaller a market?' I asked, not knowing whether to be grateful for his advice, or slightly offended.

'Tony, it takes a long time to get respect in this town. People will be nice to you, but they won't take you seriously. Not when your entire catalogue is made up of a song about birds' eggs.'

It was obvious, and he had a point.

'Don't forget "Chicks'n'Trucks'n'Rock'n'Roll",' I chipped in, somewhat irrelevantly.

'Well, whatever. The point is that you're going to have to move out and live here if you want to make anything happen. Are you prepared to do that?'

'Not really.'

'Why not?'

'Cos I don't think I really like Nashville.'

There, I'd said it.

And that was the bottom line. I didn't really like it here. However much of a joy-bringer music can be and however much a song can lift your soul or touch your heart, this town was all about the music business, and people took their business seriously. And here I was, someone who'd spent the last five years discovering what a joy life was if you took it *less* seriously. How much happiness was I going to find in this environment?

When Carol from the Writers' Boarding House gave me a lift to the airport, I unloaded some of my feelings about the trip, and she was sympathetic.

'I must say Tony,' she said, as we crawled up the busy interstate, 'that you always seemed a little too gentle to be taking on this town.'

'You need to be tough then?'

'You need to be tough to compete. Why have you taken this bet on? I mean *really*?'

It was a good question and there were two answers. I didn't really want to give the one that involved using the words 'Victoria', 'bit drunk' and 'quite wanted to get off with', so I opted for the other.

'I suppose it all stems from an interview I once heard Paul McCartney give,' I offered thoughtfully, 'in which he talked about the thrill he once got from overhearing a milkman whistling the song "Yesterday". I was amazed that in spite of all the millions of copies it had sold, and all the cover versions that hundreds of artists had recorded, this still meant so much to him. For him, there was no greater proof that he had written a song that people really loved.'

'And you want to write a song that people really love?'

'It would be nice, yes.'

I looked out of the window and saw the airport terminal come into view.

'So what are you going to do next?' asked Carol, busily looking around her for a parking spot as we reduced speed at the airport's drop-off point.

'I'm going to change direction.'

'And do what?'

'Not sure yet, but it's definitely time to put a different coat on.'

Carol laughed.

'I agree. Dad's never did suit you.'

PART II
WE ARE HAPPY

Our visitors are here

We are happy

Our visitors are here

We are happy

CHAPTER 7 A SONG FOR SUDAN

'You've got to expect the unexpected,' people say. People who've never thought this through properly.

You can only *expect* the expected, and *not expect* the unexpected. That's just the way it is, otherwise the words just don't make sense any more. Nevertheless, I will admit that I do know what these people mean, these people who say we've got to expect the unexpected. And what's more I have to say that they're actually offering some half decent advice.

Certainly, I was a little surprised to find myself heading for Heathrow Airport, with only a smattering of knowledge about the African country I was about to visit.

After my ultimately disappointing trip to Nashville I'd been anticipating spending a period of time in London, working on some new songs and searching for the gap in the pop market into which I might gainfully slip. However, when the envelope had arrived on the doorstep bearing the UNICEF logo, I'd found the offer contained inside it far too tempting for refusal. Would I like to visit the wartorn region of Sudan, and then write something about it for a fundraising project?

Yes, please.

'What angle do you want me to take?' I asked, when I called to find out more.

'Any one you like,' came the reply.

'How safe is it?'

'Safe enough.'

'All right, I'll do it,' I said charitably, fighting the urge to ask if they had much of a pop scene there.

I knew it was a long shot, but maybe, just maybe, the source material for my hit record was waiting for me within the battle-weary borders of Southern Sudan? My logic was sound enough. Paul Simon had popularised the sounds of Africa with his stunning million-selling album *Graceland*, and Peter Gabriel had drawn on African rhythms and vocals for much of his latter work. If that wasn't evidence enough of the commercial potential of the sounds of Africa, then I could also point to Damon Albarn from Blur, who'd just become involved in a musical collaboration in Mali. Why not the comedian and author Tony Hawks too? Especially if it helped him to win his bet? To borrow the Nashville vernacular – 'Africa was hot right now'. In more ways than one.

The Sudan had been a British colony which had established its independence in 1956, only to become embroiled in a series of civil wars, the last of which has been waging since 1983. The conflict is broadly drawn along the battle lines of Arab Muslim north v. African Christian south, but there are as many as twenty different sub-conflicts going on within it, mostly of a tribal nature, which complicate the issues still further. Simply getting permission to gain entry to the country had been something of a palaver. Our party had been granted special passes by the SPLM and the SPLA, who are the Sudanese People's Liberation Movement and the Sudanese People's Liberation Army, respectively. (Neither should be confused with the SNCF and YMCA, which are the French railway system and a pop song, respectively.) I was now one of a privileged few permitted to enter a sensitive war zone. Not that most people are that keen.

At the airport I met my fellow travelling companions by the desk for the Kenya Airways flight to Nairobi. These were fellow authors Victoria Glendinning and Irvine Welsh, a journalist and photographer from the *Daily Telegraph*, and two representatives from UNICEF. Oddly, I was the only one of us who was checking in a guitar. Maybe the others weren't particularly musical.

There was, of course, the possibility that I was the only one who seriously wanted to have a go at composing music with a Sudanese tribesman. Perhaps too, I was the only one who was carrying a professional standard mini-disc recorder to capture and sample the magical African sounds so that they could form the thematic element for a stunning dance track.

During the long flight I read some more about UNICEF's work in the Southern Sudan and discovered that as well as basic humanitarian aid to the innocent victims of war, it had a more long-term goal of showing the benefits of peace to a people who had only ever seen conflict. However, it does rather say something about me that I got most excited when I discovered that UNICEF's deputy executive director was called Karin Sham Poo. I studied her photo to see what her hair was like, and was relieved to see that it was presentable. With a name like that, the poor woman really had no excuse for a bad hair day.

When we landed in Nairobi we were collected and driven across the city to Wilson Airport, where we were to take an internal flight to Lokichoggio in North-Western Kenya. As we sped through the bustling capital, I looked out of the side window of the mini-bus, mainly because it was much preferable to looking ahead. Our impatient driver was weaving in and out of traffic with a wanton disregard for the rules of the road or, more importantly, my safety. It seemed a great irony that, although we were about to head into one of the world's war zones, statistically this was probably the most dangerous part of our journey.

Nairobi was not a pretty sight. Occasionally we'd see glimpses of jacaranda trees and areas of green parkland, but for most of the drive we were surrounded by huge lorries coughing out pollution by the CO_2-load, tatty concrete tower blocks, crumbling advertising hoardings, and a tense and overcrowded population scrambling around in search of the next Kenyan shilling. In the more salubrious areas, the properties came with the neat trimmings of barbed wire and security cameras. Nairobi is, after all, a very violent city. Laura from UNICEF told us about the all-too-frequent practice of car-jacking, in which the driver is held up at gunpoint, bundled into the boot of his own car and driven miles out of town and dumped by the roadside, at which point the assailants make off with the vehicle. The poor victim is left to walk home, having involuntarily become an expert on the design and contents of his own boot. I decided that there must have been occasions when the car-jackers became ambitious and went for a bit of minibus-jacking. It was the only plausible explanation I could find for our driver's refusal ever to allow his vehicle to become stationary.

Wilson Airport, we soon discovered, was one of those which had been designed to make the nervous flyer feel positively suicidal. Since this was an airport which specialised in short flights to unpopular destinations, the airlines evidently saw no need to supply any aircraft which had been built after 1950. The airstrip was dotted with antiquated flying machines with which goggles, leather hats and long flowing scarves would not have seemed out of place. The presence by the side of the runway of the burnt-out wreck of a plane, from what could only have been a previously unsuccessful landing, did little to inspire the confidence of the waiting passenger. Perhaps they might have tidied that away, I thought to myself, as I viewed its scarred remains before moving beneath the tired-looking propellers of our own sixteen-seater plane. I drew a deep breath as I readied myself to climb aboard and entrust my life to the couple of strangers in faded uniforms who were chatting together up in the cockpit.

The flight was actually less scary than I had imagined it might be. There is something rather soothing about the open-plan layout of these aircraft. Every time there is a slight wobble you can simply look forward to seeing the pilots' reaction before deciding on yours. If they are still playing Scrabble then you feel pretty comfortable that everything is OK; however, if they are shouting 'shit! shit! shit!' and desperately composing notes to their loved ones, it's probably a good idea to fasten your seat-belt and devote a quick couple of minutes to your relationship with God.

As we flew, Kenya sprawled beneath us. The land appeared to have been cultivated in an ordered manner and with the benefit of old colonial money. The healthy greens suggested that 'irrigation' to the farmers was not just a tricky four-syllable word, and the straight lines of fences and hedges implied that the fertile land had been divided up between the wealthy and the privileged. I firmly expected the landscape to change dramatically once we crossed the border into wartorn Sudan. Apart from a brief struggle securing its freedom from Britain in 1963 Kenya had been free from violent strife. However, the particular burden that Kenya's people had to bear was a massively corrupt government. I'd been told that a group of academics had recently collated enough data to publish The Top Twenty of Corrupt Governments, and Kenya had made a strong showing at number nine – although we can't be entirely sure that they didn't use backhanders to buy their way into that position.

After a brief flirtation with some small mountains, which happily the pilot noticed before I had to point them out, we landed on what appeared to be an airstrip in the middle of nowhere. All around it were huts, tents and compounds resembling army barracks.

This was Lokichoggio.

Until the crisis in Sudan, Lokichoggio hadn't really existed. Until then the land had been occupied by the nomadic Turkana tribe who'd conducted themselves decently enough, wandering around raising livestock while occasionally indulging in cattle-rustling against their neighbouring tribesmen, the Toposas in Southern Sudan. With the arrival of the Western aid agencies and the setting up of the camps which constituted Operation Lifeline Sudan, most of these tribes people had descended on this area, drawn by the lure of money, material items and an easier lifestyle.

When we finally dumped our bags inside the highly secure UNICEF compound, some of the dangers which this situation had created were explained to us by Ruben, a member of the security team.

'The problem,' he began, 'is that a lot of the Turkana people see all this food and aid arrive here and then watch it being airlifted into Southern Sudan. This is frustrating for them because a lot of them are hungry and they could really use it themselves. The situation is made worse by the fact these people hold a large number of illegally acquired firearms so this means that in the surrounding area there is a great deal of highway banditry, armed robbery and rampant night firing.'

'So it's probably not a good idea to wander around outside the camp after dark?' I pondered out loud.

'Let's put it this way. This year alone, there have been 37 shooting incidents in and around Lokichoggio; 18 people have been killed and 19 seriously injured. We tend to encourage our OLS staff to stay in at night.'

I had to admit, a nice early night did suddenly seem very appealing.

Following our rather sobering meeting with Ruben, we were now led into another small conference room where a man called Patrick Fox briefed us on the security situation in the Southern Sudan. Patrick just had to be an ex-army man, someone I imagined fellow officers referring to as 'a thoroughly good chap'. It was rather disappointing that he didn't begin each sentence with 'Right men, now pay attention ...', but somehow this was implied in his tone of voice. As well as updating us on the state of the war and pointing out the areas of the country where we were most likely to be bombed, he passed us each a security aide memoire which, among other things, outlined how best to behave should we be taken hostage. Being someone who's always anxious to act with decorum in every social occasion, I took a moment to study the instructions in detail.

1. Obey orders.
(This made sense to me. Especially if my captors had a gun and I didn't.)

2. DON'T speak unless spoken to.
(Absolutely. Being too chatty might get on their nerves.)

3. DON'T whisper to fellow captives.
(Sensible. I'd always been taught that it's rude to whisper and the chances are my captors would have been taught the same.)

4. DON'T look captors in the eye.
(Bit of a surprise this one. I would have thought that looking away from them would have made one appear shifty, but there you go.)

5. DON'T offer suggestions.
(So you'd have to work hard to suppress remarks like 'Wouldn't the sofa look better over by the window?')

6. DON'T argue, threaten or draw attention to yourself.
(Couldn't agree more. This is no time to start carrying on like a spoilt child.)

7. DON'T make any sudden moves – ask first.
(I'm a bit dubious about this one. Can't see much point in asking 'Could I make a sudden move please?')

Patrick explained that I was going to be air-dropped into a place called Yambio, in the Western Equatoria region. This had been given a Security Level of Two. Level One was a *Normal Operational Situation* but alas, this didn't exist in South Sudan at the moment. Level Two was a *Medium Operational Situation* which meant that we would have to make radio contact with the Lokichoggio base twice a day, and only make day trips from our base. Level Three was a *Tense Operational Situation* which meant radio contact three times a day and no travel outside base. Finally, Level Four meant that you had to get the hell out. Basically, hang on somewhere safe until a UNICEF plane came to airlift you to safety.

'It is extremely unlikely,' explained Patrick, in his soothing public school delivery, 'that the security level of Yambio will become a Level Four while you are there. It has been firmly in control of the rebels for ten years and the Sudanese government have more or less accepted it as a lost cause. Unlike many of the populated areas in the South which are regularly terrorised by random bombings, it hasn't been on the receiving end of any enemy shells for some four years. Any questions?'

'Yes, what's the music scene like in Yambio?'

This had been the question on my lips but I hadn't had the courage to ask it. I felt it would have trivialised all which had gone before, and besides, I suspected that it wasn't an area where Patrick was likely to have any great inside knowledge. Most of his life had probably been spent briefing people with more than guitars as their first line of defence.

Following Patrick's security briefing we were taken to a huge warehouse and briefed on what aid was going where, then it was off to the radio room for a briefing on operational procedures, before finally being led to a courtyard in the centre of the camp where, along with the rest of the staff on the camp, we were briefed on the latest security situations throughout the Southern Sudan. Goodness, more briefs than Marks & Spencer. I was now one of the world's leading experts on how to run an aid operation in a warzone. I felt over-qualified for someone who only really wanted to strum a guitar in a mud-hut with a mildly interested local.

One evening in the UN camp in Lokichoggio is enough to alert you to the fact that a long stay here might be quite tiresome. Two main factors worked against it, the fact that going out in the evening might result in death, and that staying in was deathly boring. Having eaten supper and sat around in the bar, I felt I'd pretty much exhausted all the available leisure options. I'd heard whispers that aid workers created their own entertainment by indulging in a fair amount of 'tukul hopping' (tukuls being the little straw huts which workers slept in), but I didn't feel up to any of that tonight, and anyway I needed to channel all my remaining energy into putting up my mosquito net.

Back in Blighty the doctor had told me that the mosquitoes in this part of the world packed something of a malarial punch, so I was going to take every precaution I could. I'd already gone through the trauma of deciding whether to take Lariam or not. According to government health sources, Lariam is the only drug which offers you decent protection against malaria in this part of the world, but unfortunately it is also the drug which, when you announce that you are taking it, causes people to take a sharp intake of breath, shake their heads and list all the horrific side effects which it has induced in them, and all of their friends and loved ones. After much deliberation I'd opted to take the bloody stuff but thankfully, thus far, I'd suffered no ill effects. I'd taken the pills once a week and I'd followed all the instructions on the box. 'Keep Away From Children', it had said. Well, I'd certainly done that. Apart from brushing past one in a super-market, I hadn't been near a child for weeks.

However, there still remained the risk that I might fall victim to one of the possible side effects listed on the accompanying leaflet. The most common ones were: sickness, dizziness, vertigo, loss of balance, headaches, sleepiness, diarrhoea and

A SONG FOR SUDAN

stomach ache. Less common ones included unusual changes in mood or behaviour, feelings of worry or anxiety, depression, feelings of persecution, crying, aggression, restlessness, forgetfulness, agitation, confusion, panic and hallucinations. As if this wasn't enough, it went on to list the possibility of visual disturbances, ringing in the ears, co-ordination problems, shaking of the hands and fingers, changes to blood pressure or heart rate, palpitations, skin rash, itching, hair loss, muscle cramps, joint pains, and loss of appetite. As far as I could see, they might as well have put a sign on the side of the box saying:

WARNING, THE EFFECTS OF THIS DRUG
MAY BE CONSIDERABLY WORSE THAN MALARIA

I woke in the morning, relieved to find that I hadn't been bitten by any mosquitoes or attacked by any disgruntled gun-wielding Turkana. Consequently I was fighting-fit and ready for the next leg of this somewhat elongated journey. This involved climbing on to a yet still smaller aircraft, a six-seater Cessant Caravan which was going to whizz us to our destination at a top speed of 140 mph. In two and half hours' time the pilot would land us on a mud airstrip hewn from equatorial rainforest. All feelings of fear were superseded by a sense of importance, because I knew that presidents and billionaire businessmen did not dilly-dally with Jumbos. No, the rules were clear: the smaller the plane, the more consequential the passenger. I looked around me and saw that for some of my fellow passengers this sense of buoyed vanity was not enough to dispel all concern about the journey ahead. Sue, the *Daily Telegraph* journalist, had a pallor and grim demeanour which suggested she was fully aware of what the results of being important had been for Glenn Miller, John Denver, and Payne Stewart and the like. I attempted to offer her a comforting smile, immediately realising that the fear-stricken are not easily consoled by such feeble gestures of support.

Unlike commercial passenger aircraft which provide a one-sided, port-hole-sized aspect of the journey, Cessant Caravans offer excellent views simply by virtue of being so small. Seated as I was, directly behind the pilot, I was afforded a full panoramic vista of the Southern Sudan, which I soon discovered to be a little disappointing since it was so uncompromisingly flat. Perhaps the only relief in these parts was humanitarian after all.

Forty minutes before we were scheduled to arrive in Yambio, the countryside beneath us changed dramatically, becoming surprisingly lush and verdant. Unlike most of Southern Sudan, Yambio County is a tropical rainforest characterised by tall trees as well as some savannah grasslands. There is plenty of rainfall, and fruit and vegetables are in good supply. All this was clearly visible from the sky and it made for exciting viewing. I looked down on the miniscule mud-huts and the tiny moving black figures which represented the first glimpses of civilisation, and I felt a rush of excitement. The simplicity of what was below me was somehow humbling. I was hovering over a part of the world which had not been party to the development of the one which I inhabited. What was I going to discover? How had life here been affected by its isolation from people and progress? And what would the music be like?

Soon Yambio's muddy airstrip appeared on the horizon and the pilots, who thankfully had finished with the papers, fiddled around with buttons and knobs in preparation for landing. I felt like a kid in an amusement arcade watching a video game over a bigger kid's shoulders. Of course, the difference was that we were involved in a version of the game where if we messed up we couldn't just put more money in the machine and have another go. I glanced at Sue who didn't appear to need reminding of this.

We hit the mud at what seemed like enormous speed and wobbled a little. At once I became aware of how important it was for the airstrip to have been properly maintained. Had the wheels of our aircraft hit a small rock then we would have been tipped clean over and my musical career would have acquired at least one similarity to Buddy Holly's. However, there was no such calamity, just a smooth and successful touchdown.

I felt like applauding. I'd been on a charter flight to Spain a few months previously and had been delighted to find a good proportion of the passengers had been unrestrained enough with their emotions to be able to applaud enthusiastically following the successful landing of the aircraft. Of course, if one takes the time to analyse their actions, what those passengers had really been doing was applauding because they weren't dead. *

As the Cessant Caravan's propellers made their final transition from a whirring blur into gently spinning blades, the cabin door of the Cessant was thrown open and we were hit by a wave of equatorial heat. We had landed in the Southern Sudan. I stepped out on to the red soil of the airstrip and into a warzone.

I was ready for anything. After all, I was armed with a guitar.

---

* *I'm pretty certain that's also why people applaud at the end of Neil Sedaka concerts.*

CHAPTER 8 STAND BY ME

The first few hours in Yambio didn't promise much with regard to the accomplishment of my personal mission in this country. The political figures who had authorised our entry into their territory had organised a complete itinerary for us, nothing of which involved any allotted time for musical collaboration. Instead we were to be whisked from place to place in order to be shown how responsibly their society was spending the aid money of which they were grateful recipients.

We were driven to the first of these rather formal meetings in a four-wheel drive with the letters U and N emblazoned on its side, clearly marking us out as benign and well-meaning sorts. Whether we'd been displaying the distinctive bright blue letters or not, most would have known our identity given that the UN were the only ones with any vehicles at all in this area. Ten years previously many Arab Northern Sudanese would have been driving around on these mud-tracks which served as roads, but they had been forced to flee when Yambio had been 'liberated' by the SPLA, and with them had gone all motorised forms of transport. Once 'set free', Yambio, which had never been much more than a relatively under-developed market town, suddenly had to adapt to a life with all its former supply lines cut off. Like it or not, it was back to subsistence living for its inhabitants, just as it had been before the opportunistic British and Arabs had first arrived a century or so earlier. A derelict petrol station, with rusting pumps and crumbling forecourt, served as a faint reminder of Arab prosperity, and the shell of a burnt-out bus bore grim testament to how these former overlords had been removed.

I looked around me and saw nothing but decay and neglect,

which would have made the place feel like a ghost-town had it not been for the antlike procession of villagers heading for the main market square, eager to trade whatever they could manage to carry there. These people were extraordinary. Each jet-black face, whether male or female, young or old, displayed a mysterious combination of intensity and warmth, of gravity and accessibility. Occasionally my intrusive stare would be returned with one of an even more penetrative and inquisitive nature, amazed no doubt, by my whiter than whiteness. After all, they didn't see many of my type – one of the few advantages of being entrenched in a bloody civil war being that you are spared adventurous backpackers from Oz parading up and down the main street in search of the youth hostel. From time to time I waved to one of my co-starers, and on each occasion I was greeted with a huge toothy smile followed by self-conscious giggling. Happiness appeared to be all around us. A little odd. These people had suffered greatly, so why weren't they showing it?

I sat by the van window, spellbound by the magic of the women outside who went about their business with such nonchalance, displaying the skills of circus performers as they strolled with huge baskets of vegetables balanced on their heads. I suddenly felt genuinely excited and privileged to be here, reaping the rewards at last of the exhaustive journey.

Presently we arrived at Freedom Square, so-called I assume, because of its freedom from any similarity to conventional squares. It was little more than a knackered old football pitch where desperate grass fought a losing battle against the elements. Beyond it was a single-storey building which looked like it was the recipient of as much maintenance as an alcoholic's ex-wife. This, we were told, was the Commissioner's Office.

Inside we were lectured on the Sudan's recent history by a confident and prosperous-looking man who introduced himself as Pascal, the Minister of Agriculture. After an initial gracious preamble, his expression hardened and he began to outline some facts which he obviously felt we needed to know.

'The suffering of the last 53 years has been caused by Britain,' he declared with a sudden severity.

I glanced out of the window and saw two moody teenagers pacing around with guns, watching our building.

'Our people,' continued Pascal, with more than a hint of the ruthless dictator about him, '... our people have been killed like flies since the British deserted us to the Arabs.'

I felt a momentary shudder of fear and quickly reminded myself of the hostage procedure, taking care not to look anyone in the eye while I did so. Being on the receiving end of all this anti-British rhetoric, I wondered whether it might not be a bad idea to have an Irish accent ready.

'Ah Jeez, now there's a ting, Pascal, 'cos if it wasn't the Brits who shafted us too!'

It was a relief to discover that instead of having us arrested, the Minister wound up his speech and introduced us to the Commissioner, a more frail, modest figure to whom he referred as 'His Excellency'. This was the first time in my life that I had been in the company of a 'His Excellency', the closest until now having been the Fixtures' Secretary at the tennis club. (The difference between the two being that this one was more humble, and you didn't have to kneel before him.)

'You are most welcome visitors here,' began the Commissioner, who I assumed was distinct from most of the other 'His Excellencies' in the world in that he didn't have any laces in his shoes. 'I hope that you enjoy the programme that we have arranged for you.'

His Excellency then outlined this programme which he and his colleagues had gone to considerable trouble to arrange for us. To me though, it sounded extremely dull, and unlikely to bring me any closer to any Sudanese musicians – although I realised that this probably wasn't the best moment to point this out. Lunchtime, however, after a visit to a school, an agricultural college and then a teak plantation, was.

'They're treating us like visiting politicians,' I moaned to a patient Laura as we tucked into an unexpectedly wholesome meal back on the UNICEF compound. 'They seem to think that we're more important than we are. Can't you tell them that Irvine wrote a novel about heroine addiction and I hitch-hiked round Ireland with a fridge?'

'I know, I'll talk to the powers that be,' replied a concerned Laura. 'I'll see if I can organise a shift in emphasis.'

~

Whatever tack Laura had taken, it had been a success. Two hours later we were taking a gentle stroll to Yambio's market, chaperoned by three locals who were there to oversee our safety rather than provide us with propaganda. Rather optimistically I was carrying my guitar, ever eager to seize an opportunity for collaboration, should the moment arise.

'Please, I can take that for you?' asked Justin, the most enthusiastic of our chaperones, pointing to my guitar.

'No, it's OK, I can manage,' I replied, eager not to replicate any of my colonial ancestors' desire for native servitude.

'Please, let me take your guitar,' urged the fresh-faced and eager Justin, oblivious to my concerns.

'It's all right.'

'No, I take.'

'Oh well, if you insist.'

I handed him the guitar, for a split second wondering rather shamefully if he might run off with it as soon as it was in his hands. Instead he smiled meekly and alerted us to the fact that the little path we had taken had now brought us once again to Freedom Square.

'Is there a bar anywhere in the town?' asked Irvine, his accent sounding all the more pronounced and incongruous in this environment, although to my ears the nature of the request did seem to lend itself to his Scottish brogue.

'Yes, there is one,' replied Justin.

'Great,' declared a beaming Irvine.

'Would you like to go there?' asked Justin naively, presumably not having met that many Scotsmen to date.

'I most certainly would,' replied Irvine without hesitation.

'OK, I take you there.'

Justin looked to me to be in his mid-twenties, a neatly turned-out young man who definitely took great care with his appearance, despite wearing Western-style garb which was palpably not his size. His outfit was far more likely to have been a handout from an aid package than the product of numerous return visits to a clothing store's fitting room. I smiled to myself, momentarily warmed by the thought that all those clothes-filled binliners that we dump on the doorsteps of Aid shops really do have a life beyond the two old ladies who first sift through them.

It was nice to know that Justin and his like could return them once more to the cutting edge of fashion.

Justin's Christian name was exactly that, a Christian name. Sure he was one of the Azande people from Southern Sudan, but he was a Christian, so he'd been given a name which made him sound like he came from just outside Esher. That's how it worked. He led us along the narrow mud paths, past a constant stream of energetic and eager villagers who were each as fascinated as the next by our extraordinarily pale skin. Soon we reached a point where the mud-tracks widened and became the closest thing to a set of crossroads that this part of the world could offer. Ahead of us there was a dilapidated shack with a sign outside which read: KABASH'S INN. Irvine beamed and led us inside where we discovered that its innlike characteristics didn't stretch much beyond a few tables and chairs. The bar was little more than a counter with a few bottles stashed behind it. African music blared from an old music-centre which was powered by a solar panel which lay in the sun on the porch outside.

'What a terrific idea,' observed Irvine, pointing to the contraption which was eagerly harnessing the sun's rays.

'Yeah,' I replied, 'although it must be a bit of a bummer if it gets cloudy. Presumably the music stops.'

'Hmm,' responded Irvine thoughtfully. 'Maybe that's why you don't see many of them back home in Scotland.'

The beers were ordered easily enough but there was a problem when it came to paying for them. Since the only economic connection the Southern Sudanese had with the Khartoum regime in Northern Sudan was funding an armed struggle against them, Sudanese currency was not readily accepted. We'd been told in Lokichockio that US dollars were what locals were after but we were now being asked to pay in either Kenyan or Ugandan shillings, and none of us had any. Perversely we were in the embarrassing situation of being unable to pay for a drink in a region where we were supposed to be the providers of aid. The owners of Kabash's Inn were giving us suspicious looks. Maybe they were expecting one of us to tip them the wink, tap our noses conspiratorially and say:

'Let us have the drinks for free and we'll sort you out with a nice tractor, OK?'

I couldn't understand why they weren't mad keen for our American money.

'Justin, why are they waving our dollars away?' I asked.

'Because you have too much,' he replied.

It seemed an odd moment to pass comment on the economic injustices which meant that we probably had enough spending money in our pockets to feed an entire family here for three years.

'What do you mean we have too much? We're trying to redistribute some of our wealth here and they won't let us.'

'It is that you have only twenty dollar bills. They cannot give you any change – they do not have any dollars.'

'Oh, I see. Well, tell them not to worry about change. We will buy everybody here a drink and they can keep any of the money left over.'

Justin got to his feet with a twenty dollar bill and explained this proposal to the tall, thin lady who seemed to be running operations. The marked change in her expression suggested that this arrangement was not a disagreeable one. In fact she had quite a spring in her step as she reached for the beers from the solar-powered fridge.

'You're lucky to have bottled beers,' explained Laura as they were delivered by the beaming proprietor. 'Yambio is near the border so they get goods like this from Uganda. If we'd taken you to some other places in Southern Sudan you wouldn't have had luxuries like this.'

The beer hit its mark and it felt good. I looked at Justin who was drinking like a naughty teenager, not normally allowed alcohol.

'Are there many musicians here in Yambio?' I asked, making a token effort to get my visit back on track.

'Yes, there are many.'

'Could you introduce me to some?'

'I think so, yes.'

I was quickly growing to like Justin. I felt there was room for our relationship to develop beyond one merely between would-be composer and guitar carrier. But that would have to wait. As we got to our feet to head off for a stroll around the market area, Justin made a dive for the guitar and held it to his chest like a mother might a small child.

There is an urgency and earnestness about market places in the Third World which sets them apart from anything we experience in the West, such is the importance of each transaction. I found myself quite enthralled by the vibrant atmosphere of this one, bustling as it was with the irresistible energy of traders with an indisputable vested interest. Many had walked miles to sell their wares, the proceeds of which would provide food for their children and next of kin. Little wonder that emotions ran high and that shopping was done at volume and with passion.

Expectant merchants sat cross-legged on the dusty ground, their particular specialist fruit, vegetable or spice spread out before them for the passing shoppers' perusal. Little money seemed to be changing hands, the barter system understandably being favoured in a land where economic stability had gone out of the window the day the bank had been blown up. As I watched a particular deal being struck, I became somehow envious of the simplicity of it all. As someone who has always been too lazy or stupid to have ever properly grasped how money *really* works, there was something irresistibly gratifying and somehow romantic in watching a bunch of bananas being exchanged for some grain. And not a Reward Card in sight.

What impresses me most about the barter system is the way it excludes outside influences. The value of the currency, in this case bananas and grain, cannot be decided by anyone other than the buyer or seller. Its value is entirely subjective and therein lies its beauty. Unlike in our system where the worth of our currency is often decided by the actions of financiers in the City or on Wall Street, no decision on a distant trading floor can alter the value of those bananas to their owner. Better still, the problem of counterfeiting never raises its ugly (and almost identical) head. After all, who in their right mind is going to forge a banana? Apart from anything else it's bloody difficult, and the equipment needed is expensive and only available over the Internet.[*] Certainly, the presence of forged bank notes within our society has led to the most annoying practice of the staff on supermarket checkouts of holding our twenty pound notes up to the light to check the validity of their water marks. I deeply resent this,

---

[*] *www.forge-a-banana.com.*

and whenever it is done to me I pick up each item of shopping from my trolley and hold it up to the light, in a similarly untrusting manner. Frankly, if they think my twenty pound note is dodgy then I'm hardly going to head home with my groceries until I'm absolutely certain that they haven't tried to fob me off with some counterfeit Shreddies or Marmite.

'Why don't you give them a song here, Tony?' came Irvine's suggestion, rather jolting me from my profound thoughts on world shopping.

'What? Here in the market place?'

'Yep, right here. Why not? I reckon you've got to put yourself on show. If you want the Sudanese Paul McCartney to come out of the woodwork, then he'll have to know that his John Lennon is in town.'

Fortunately I was tuned into the same wavelength as Irvine, and his irrational logic made perfect sense to me. I knew he was right. My instinct was telling me that if I wanted to make something musical happen here then I would have to take the initiative, and so I asked Justin to hand me the guitar. I began taking it out of its case and a crowd immediately began to develop. Well, why wouldn't it? One of the white people was producing a strange-looking instrument from a bag, and it looked like he was going to begin playing it.

An expectant throng gathered before me and I became suddenly very nervous. I was about to make a performance for which I was totally unprepared. I still had absolutely no idea what I was going to sing. And once I'd decided on it, how would it be received? Would my actions be offensive to the local culture? Maybe producing a guitar and singing uninvited in the middle of the market might be a great insult? Would I be arrested, reported to the commissioner, or worse still, completely ignored?

The butterflies whizzed around my tummy more than they had done for years. The odd thing was, I liked this sensation. Masochistic though it may have been, I found this feeling of discomfort reassuring in that it was confirmation that I was stretching myself, and not settling for the comfortable, easy path. These are the sort of moments that stop life being boring. Here, with an audience of fifty or more South Sudanese villagers assembling before me in expectation of something special, I knew one thing. I was alive. I reminded myself of how nervous I'd felt at the Guitar Pull too, and the feeling of exhilaration which had seamlessly followed. It was time for some more of that.

How do you choose a song in a situation such as this? 'Bird's Egg' wasn't going to work here, certainly, and I was denied the *Here's one that everyone will know* option, given that these people had been completely cut off for years, and had therefore been lucky enough never to have had to endure buskers singing 'American Pie' or 'Streets Of London'.

Quite why I elected to go for 'Stand By Me' I can't really remember, but I strongly suspect that it was because it was the only song I could think of at the time. As I played the introductory chords there was a buzz of anticipation among the fascinated onlookers. There I was, the white man beneath the jacaranda tree as dusk fell, strumming away much like a busker on the London underground. Except that I was much more of a novelty here. Extremely special in fact, in this location and against this backdrop. I drew my breath for the first line, and with my heart pounding I launched into song. Nothing could have prepared me for what was to follow.

When the night has come and the land is dark ...

With the first line of the song barely over, my audience fell about laughing. Not gentle tittering or embarrassed giggling but full-blown guffaws and hysterical side-slapping. These people were, to use the vernacular, pissing themselves laughing. It was not quite what I'd expected, and a little bruising for the ego. What made matters worse was that the response of the locals was so unusual and in itself so amusing, that Irvine and the rest of our party also began to lose themselves in laughter. My singing had never produced such mirth before, even while performing a comedy song when that had been the intention (more's the pity). It was so disconcerting that it felt pointless to proceed with the song, especially since none of it would have been audible above this mirthful and overwhelming cacophany. The sound must have been carrying for miles around, confusing humans and frightening the wildlife.

After having vamped on the same chord until the laughter had subsided (it may have only been a minute but it seemed much longer), it was time for the singer to resume the song, albeit with an entirely different set of expectations.

... and the moon is the only light you'll see

More hysterics, this time slightly tempered by general exhaustion from the first outburst. I elected to continue regardless, and by the time I'd made it to the first round of 'Stand by me's, the listeners' laughs had dwindled and become smiles which occasionally broke into the odd titter.

By midway through the second chorus there was something approaching complete silence and there was definitely room for suspicion that the sounds I was producing were genuinely being appreciated. Then I made a mistake. I had come to the section in the song where a long solo begins and I was faced with the choice of either humming it (not really an option, I mean how hysterical were they going to find humming?) or thinking of something else. That something else was to have a go at a spot of audience participation. I began to sing a round of choruses without guitar accompaniment, urging my audience to get involved by raising my arms above my head and clapping, much like desperate old rockers do at the conclusion of their regular comeback gigs. Instead of recognising this gesture as an invitation to share in this memorable performance, my fans regarded me with confusion, before a bold few took this as a cue to burst into a round of applause.

The rest followed.

My music was now drowned out by an audience applauding enthusiastically, regardless of the fact that I hadn't yet finished. This time the sound was too much to fight against so I had little choice but to throw in the towel and wind up proceedings with a bow. On seeing this new signal from me, the crowd at once ceased applauding and began watching me with interest to see what I would do next. Thus, the conclusion to my epic performance was greeted with complete silence.

Well, almost. If you listened carefully you could just hear the sounds of a small group of white people desperately trying to suppress laughter.

'Thank you, Yambio, and good night!' I exclaimed in ironic homage to the old rockers everywhere.

The titters of the white people gave way to loud guffaws.

It really was turning into quite a busy day. I mean, hadn't I done enough already without getting involved in a game of football? I suppose I would have had the sense to turn the offer down, had I not still been reeling from the shock of the 'singing' experience.

'Why don't you and Irvine join in with the game?' we were asked.

'Because I'm wearing these silly sandals,' I'd replied.

'Yes, but most of them are playing barefoot, look!'

I looked and I saw. Freedom Square was now hosting a spirited football match which was being contested between two youthful teams, most of whom were happily competing without any footwear. It didn't matter though, because the soles of their feet were as tough as old boots. Considerably tougher, as it turned out, than my designer sandals.

Irvine and I were quickly assimilated into proceedings. The addition of one more player to each team didn't make much difference when there were 17-a-side already. A hundred or so excited onlookers were watching a game which was being played in a competitive spirit even though it was little more than a friendly kick-around. It was just bad luck that the only player on the pitch who had failed to grasp the meaning of the word 'friendly' was the one who had chosen to mark me. When the ball first came to my feet, I attempted to control it with my back to goal before laying it off to one of my team mates. However, before I could do this, I felt a shooting pain in the back of my calves as my legs were scythed from beneath me and an opponent's body shot out from underneath my feet, taking the ball with it.

I collapsed on the rock-hard ground in an uncomfortable heap. I had just been the victim of a Sudanese tackle from behind (they don't come any worse, check with FIFA if you don't believe me). Then I heard a familiar sound. I did not recognise it at first, still being a little dazed from the severity of the tackle and subsequent tumble, but I knew it, I definitely knew it. What *was* it? Ah yes, I recognised it now – hysterical laughter. Of course! My fall had been the funniest thing the crowd had seen in their lives to date (their presence at this game meaning that this lot had missed out on my earlier singing) and the obvious response was to shriek with laughter. To call these people uninhibited would be a gross understatement. They were producing the kind of sounds that most of us could only make following dangerous levels of drug consumption. The readiness of these people to explode with such demonstrative expressions of mirth was remarkable, not least given the hardship and suffering which recent history had forced them to endure, but it was personally a little disappointing that I should be the one who seemed to instigate these emotions, especially when I'd been attempting to do something serious.

The game continued, and so did my marker – with the same unbridled ferocity. Perhaps Pascal, the Minister of Agriculture, had explained to this lad exactly how badly the British had messed things up around here, because there was scant evidence to suggest that he saw me as someone who was in the region to help his community. After being on the receiving end of a fifth bookable offence, I decided that it would be dangerous to carry on, or else one of the crowd would have almost certainly died laughing. I limped from the pitch to huge cheers, and with every possibility of being promised a testimonial match late next season. I slumped to the ground on the sidelines, nursing my wounds and cursing the Aid organisations. OK, I thought, they might do sterling work in the area supplying engineers, teachers and doctors, but would it hurt to ship out the odd referee as well?

That night Justin took us to a small bar which bore more of a resemblance to someone's house, and one which had clearly been opened especially for us (I guess not having anything smaller than twenty dollar bills can open doors for you in this part of the world). A lady emerged to take our orders, looking rather like we'd just got her out of bed.

'Why don't you try some Sukusuku?' Justin asked me. 'It is the alcohol which they make here in Yambio.'

'Er, no thanks,' I replied unadventurously. 'I think I'll just stick to a bottled beer.'

'Why don't you just try a little?'

I remembered having read newspaper reports back in Nairobi

which detailed some of the horrible consequences of drinking local home made alcoholic beverages. Blindness and death had been two that hadn't appealed greatly.

'Thanks, but no,' I said, feeling a little like a prim convent girl refusing a kiss. 'Not tonight. Really, thanks but no.'

'It is strong, but it is good.'

'I'm sure it is, but I'm happy with a beer.'

For the second time in the evening I was being rather churlish with regard to the hospitality which was on offer, but ultimately I was comfortable with my decision. It wasn't very British, but by my reckoning it was better to risk appearing rude than to go blind or die.

'Justin, tell me about your family,' I requested, just after I'd ordered the considerably safer option of a beer.

'I never knew my father,' he explained. 'Nobody talked about him and I think perhaps nobody knew who he was. My mother died when I was two days old. I was brought up by her sister but she died when I was twelve years old and then I had to remain alone.'

'And how did you manage?'

'I had to absent myself from class so I could go and try and find work to get money. It was a condition which forced me to get married. I am 29 years old now and I got married in 1991 but this was too early for me.'

'How could getting married help?'

'A wife could at least contribute to looking after me and help me to complete my studies. Women have many techniques for getting money here. They can brew beer which they can distill and then sell. They can cultivate the garden and plant some things which can help get money.'

'So you married for money, not for love.'

'I married on a condition basis,' said Justin rather shiftily, almost sounding like a politician. 'Once you have a wife she can help you in different things.'

I knew that in the past a woman had been considered to be of such value to the Azande people that marriage was usually contracted by the gift of about twenty spears by the bridegroom to the family of the bride. I wasn't sure if this tradition was still observed but I was aware of what trouble I'd have over here, having carelessly let my spear collection dip to as low as six (two of which were slightly damaged and buried somewhere up in the loft). I also knew that girls here married very young, sometimes being betrothed only a few hours after birth, presumably to someone who'd been very careful not to throw their spears without being sure of their safe retrieval. Polygyny was also practised – this being the rather unfair system in which a man can take as many wives as he wants. It had been common for nobles to have taken so many wives that there hadn't been enough to go around and other men hadn't been able to marry, regardless of how many spears they'd managed to accumulate. What a bummer.

I learned that Justin's wife had been 14 years old when he married her and that now she had given him two healthy children. Unfortunately she was suffering from appendicitis and was in the hospital awaiting an operation.

'The doctor will not operate,' he explained. 'She is anaemic and she has to build up the strength of her blood. It is difficult for me right now because I need to find the money to bring her the food which will build up her blood, and the hospital already is expensive. You have to pay for the admission card, and then for the bed and for the person who washes the bed clothes. On top of that you have to pay for the operation.'

'It seems that things are tough for you, right now.'

'Yes, I think that I am unlucky.'

'*Have been* unlucky,' I corrected him.

'What do you mean?'

'You *have been* unlucky. Who knows, you could start being lucky from today onwards?'

Justin looked blank. Maybe this was just too implausible for someone who'd been through what he'd been through.

'We have to go now,' announced Laura. 'The man in the UNICEF truck says that the main base in Lokichoggio have been radioing and they are becoming concerned that we are not back within the compound. They would like us to return there.'

And so it was that we finished our beers like naughty children who had stayed out too late, and we jumped into the school bus to head home. As we alighted at the compound, I shook Justin by the hand.

'Thank you for looking after me,' I said.

'It has been my pleasure.'

'Perhaps tomorrow you could take me to the hospital to visit your wife.'

'I will arrange it. No problem.'

'And I need to record some people singing – do you have any ideas?'

'Yes. I have some ideas,' he said rather formally, before adding a 'goodnight' and a 'sleep well', just when I thought he was going to tell me what these ideas were.

I hoped they were good.

CHAPTER 9 WE ARE NUMBER ONE

I awoke in my tent in the morning having obediently followed Justin's instructions to sleep well. At breakfast, Justin outlined the day's schedule which was to incorporate his 'idea'. This was to visit a girls' school where he was fairly confident they would sing songs of greeting for me. After that we would spend the day cycling around the mud tracks and among the tukuls of Yambio, getting a real feel for the place and hopefully visiting the home of a musician with whom I could set up some kind of writing session.

'What kind of music are you hoping to write?' asked Sue, as she tucked into some exotic fruit.

'I really don't know,' I replied honestly. 'Hopefully we'll end up with a fusion of Sudanese tribal music and good old-fashioned pop.'

Silence around the breakfast table. I guess everyone was trying to figure out what kind of a sound this might be, and indeed, whether anyone would really want to listen to it.

'I suppose I'm really more interested in the process than the actual result,' I said, feeling the need to fill the embarrassing silence which had suddenly descended over the table.

'Well at least you're going to have a go,' offered Irvine, supportively.

I never really feel comfortable on a visit to a school or hospital. They invoke too many memories. Like the time I was stood in a corridor as it was explained to me, in no uncertain terms, that one of my organs was going to have to be removed. That was, it has to be said, a particularly bad day at school, that one.

The school I was visiting this morning was so different to any I'd ever seen before that it triggered no memories, painful or otherwise. At the end of a long mud-track Justin and I were greeted by the headmaster who led us into the large dusty court-yard. This lay beyond the narrow, single-storey building which constituted the school itself. The building, we were told, only really served as an administrative centre, most of the lessons taking place beneath the surrounding jacaranda trees. The head-master explained that he was unhappy about this and longed for classrooms, but for me it all seemed so romantic. I remembered being stuck in a dingy classroom suffering double-geography lessons with Mr Baxter.

'In our society we don't sit under trees as much as we ought to,' I said, trying to be profound.

Just as I was beginning to regret the pretentiousness of my remark, we were interrupted by one of the most beautiful sounds I'd heard for a long time. At the far side of the courtyard, I saw the source of this music – a large gathering of maybe fifty or sixty girl pupils, all in a neat blue uniform, who had begun singing. As I moved closer it became clear that they were doing so specifically for me – for it was a song of greeting:

WE ARE HAPPY, WE ARE HAPPY TO RECEIVE YOU

The voices were shrill, but extraordinarily musical, and the sound cut through the air with a great power which arrested the senses. The metre of the song was complex, the singers occasionally pushing a beat rather than singing to the uniformed beat of a metronome. We made our way towards the source of the sound. They accompanied their singing by gently clapping on the down-beat, providing a crisp, percussive energy to the performance, actively driving it along. At once we all stood still and watched intently, mesmerised by the joyous sounds emanating from these hundred and fifty or so girls, who must have ranged in age from five to fifteen. Then, remembering the nature of my mission here, I quickly produced the mini-disc recorder from my bag and moved towards the girls to begin recording this spectacular aural treat. These sounds, I knew, could provide the inspiration for a piece of music which might in turn lead to a successful conclusion

to my bet. Adjusting the levels on my small machine and pointing my microphone towards the children as I was, I must have
appeared like a strange alien who had infiltrated their world. And
in some ways, I was.

We were treated to four songs in all, the lyrics mostly being
English but nonetheless difficult to comprehend given only the
approximate pronunciation of the words. Of the discernible
lyrics, my favourite was the simplest:

> *NUMBER ONE,*
> *NUMBER ONE,*
> *WE ARE NUMBER ONE*

The music was so beautiful and captivating that I found myself,
almost trancelike, drifting off to another world. Away from the
poverty, to a place where there was no danger, and where I was
a man whose only role in life was to listen and be soothed by the
mellifluous sound that was now enveloping him.

'We have to go now,' announced Justin, cruelly curtailing any
further exploration of this magical and, for me anyway, unchar-
tered dimension. 'We have to return to the compound for lunch.'

Oh yes, lunch.

'Are you going to be all right on that thing?' asked Irvine, as I
wobbled around on the bicycle which Justin had just wheeled
into the UNICEF compound.

'Yes, I've just recently been to Nashville to brush up on my
cycling skills,' I called back, as I pedalled off, leaving a baffled
Irvine behind me.

Bicycles, I've decided, are brilliant things. They don't cough
pollution into the atmosphere, and they provide you with excellent aerobic exercise. Not only that, but when in motion they are
pleasing on the ear, and they neatly obviate any need to place
trust in garage mechanics. Along with the pumps for fresh water
supplies and the introduction of medical vaccinations, these little contraptions had to be one of the more valuable contributions which foreign aid had provided. Yambio's muddy, bumpy
tracks were packed full of a furiously pedalling population, most
of whom were sporting large grins. It made quite a contrast with

the expressions of car drivers, whose stress levels force them towards the obscenity of 'road rage'. Where I was right now, perched on my neat little saddle, the prospect of witnessing any 'bicycle rage' did indeed seem distant.

'Do people have padlocks for their bikes?' I asked Justin as we pedalled our way up a busy artery which was leading us to the hospital.

'No, there is no need. People do not steal.'

This I liked. The concept of a padlock-free society – not least because my experience in Nashville had proved that I didn't know how to work them. I asked Justin if there was any crime at all.

'Yes, there is a prison'

'And who is in it?'

'People who have taken others' lives. And adulterers.'

Immediately I thought of our overcrowded prison population in the West and I wondered whether our town centres would have room for anything other than prisons if we counted adultery as a felony.

We cycled past roadside (or, more accurately trackside) traders, who were selling seeds, herbs and fruit. To most of these merchants, the sight of a white man on a bike was most unusual, but it was funny too, and while some smiled and waved, most of them laughed heartily. I should have expected as much. Although I wasn't singing or playing football, I had another act up my sleeve as a comedy cyclist, and that could still get the punters rolling in the aisles. Never before had a combination of pedalling and sweating caused such unbridled laughter, but then not everyone had my comic timing. As I listened to the shrill sounds of the laughter reverberate through the trees of the surrounding rainforest, I resigned myself to the fact that whatever I did here was going to be the source of immense amusement, unless of course I'd stood on a box and delivered my stand-up comedy routine. Ironically, that probably would have left my audience stony-faced and confused. (Tragically, it wouldn't have been the first time.)

'We turn right down here for the hospital,' announced Justin, breaking suddenly to avoid overshooting the turning.

After a hundred yards of narrow path we found ourselves dismounting in a courtyard which was full of people seated in the shade of its four large trees. They were silently and patiently awaiting treatment, with an air of resignation about them, many not being able to afford the limited medicines and treatments which the hospital could offer. Justin led me into one of the four shacks which surrounded the courtyard and into a sparse room which served as a hospital ward, the complete absence of medical equipment meaning that the sick people were the only clue as to its identity.

Visiting any hospital is a humbling experience primarily because it invariably involves seeing those who are suffering when you are in a relative state of good health yourself. This one, however, left me with a new feeling of numbness. Although a Norwegian aid agency provided assistance to operations here, there seemed to be little evidence of it anywhere in the immediate environs of Justin's wife, who was perched on one of the few beds in the ward.

Many of the patients simply lay stretched out on the floor.

The pungent smell of sickness momentarily threatened to overpower me and I had to work hard to stop myself from retching. As she was introduced, Justin's wife shook me weakly by the hand and tried to smile. Two things were immediately clear to me – she was in a lot of pain and she needed help very badly. I felt frustrated at my powerlessness and after a brief and stilted conversation with her, I decided that enough was enough.

'I think we should go now,' I said uncomfortably, turning to a dulled Justin.

'OK.'

Just for now, there was nothing more to say.

'I will show you where I live now,' announced Justin, as the motion of our bikes began to revive the senses which had been numbed by the hospital visit.

An eagle circled above a banana tree, and the sun's rays smothered us like a gigantic hot towel. I wobbled on my bike as I took a sip from my bottle of water. A group of young girls giggled. I felt better. The world of suffering was five minutes behind us now. Time the great healer was already working its wonders on me, but I just wondered what it might do for those who we'd left stretched out on the hospital floor.

The twenty-minute cycle to Justin's home involved the negotiation of a labyrinthine sequence of twisting, bumpy, potholed paths among which Yambio's dwellings were dotted. These constituted a circular plot, around which four or five mud-huts were neatly arranged. I was afforded a unique glimpse of another world as I peered into these primitive domiciles. Mothers toiled, very often weighed down with a baby or two strapped somewhere about their person, and children were playing. The Azande are an attractive race with strong bone structure and an open and welcoming physiognomy, but their kids are just stunning. Barefoot and beautiful they ran, beaming and joyous among the tukuls, oblivious to their dubious destinies. They smiled and waved at this strange pallid onlooker, who felt privileged and exhilarated to be seeing what was unfolding before him, like he'd been allowed to step into the past. Apart from tattered Western clothes everything was as it would have been for centuries. I imagined myself to be one of the first white explorers – a benevolent one who wasn't going to foist his religion and culture upon the people. I'd just give them a bar of melted chocolate and then move on.

'This is it,' called Justin to the explorer behind him. 'This is where I live.'

We dismounted in the middle of the charming and well-kept ring of tiny mud-huts and I was invited into the furthest one on the left. Inside this small circular space which was presumably the reception area, we took a break from the power of the afternoon sun. Justin offered me a refreshing drink but I refused, fearing that my stomach might not have the requisite fortitude to withstand an onslaught of Sudanese water. I felt it unlikely that 'Yambio Spring' would compare favourably in tests alongside Evian, Perrier, Highland Spring and the rest.

'How many people live here?' I asked, pointing to the four other huts which were distributed evenly around the neat little plot.

'Me, my wife and our two children, and my wife's two sisters and their three children.'

'So there are nine people in this small area,' I said a little hesitantly, unsure of my maths.

'Yes. Nine. But it is OK.'

'Why aren't the husbands of your wife's two sisters here?' I asked, half expecting to hear that they'd been killed in the conflict.

'They left Yambio when it was liberated by the SPLA. We think that they have gone to one of the neighbouring countries but I have no way of knowing where they are.'

'Why did they leave?'

'They are refugees of the war.'

I questioned Justin on this subject for a further five minutes but failed to get a satisfactory answer as to why his brothers-in-law had fled. It would have to remain one of the mysteries of this complex war, but whatever the uncertainty surrounding the reasons for their disappearance, the real victims of it were skipping around just outside. The children.

'Justin, did you fight in the war?' I asked.

'No,' he replied. 'I did not have to because the chief knew my position.'

'What do you mean?'

'The way we find our soldiers is not done politically and we do not have subscription. When the army need support then the commanders call on the chief and he does the recruiting. If you are a father and he has already taken one of your children to fight, then he will not come and take another. If you have two or three then he will take one. For me, the chief knew that I was an orphan already, and he will not take me today because he knows that there would be no one to look after this family.'

Had Justin been lucky? It was a difficult call. His circumstances had meant that he'd avoided being a part of the horrific dehumanising atrocities of war, and yet he'd been denied the love of a father or mother, or even a surrogate stepfamily. His had been a solitary struggle into adulthood. And here he was as an adult, entertaining the inquisitive white visitor in his front hut.

'When would be a good opportunity for you to introduce me to a musician?' I asked, rather abruptly changing the subject. 'I have the girls singing but I would love to try and do some writing with someone who lives here.'

'I think it would be better to do it tomorrow.'

'Is that not leaving it a little late? I only have two more days here.'

'Tomorrow is good because there will be musicians everywhere. Tomorrow is the tenth anniversary of our liberation from the Khartoum government. There will be a party all day and musicians will be a big part of that.'

'So you could introduce me to some and we could see if anyone was interested in writing with me the following day?'

'Yes, this is not a problem.'

The problem, I was yet to discover, was to be an altogether different one.

I awoke the following morning with a fever and an aching body. I couldn't move. I lay there, hurting, not just physically but emotionally too. This was nothing short of a disaster. Instead of meeting Sudanese musicians, I was going to spend the day wretched and bedridden. How could this have happened? I'd been so careful not to drink the water and I'd eaten pretty much the same as everyone else, and yet something had reformed my constitution. Damn.

The concerned visitors to my tent offered their sympathy, along with an array of unsuitable medicines from their personal first-aid kits.

'How do you feel?' each one would ask, as they stooped to enter the tent of the sick one.

'Awful,' I replied, shortly before the visitor offered their theory as to why I'd ended up feeling that way.

'Maybe you overdid the cycling in the Sudanese sun.'

Yes, maybe I had done, but frankly that was an irrelevance now and all that mattered was that I felt awful. Too awful in fact to tell people how unwanted their theories were.

The worst diagnosis was yet to come, and it was given by a local doctor who'd been summoned to my tent after having been spotted making his way to the tenth anniversary celebrations. He made a brief examination and asked the same old routine questions which are so basic that they do leave you wondering why doctors spend years qualifying, instead of just a couple of months.

'I am afraid that you have malaria,' he finally declared, almost triumphantly.

'But I can't have malaria,' I replied in disbelief.

'You have all the symptoms,' he said, reaching into his bag. 'You should take a course of anti-malarial tablets.'

'But I don't have malaria.'

'I see. You have decided this, yes?'

'Yes, I have decided this, yes.'

The doctor made his way from the tent and I heard the short exchange which took place outside.

'So doctor, what do you think?' asked a concerned Laura.

'I think,' he replied, 'that the patient has malaria. The patient, however, does not.'

I had pretty good grounds for doubting this medic. Not only had I been taking the anti-malarial drug Lariam, I was also pretty certain that I hadn't actually been bitten by a mosquito, and anyway, even if I had, I'd definitely read somewhere that malaria takes a minimum of nine days to develop after you've been the reluctant recipient of the bite. Even in my present state of delirium I knew that this quack's maths were suspect.

Malaria or not, my visit to this place was pretty much over. The spectacle of Yambio in celebration was to remain unseen, and its musicians would play without the scrutiny of my watchful and opportunistic eye. In the distance I could hear the sound of drums and occasional gunshots, but unlike my travelling companions who had departed to immerse themselves in this rich cultural experience, I was left in my tent to sweat profusely and wallow in the damp sheets of self-pity.

Occasionally I'd break the monotony by throwing up.

'How are you today?' asked Justin, having returned from ferrying the others into Freedom Square.

'Not good, I'm afraid.'

I explained my symptoms and was more than a little frustrated by Justin's response.

'I think that you have malaria.'

'*I don't have malaria!*' I shouted, foolishly squandering precious resources of energy.

Poor Justin looked a little hurt, but not like someone who'd just made a mistake. It was as if my quick outburst had made him even more certain of his diagnosis. Flying off the handle and denying that you have malaria is probably one of the more recognisable symptoms of the disease.

'Here,' he said, offering me a glass of water. 'You must drink lots of this today.'

I was touched by Justin's concern. He stayed with me for a full half hour, mainly just sitting quietly, but occasionally uttering some quiet words of commiseration. I was in too much discomfort to offer any responses. At one point he leaned forward and pointed to my guitar which was propped up rather forlornly against the bed.

'May I play?' he asked.

'Do you know how?' I managed, with a groan.

'Yes, I learned it in the church.'

I made an attempt at a nod in the direction of the instrument, and Justin picked it up and began to strum a rhythm and sing a few lyrics, presumably in his native Azande dialect. It was not bad at all, and he clearly had a reasonable guitar technique (although from his singing you might have thought that he was the one with suspected malaria, not me).

I was suddenly struck by the irony of the situation. Here I was, a man who had made it his mission to find someone in Yambio with whom I could collaborate musically, and the very person I'd charged with finding this potential co-writer had turned out to be precisely that man himself. There was probably a moral in there somewhere, but I was definitely too ill to work it out. In my present state all I could do was listen to Justin's lilting renditions, and lament the belated discovery of his musical prowess.

'Justin, that was very nice,' I said, when he had finished the song. 'Now please could you pass my bag over to me?'

He did so, and I rummaged around in it until I found my wallet.

'Here,' I said, thrusting some dollars in his direction. 'This is for your wife's operation.'

Justin looked at the money and then gently leaned forward and took it.

'Thank you. Thank you Tony,' he said softly. 'This will make things much easier for me and for my family.'

I had been considering making this gesture from the moment I'd seen his wife suffering quietly in the hospital, but until now

I'd not wanted to unbalance our relationship by doing so. For me, it was not a huge amount of money – no more than the cost of a meal for two back in London – and yet I knew that here, on the front line, it was going to make a substantial difference.

'It is my pleasure,' I said. 'I hope that things continue to get better for all of you.'

I had been anticipating this moment for some time, and it felt good finally to be doing some giving. Something in me, however, had expected this to be a warmer and more emotional moment. In spite of Sudan's heat and the warm-hearted nature of the transaction which had just taken place, there was a cool atmosphere in the tent. It was difficult to fathom.

I was still awake at 4 a.m., and it wasn't just my relentless fever which was preventing a peaceful slumber. The people of Yambio had decided to rub salt in my wounds by partying into the night. The distant sound of drums seemed to mock me as I lay there wondering what exciting opportunities would have been opening up for me had I not been ambushed and assaulted by this wretched fever. I longed for the snugness of my own bed, and other familiar comforts of home. I knew only too well that for all the positive observations I had made about life here – the laughter, the sense of community, the lack of cars or padlocks, the stress-free simplicity of life – there were much better places in which to fall ill. Unlike the unfortunate occupants of the hospital and those waiting in the courtyard outside it, three different aircraft were soon going to whisk me to a place where I could feel cosy and unwell, instead of just unwell. I reminded myself how lucky I was. Yep, I felt like shite, but I was lucky.

Justin came to my tent in the morning.

'Are you feeling better today?' he enquired, sensitively.

'A little.'

He ambled over to the far side of the tent and looked down at my belongings which were untidily strewn all over the ground.

'This is very fine,' he said, picking up and studying my camera. 'We cannot get these here.'

There was a pause. He looked uncomfortable and a little restless.

'What's the matter?' I enquired.

'Do you need this camera?' he asked.

'What do you mean?'

'This could be very helpful to me in finding money for my family.'

'How?'

'There are people in Yambio who would like to have their families photographed. I could take their pictures and sell them the photos.'

'But where could you get the film developed?'

'This I would have to do in Uganda. But I have ways of getting this done.'

What a rigmarole, I thought. Personally I would have waited until 'Snappy Snaps' had set up in Yambio.

'There is a problem, Justin,' I said after a moment's reflection. 'I really want to take pictures documenting my journey back to England and I need the camera for that.'

'Oh.'

'I'm sorry.'

'It would be very helpful to me and my family.'

'Justin, I'm sorry but I need it.'

I didn't actually need it as much as I was making out. I could easily have got duplicates of photos taken by my fellow travellers, but I was confused by what I felt about this latest request. Hadn't I already helped Justin enough? Wasn't he being a little greedy here? After all, I'd paid for his wife's operation. I needed time to think about this one, and in my position of supine immobility, I had plenty of time to do just that.

But time, as it inevitably does, ran out.

'So Tony, what a bummer you being ill,' sympathised Irvine, as we stepped from the mini-bus on to the red mud of Yambio's makeshift airstrip. 'It means you didn't get what you wanted from this trip, did you?'

'That's not necessarily the case,' I replied, tapping my mini-disc player which was hanging round my neck. 'I have the girls from the school singing. I'm going to take this into a studio and see if I can't do some kind of collaboration with them.'

'A collaboration which they know nothing about?'

'Yes.'

'That's the best kind of collaboration, if you ask me.'

There was a short delay while twenty or so villagers unloaded what looked like a tractor engine from the waiting Cessant aircraft. Still feeling well below my best, I sat down in one of the seats which had been removed from the plane, and waited for the first leg of the journey back home to begin. When Justin approached me I thought that he was going to thank me and wish me a pleasant and safe return journey.

'Tony, I know that you said before that it would not be possible,' he began. 'But I wonder if you have been able to change your mind?'

I shrugged, implying that I did not know what he meant.

'Do you think it might be possible for me to have your camera?' he asked, almost in an apologetic whisper.

My heart sank. I had forgiven Justin his previous over-zealousness in this matter but now his persistency was beginning to make me question my whole relationship with him. Had Justin had an agenda from the moment he took my guitar from me a few days before? What had his motives been for visiting me in my tent and generally looking after me? Did his bold request stem from a genuine need, or was he something of a chancer?

I had a strong feeling that I should be firm with him and refuse his entreaty. But then again, another part of me didn't want to be mean. Didn't I have a responsibility to help this man and his family? After all, one of the reasons I'd accepted the offer of this trip to Sudan was because I'd wanted to make a difference, and here I was with a real opportunity to do exactly that. How could I be sure that the root of my uncomfortable feelings wasn't linked to my own ego, and that what I'd wanted was for this man to have been so moved by my initial gift that he should have felt too humble to have broached the subject of another?

'Justin, if I give you this camera, are you certain that it could improve things for you and your family?' I asked, when the expeditious soul-searching was over.

'Yes.'

'And you can really get the film developed in Uganda?'

'Yes.'

'In that case, I want you to smile while I finish off this film with pictures of what you looked like immediately prior to becoming the owner of a new camera.'

And so the final photographs I would shoot with this camera featured a man grinning from ear to ear. I didn't even need to get him to say 'cheese'.

Heathrow was cold and unwelcoming. It seems that the hotter the climate of the country from which one has begun one's return journey, the more damp, grey and blustery the climes provided by England's awaiting airport. That's just the way it is – I guess it's some kind of unwritten law of nature, but personally I prefer to blame it on New Labour.

The last two hours of the journey had left me restless and confused. The reason had been the conversation I'd had with Abi, the *Telegraph* photographer.

'You know you said how wonderful it was that Yambio was a town with no padlocks?' she'd said. 'Well, I noticed when I was taking pictures at Justin's home, that he had a padlock on one of his tukuls.'

The revelation had sent my mind racing. A padlock? What did he have to lock away? Hadn't he told me there was no theft in Yambio? I became worried that I'd been duped into giving to a kind of Southern Sudanese 'Del Boy'. Well – he had a lock-up didn't he?

I began to wonder if I had engaged in the wrong kind of giving, and I devoted my thoughts to this matter as we had completed the final leg of our retreat to England, the land of a million padlocks. I wondered if the best kind of giving was something that was done on an everyday basis, not just on special occasions like trips to Sudan or big charity events. Perhaps if we all gave a little more to those around us, in terms of time, consideration and love, then the world would be a better place. Hey, I could feel a cheesy song coming on ...

'Gor, you look brown mate,' declared the chirpy taxi driver, as I climbed into his cab. 'You been somewhere hot?'

'I've been to a place called Yambio,' I replied.

'Never 'eard of it? Where's that?'

I was tired and I really didn't fancy getting into a conversation with this guy.

What I really wanted to do was begin thinking about what should be done with the mini-discs of the schoolgirls' singing which I had in my bag. But wait. Wasn't this the perfect opportunity to do some real giving? If I made a bit of effort, perhaps I could lift his day a little by sharing some of my recent experiences. Fatigued or not, it was time to put my theory into practice. It was time to go that extra mile for someone else.

'Yambio is an amazing place,' I replied. 'It's in Southern Sudan.'

'Blimey, what were you doing in a shit-hole like that?'

It was Jakko to whom I turned for assistance – the man who enjoyed the dubious honour of having produced all my hits to date, and the man who'd hosted the dinner party which had given rise to this whole challenge in the first place. I'd decided that he was going to be the one who would help provide me with my hit record. He'd done it before – so why shouldn't he do it again?

So, once my malaria/flu/mystery illness had cleared up, I headed straight round to his place to play him the mini-discs of the Yambio schoolgirls singing.

'Jakko,' I said, 'we have a hundred per cent track record in the music biz. Isn't it the case that everything we've worked on together has made the Top Five?'

'Well … yes,' he said nervously, obviously aware that I was soon about to try and enlist his help. 'But it's worth remembering though that we've only ever worked together on the one track.'

'Exactly!' I exclaimed. 'So can't you see that a return collaboration is long overdue?'

'Tony,' said Jakko, 'I'm a serious musician. I decided a long time ago to limit my involvement in comedy records to just the one.'

'Which is why you're going to love this idea,' I said, with a big smile.

Jakko listened patiently while I explained about the Sudan trip and the wonderful girl singers from the school, and I could see his enthusiasm growing. By the time I'd finished playing him the mini-disc samples, he was completely sold on the project.

'All right, let's do it,' he said.

'Do you reckon we can turn those Sudanese children into pop stars?' I asked.

'We can but try,' he replied.

In the coming weeks Jakko used a combination of musical skills and computer wizardry to help create the song 'We Are Happy'. Keyboards, guitars and drums were added, but the *pièce de résistance* was yet to come. Having formerly been the guitarist with Level 42, Jakko was able to call up the band's maestro – Mark King – and ask him if he'd play bass on the track. And Mark King, being a good bloke, said yes.

Following an inspiring afternoon in Mark's home studio, Jakko and I came away with the song now greatly enhanced by the distinctive pumping, driving, slapping bass-line delivered courtesy of one of the world's foremost bass players.

I started playing 'We Are happy' to friends, and the general reaction was that it sounded 'just brilliant'.

'Is it a hit though?' I probed.

Invariably there was hesitation at this point, followed by 'maybes' and 'I'm not sures'.

It was time to seek some professional opinions.

My friend Jane, who'd been responsible for bringing me and Steve together for our 'Bird's Egg' collaboration, suggested that I talk to David Field.

'He's an A&R man, but he's a good bloke,' she said, as if these two didn't often go together. 'Also he's got a reputation for making hits from original source material. He was the man behind US3.'

'US3? That's a kind of submarine, isn't it?'

'Not really. It was Blue Note samples mixed with hip hop beats.'

'Oh yes. That's what I meant.'

As David stood by the window of his ninth-floor offices, surveying the vast and heavily populated capital which stretched out before him, it felt strange to hear the voices of the children from the Yambio school. On Jane's recommendation he'd agreed to listen to the fruits of mine and Jakko's labours. As the children's piercing voices cut through the hum of the office's air conditioning, my mind flashed back to the classes of girls beneath the jacaranda trees, birds of prey hovering overhead, their teachers strutting like stage actors, struggling to be heard above the constant click clicking of insects. How odd that the musical efforts of these children should now, totally unbeknownst to them, be the subject of analysis in a west London office block. I allowed their singing to lull me into a state of reverie, and I imagined myself on a return visit to their school where I interrupted a lesson to inform them that they would be required for a *Top of the Pops* appearance the following Friday.

When the track finished, David turned around slowly, seemingly touched by the sounds he'd just heard.

'Yes,' he said, nodding approvingly. 'It certainly has something.'

He paused, his face contorting for a moment. He was clearly struggling to articulate what he felt.

'The trouble is,' he continued, 'there's also something missing. And I'm not sure what it is.'

David walked back over to the window again and looked out across London, as if the answer might lie there, somewhere on the polluted, bustling streets. 'Maybe you should play it to Ben,' he said, spinning round quickly, as if he'd found what he'd sought from the window's vista. 'Yes, I think Ben should hear it.'

I met Ben Turner in a trendy West End bar. The kind of place where the barman gives you your change on a small tray or side plate, and where the clientele have thought about what they're wearing, and what it says about them, at least four times a day. Or possibly even four times an hour. Ben, who was founder and editor of *Muzik* magazine and had written extensively about the Ibiza club scene, was far more down to earth than I expected, and we shared a relaxed beer and the kind of chit-chat you might have overheard in a local pub. But then I changed all that when I produced my portable CD player from my jacket pocket.

'Have a listen to this, Ben,' I said, as cool as you like. 'And let me know what you think. Honestly.'

Ben put on the headphones and hit the play button. I was getting used to this now. The three minute wait before people passed judgement was becoming less agonising. On this occasion I was even able to think about other things. Did I need to get some margarine on the way home? How was it that bowling shoes had become fashionable? Did anyone watch BBC Choice out of choice?

'I think it's great,' said Ben, whipping off the headphones and reaching for his beer.

'Really?' I said, slightly stunned.

'Yeah,' he continued, after a smooth sip of fashionable foreign lager. 'I actually think it's got massive potential. Those vocals send memories flooding back of Transglobal Underground's timeless Temple-Head record. Don't you agree?'

'Er … well—'

'The piano part is a little pedestrian,' Ben continued, thankfully, before I could fail to comment. 'I reckon that you should go for a more chilled down tempo vibe with lush strings and synths.'

'Right. Yes, good idea.'

'The elements are there, it just needs a cinematic soundscape embedded underneath.'

At this point I began to realise just how out of touch I had become with the common parlance of the current music scene. I wanted to pass comment but all I could do was grin.

'With the right remix, I think this could be a hit in Ibiza,' added Ben, whom I was beginning to like more and more with each overwhelmingly positive statement he made.

'Really?'

'Yes.'

'Right, well let's try and get it out there this summer.'

'Well, I'm afraid you're too late for this year though. To do these things properly these things need pre-planning. Leave it with me, Tony. I've got a few people who I think might be able to do a good job on this.'

'So it has hit potential?'

'Absolutely.'

The best thing seemed to be to leave things in Ben's hands. As hands go, they seemed very capable.

So, my time in the Sudan had not been wasted after all.

PART III
WHAT DOES A PIXIE DO?

I'm the only living pixie as far as I can tell
But I got no motivation stuck inside my pixie shell
So tell me what does a pixie do?

I'm the only living pixie and I was born that way
But I'm really having trouble filling up my pixie day
I'm the only living pixie and they tell me I'm a cult
But there is no pixie manual with which I can consult
So tell me what does a pixie do?

I'm the only living pixie you can check the pixie news
You can ring my bell anytime you'll find it on my shoes
I'm the only living pixie consumed with pixie lust
Oh to find a Tinkerbell to sprinkle with my dust
So tell me what does a pixie do?

Vocation frustration, ideas above my station
I could lose my concentration, I'm a pixie after all
My mission — transition to an easier position
Gonna wake up other pixies with my secret pixie call

I'm the only living pixie as anyone can see
With button up pixie trousers there ain't no flies on me
I'm the only living pixie you can get inside my head
Just visit pixie-love.com on the worldwide pixie web
So tell me what does a pixie do?

CHAPTER 10 MIDGET, DWARF OR DWERG?

The only problem with Ben's enthusiasm for the Sudanese track was that it left me powerless. All I could do was wait. Wait and hope that he came through with the goods – and even if he was able to find the winning remix, it would be over a year before we could exploit the following season's Ibiza dance frenzy. I began to realise that relying too heavily on this track was a risky strategy, and in the coming weeks I started to consider other options. Although I longed to have a hit record which would have some 'credibility', I wondered whether some distant relative of my former smash 'Stutter Rap' might be needed.

Some kind of novelty record.

Some kind of novelty record in Europe.

I had an irrational hunch that the European market would provide the backdrop for my eventual victory, and I wondered if I should consider writing a nonsense song with catchy tune and thumping mesmeric bass-line which would prove irresistible on the dance floor. I'd always had this nagging respect for Euro pop, even though many of its biggest hits often left me feeling nauseous. I suppose this was because I was so impressed that the songwriters had managed to come up with a lyric in a language which was not their mother tongue. The phenomenon began in the seventies and soon these writers had created an entirely new genre of song lyric in which there were no glaring grammatical errors, but in which the artist was required to sing words which you never would have heard from a native English speaker.

In 1977, the talented Spanish female vocal duo Baccara sang:

Yes sir, I can boogie but I need a certain song
I can boogie, boogie woogie all night long

In mainland Britain people had ceased using the word *boogie* in 1972, and no-one had ever talked about *boogie woogieing* all night long. Ever.

The German Band Boney M had returned an impressive array of uptempo smashes, most of which made little or no sense. Their all time classic song was 'Rasputin' which rather ambitiously chose to document the life of a powerful priest who had infiltrated the court of the Russian Tsarina, and who was eventually murdered by jealous rivals. All this delivered in the genre of an upbeat disco track. No wonder they lost their way occasionally.

There lived a certain man in Russia long ago
He was big and strong, in his eyes a flaming glow
Most people looked at him with terror and with fear
But to Moscow chicks he was such a lovely dear

The feeling was mutual because Rasputin was quite partial to the Muscovite chicks too, it seems.

In all affairs of state he was the man to please
But he was real great when he had a girl to squeeze

Poetry.

Of course the greatest exponents of foreigners writing in English have to be the Abba boys, Benny and Bjorn. These guys were good. Very good. But there were occasions when our Swedish heroes clearly had difficulty coming up with lines which provided the requisite number of syllables to complete a line, and as a consequence they left Agnetha and Frida singing things which no native English speaker would ever really say. The opening couplet of the second verse of the song 'The Day Before You Came' was one of just many of the gems which can be found within this one piece.

I must have lit my seventh cigarette at half past two
And half the time I never even noticed I was blue

Only someone who'd just finished boogie woogieing all night long would talk about 'noticing they were blue'. However, my favourite line is in verse three:

> There's not I think a single episode of Dallas that I didn't see.

Well, what can I say? Except that there's not I think a single example of better lyrics that I didn't see. Or do I mean the opposite? Well, one or the other anyway. What does it matter as long as it's got a catchy tune?

'What do you mean by *nonsense lyric*?' asked the long-suffering Willie, whom I hadn't seen since we'd recorded the 'Bird's Egg' track together, and whom I'd once again cajoled into being a musical accomplice.

'I'm not entirely sure,' I replied. 'You know what all those Euro-dance hits are like. They just sing about whatever they want and don't worry in the slightest whether it makes any sense or not.'

'And you want the two of us to write a song like that?'

'This very afternoon.'

'I see.'

'Are you up for it?'

'Depends. What's it going to be about?'

I hadn't really thought too much about this. I was hoping that the inspiration would just come and that the subject matter would emerge from my subconscious at the moment. Extraordinarily, it did.

'Pixies,' I said, with a surprising earnestness.

'I beg your pardon?'

'Let's write a song about pixies,' I offered enthusiastically. 'Well, one pixie. A pixie who doesn't know what he's supposed to be doing.'

'How do you mean?'

'He's a pixie, right?'

'Who is?'

'The hero of our song.'

'... Right ...'

'And he was born a pixie – but he doesn't know any other

pixies and he just doesn't know how he ought to be ... er ... filling his day.'

'Tony, have you ever thought of seeing a counsellor?'

'Certainly not, they might spoil my fun.' I took a sip of my tea. 'Are you on board then?'

'Hmm, I suppose so,' he mumbled with a not totally convincing reluctance. 'I'll go and get the beers.'

The process which followed afforded us much amusement. I identified an annoying little riff on the keyboard which Willie approved of, in a disapproving kind of way. (His exact words were – 'That'll do. That's exactly the shit they like.') Then Willie combined his musical and technical skills using his magical machines to provide an authentic drum sound and a muddy, thuddy bass-line. Then, before you could say 'long live the Venga Boys' we were on to the lyrics.

Once I had written the opening few lines, we both understood exactly what was required for the rest of the song. Here, for your delectation, are the lyrics to our Pixie song.

> *I'm the only living pixie, and I was born that way*
> *But I'm really having trouble filling up my pixie day*
> *So tell me what does a pixie do?*
> *I'm the only living pixie as far as I can tell*
> *But I got no motivation stuck inside my pixie shell*
> *So tell me what does a pixie do?*

I could go on, but I think you get the gist.

The ideas flowed as freely as the beers, and it only took us about forty-five minutes to complete the entire masterpiece. Now, you may be thinking that any song which can be dashed off in just under an hour can't be up to much, but I have to remind you that they say the true works of genius don't take long to create – and God bless the people who say that, I've got a lot of time for them. (About forty-five minutes, to be precise.)

'It's a triumph!' I said two weeks later, when I'd returned to listen to Willie's completed mix of "What Does A Pixie Do"? 'The kids out there will bloody love it.'

'Hmm,' mumbled a pensive Willie, perhaps fearful that this thing might actually take off and gravely damage his reputation as a serious composer and musician. He looked wistfully across the studio to Andy, his manager, maybe hoping that a reasonably sane businessman might put the mockers on the whole thing and tell us both to stop wasting our time. He was to be disappointed.

'It's great,' said Andy. 'And I know exactly the place where it will take off.'

'Where?' ı asked.

'Holland. I've managed bands out there and this is just the kind of thing they go for.'

'Meaningless tosh?' quipped Willie.

'Exactly,' replied Andy. 'Don't you remember the Smurfs? They still make records over there and the Dutch bloody love them.'

'So what would be the best way to try and launch myself on to the Dutch music scene?' I enquired.

'Leave it with me, I'll make a few calls and get back to you.'

As Andy left, I looked across to Willie who was shaking his head incredulously. But there was definitely the hint of a smile.

Andy's game plan turned out to be that Willie and I should record two further tracks in a similar vein to 'What Does A Pixie Do?', and then I should go to Holland and perform them all at a showcase. He reckoned the best place to do this was in Hilversum.

'Hilversum is where the Dutch have based their entire TV, music and entertainment world,' Andy explained. 'The great thing about going there is that we can get a lot of people along from the industry, and if they like what you do, we could create such a buzz about the whole project that people could be vying to get your signature on a contract. But you'll need to pretend to be a band rather than a solo artist, and that band will need a name.'

'I'll come up with something,' I said, confidently.

The inspiration for the name didn't come for another week, and I ran it past Willie, who was up to his eyes in one of many remixes of the track.

'Shhh!' I whispered.

'I can't do it any quieter than this,' answered Willie. 'You need it this loud to hear the bass properly.'

'No. Shhh!' I repeated.

'What *are* you talking about?'

'Shhh! That can be the name of the band – "Shhh!"'

Willie thought for a moment and then slowly repeated it to himself.

'Good isn't it!' I said, not really giving Willie a chance to make up his own mind.

'Actually, I quite like it.'

'And that can be one of the tracks too.'

'What do you mean?'

'We do some poxy Euro dance instrumental and just pepper the track with the occasional "Shhh!"'

'Hmm.'

'No, "Shhh!"' – although we could add a "Hmm" somewhere, if you want.'

'What?'

'Then once we've recorded the Shhh! song,' I continued, riding roughshod over his confusion, 'we do a dance version of "Bird's Egg" and hey presto, we've got the three songs for our Hilversum showcase.'

'You've got it all worked out, haven't you, Tony?'

'Absolutely. And don't forget – it's going to be a triumph!'

'And at which studio are you going to record these extra tracks, might I ask?'

'I'll go and put the kettle on.'

Well, there was no point in replying. Willie already knew the answer.

'You've got to put it on,' said Willie mischievously, as the morning of my departure finally arrived.

'I've already tried it all on, back at my house yesterday. It all fits fine.'

'Tony, you're not getting away with it that easily,' persisted Willie. 'The amount of time and involvement I have put into this project means that I deserve to see you making a complete prat of yourself dressed up as a pixie. Get into that outfit now.'

There was no way I could refuse him. Time and time again I'd proposed payment to Willie in exchange for all his hard work in the studio and on each occasion he'd turned me down. 'Don't be silly,' he'd said after each offer, not realising that the time would come when that would be exactly what he was going to expect of me. That moment had now arrived, unless you don't count pulling on a pixie costume as silliness.

I struggled into the outfit – a beautiful costume made for me by my friend Liessa, who had shown a remarkable enthusiasm for such a daft project. Her passion for fabrics, design and sewing machines meant that she had created a splendid, predominantly green outfit with dashes of red, which would have been welcome on the catwalks of any of the top fashion houses (provided that I wasn't the one who was wearing it). When I was fully dressed in all my verdant splendour, I revealed myself in Willie's living room where he and his girlfriend Monika responded with much hysterical laughter. Here was the opportunity for Willie to exact revenge for the hours he'd spent labouring behind the recording desk. A short photo call began after the laughter had subsided, followed by a general discussion as to whether Dutch hoodlums might take pride in beating up over-sized pixies. Then Willie upped the ante.

'You've got to make the actual flight in the outfit,' he stated emphatically.

'No way,' I protested. 'If you were travelling with me then I might consider it, but I'm not going to walk around an airport and sit on a plane totally on my own dressed like this. It would just be too, too embarrassing.'

'All right,' said Willie in a slightly more conciliatory tone. 'But you've got to check in at the airline desk as a pixie. I'll bring the camera and film it. It could make a very funny bit for the video.'

We'd decided that 'What Does A Pixie Do?' would need a music video to accompany it, and we both felt that any shots of a strange pixie wandering around causing confusion in unlikely places would be useful to cut into the video from time to time. And so it was, with some reluctance, that I agreed to turn up at the airport fully regaled in my green magnificence, and I soon found myself standing before an extremely bemused lady at the KLM check-in desk.

'Is this some kind of joke?' she enquired, slowly inspecting my outfit.

'Not really,' I replied, as deadpan as the moment would allow. 'I'm going to Holland to become a pop star, and this is how I'm going to do it.'

The lady hesitated, unsure of how to respond.

'Would you like a window or an aisle seat?' she finally asked.

I could only assume that I had been the first pixie in search of Dutch pop stardom that she had checked in, and that it was nervousness which had driven her to resume the usual line of questioning, in spite of how much the green object before her warranted a temporary departure from it.

I plumped for a window seat and explained that, yes, I had packed my bags myself. Business was completed without another comment about my attire and I left happily clutching my boarding card for seat 7a. I then began bumbling around in the terminal, changing money and browsing in the bookshop whilst a chortling Willie eagerly filmed from a distance. The airport's other customers were giving me a wide berth, choosing to snigger at me from a distance and to avoid eye contact should I return a glance in their direction.

'We've got some good stuff there,' said Willie, after about a quarter of an hour and just when I was starting to tire of the whole thing.

'In that case I'll go and get changed then so that I can make my journey in a state of normality,' I said, and I started heading off to the gents with my civvies tucked under my pixie arm in a plastic bag.

It was with not inconsiderable relief that I began the process of shedding pixie garments in the lavatory booth.

Hat off – comb hair.

Top off – jumper on.

Pointy shoes off – long struggle with tights – trousers and socks on.

Finally, all I had to do was put my shoes back on and I'd be a regular human being again. But wait! No shoes! There were no shoes in my plastic bag, because for some reason I'd put them into my big hold-all. The big hold-all which I'd just checked on to the plane. So, I was shoeless and faced with two equally unappealing alternatives. I could either wander around the cold marble of the airport terminal in my socks or I could pull my pixie boots back on again – the bright green pixie boots with P sewn on the side in red felt – the ones with the long, pointy, curly-up toes. The bloody stupid ones. It was a stark choice between physical or emotional discomfort.

'Oh just put the pixie shoes on,' said Willie, when I emerged barefoot from the loos and explained the nature of my dilemma. 'No-one will notice, and if they do they'll just think you're super trendy.'

'Oh I don't think these are trendy,' I whined, holding the two ludicrous objects up before his eyes.

'I didn't say trendy, I said *super trendy*. You'll be making a statement if you wear those.'

'And what statement might that be?'

I never got an answer to that question because Willie had descended into fits of giggles. Whilst he cackled like an adolescent I tried to adopt a 'I'm mature and bigger than this' attitude, and I leant down to pull on the boots, struggling to get my jeans to cover the two red P's which had been sewed on to the boots' sides.

'Actually,' I said, having completed the job as best I could, 'that doesn't look too bad after all, does it?'

I looked at Willie for confirmation but he was too far gone. Hysterical laughter, tears, the full works. My obvious irritation at his reaction only served to make the whole thing even more irresistibly amusing.

'Have you finished?' I enquired in a schoolmasterly manner, having watched more than a minute of his helpless convulsions.

'Yes,' he cried, disciplining himself to bring them to a conclusion before the thought of having to terminate the laughter immediately caused him to launch back into another bout of unbridled guffawing.

'Stop it,' I said admonishingly. 'People are starting to look at us.'

'It's OK', he managed in a high-pitched whimper in a momentary break in the laughter. 'They'll just be commenting on how super trendy you are.'

And with those words he set himself off again.

'Oh I've had enough,' I declared impatiently. 'Goodbye Willie, I'll ring you when I get back.'

I tried my best to move off with as much dignity as I could muster, but the length of the shoes meant that I had to walk a little like someone in flippers and I was fully aware that each step that I was taking was sending my friend into further paroxysms.

'If he punctures a lung he bloody deserves it,' I mumbled under my breath as I inched closer to the departures barrier and the potential refuge which 'air side' would offer.

Unfortunately 'air side' offered no such respite because here I noticed that there was an extra glint of alarm in the strange looks I was getting. As I passed my hand luggage through the X-ray machines I saw two mothers physically pull their children away from me. The problem lay in the fact that there was now only one small part of me that was weird. When I'd been in full pixie attire it was clear to all and sundry that I was a man who, for some reason, had dressed up in a costume. Now that I was a bloke in sweat shirt and jeans but with the accessory of some outrageous pointy green boots, I was a far more worrying proposition, especially since I was travelling alone. I began to feel like the only chart entry I was about to make was into Interpol's Top Ten of dangerous perverts.

While waiting in the queue for foreign exchange, I noticed something extraordinary across the terminal building. Moving towards me, marching briskly towards 'arrivals', was someone whose face was very familiar. At first I felt I should immediately stop him and engage in friendly banter, until I realised that our relationship didn't warrant such action. This wasn't someone I knew personally, but it was none other than the pop superstar Sting, no doubt arriving back after promoting another platinum-selling album in some exotic location. I wondered for a moment if he might stop to convert some money back into sterling and we could fall into an inspiring conversation about life, love and exchange rates.

It wasn't to be. With every breath he took, and with every step he made, he wasn't watching me. It was a shame in a way, because had he done so he would have been able to see that I was wearing shoes that were far more suited for 'giant steps walking on the moon', than for hanging around in airport terminals. As he hurried by, flanked by his entourage, I allowed myself to believe that seeing Sting could well be a portent of great things to come. Perhaps the next time I flew to Holland I would be travelling with a manager or an assistant, having made a start in keeping the compilers of the music charts as busy as Sting had done over the years.

'Great shoes!' said the American lady in the queue behind me, disturbing me from my daydreaming.

I turned and smiled back at her, relieved to discover someone who wasn't frightened of me. Good old Americans, I thought. You can always rely on one of them to offer relief from the air of British stand-offishness which can permeate the atmosphere on occasions such as this.

'Thank you,' I replied politely. 'I'm told they're super trendy.'

'Oh they are,' she offered with a grin. 'They most certainly are. Don't you agree, Walt?'

Walt, her rather brow-beaten husband, did agree, although looking at him you got the feeling that he was a fellow who long ago had seen the wisdom of concurring with his wife's views. We exchanged cordial goodbyes and I braced myself for the next unappealing task which awaited me. I needed to go to the toilet.

In my experience most women are fascinated by the ease in which men urinate alongside each other in public urinals. They ask questions like 'Don't you get tempted to look at each other's things?' and they are generally amazed by the extraordinary lack of inhibition with which we men approach the whole procedure.

'Oh, we just get it out and point it,' we say. 'Then we give it a good shake. We don't bother about much else.'

For some reason the two males in Heathrow's gents didn't seem to be subscribers to this carefree philosophy. As I stood there at the middle one of three available urinals, manhood gently couched in my right hand, I looked around to see two men hovering around waiting for me to finish. Why didn't they use one of the vacant urinals on either side of me? Had my footwear frightened them? Did big pointy shoes with curly-up ends mean something I didn't know about? Was I unwittingly making a public signal that I was eager for a homosexual encounter in the airport lavs?

One of the men behind me chose to relieve himself in the seclusion of the cubicle, and I could hear the loud tinkle as he hit the water at the bottom of the bowl. I was deeply unimpressed. Frightening though I may have been, surely he should have had the courage not to have amended his behaviour in such a cowardly manner. Apart from anything else, peeing in the cubicle of male public lavatories is morally wrong. In my view, if you're not prepared to line up and take a leak in the same manner as everyone else then frankly, you can go elsewhere.

On leaving the toilets I discovered something new about moving about in this footwear when I was forced to climb the flight of stairs between the lavatories and the departure gate. These had caused me no problem on the way down, but the ascending journey was considerably more demanding because the extended length of my pointy-toed boots meant that they wouldn't fit on a step when pointing forwards. As a consequence of this I couldn't get sufficient body weight on to a step with a shoe facing forwards and so I was forced into side-stepping my way up the stairs. This only served to draw more attention to me, because to non-crustaceans, this kind of behaviour can look unusual.

Following some further sideways climbing, this time up the steps on to the plane (and not without suffering some playful jibes from the baggage handlers who were loading nearby), I decided that I was now officially tired of looking really very odd indeed. I negotiated my way into my seat and did my best to take advantage of the relative normality which tucking my feet under the seat in front would afford me. It was a great shame that the woman who'd been unfortunate enough to have been allotted seat 7b just happened to see my feet before the manoeuvre was completed. It could only have been a glimpse but it appeared to be enough to upset her for the entire duration of the short flight. She shifted nervously in her seat and would not allow herself to come into eye contact with me. I made one attempt at chatting but it was not a huge success.

'Are you going to Holland on business?' I asked, as the synthetic meals were placed on our trays by an equally synthetic stewardess.

7b simply fixed herself firmly and determinedly on her neatly packaged food and continued with the policy of pretending that I didn't exist. She would regret this, I thought, when 'What Does A Pixie Do?' was a worldwide smash and she bumped into me again at an airport and requested my autograph for her children.

'You shunned me,' I would reply, 'in the days before green pointy-up shoes became all the rage. Now kindly move out of my way while I deal with the world's press.'

I devoted the rest of the brief flight to considering what might be realistically achieved on this trip. If it was a success then more visits would be necessary – not least to perform on the Dutch equivalent of *Top of the Pops*. I had a fairly simple game plan. Shoot footage for the video, and perform a showcase for the Dutch record industry, just as soon as it could be arranged. Initially I was going to head for The Hague where I could take advantage of the only contacts that I had in Holland – my Dutch book publishers. They had kindly offered me the use of their offices to send faxes and emails, and make the calls needed to put everything in place. I was to be met and the airport by Roel, an editor to whom I'd spoken at length on the phone, and Sander, who was a student Roel had found for me. I was going to pay him a daily rate to act as a kind of PA – translating, filming, and gently facilitating my rise to Dutch superstardom.

Upon landing I knew that I would have the dubious pleasure of being the source of amusement for a new nationality of airport employees. However, as I waited to disembark from the plane I tried to kid myself that the Dutch would not find my footwear out of the ordinary. Weren't they heavily into clogs? My thinking was that if hollowed out chunks of wood were part of your national costume then a pair of pointy pixie boots wouldn't turn too many heads.

I was wrong. Unlike Amsterdam airport where there would have been plenty of weird-looking passengers en route for the city's infamous dope dens and seedy red light district, Rotterdam airport seemed to cater only for upright and strait-laced businessmen. As I walked through passport control and shuffled towards baggage reclaim, I prompted a range of reactions from astonished, baffled and amused, down to a wariness bordering on fear. I could hardly wait for my bag to come round on that carousel containing the footwear that would enable a resumption of a life running with vaguely normal service. I didn't want to set off on (or in) the wrong footing. Roel and Sander, my Dutch hosts, knew nothing about the 'pixie' element of my project and I didn't want to alarm them on our first meeting by turning up looking like a man who was clearly only in Holland to take advantage of the country's liberal drug laws.

Unfortunately Rotterdam airport was to prove to be an enormous disappointment to me. It was simply too small for my current requirements. I was looking for an airport which was big enough *not* to have the baggage carousel right next to a glass screen behind which people were standing waiting to greet the new arrivals. Rotterdam airport, as it transpired, let me down very badly in this regard. As soon as I arrived at the carousel I saw two men standing together beyond the glass screen, and one of them waved to me. These guys had to be Roel and Sander, and I must have been recognised from the photos which had appeared on my previous books. I waved back and as I did so I saw their gazes drop to floor level and their expressions immediately changed from welcoming to puzzled. Since I didn't have the courage to look back at them again I have no idea how their expressions may have altered during the long five minutes whilst I waited for my bag to tumble down the chute and begin its circular parade. One can only guess at what emotions they may have been experiencing, but at best there must have been a feeling of mild concern.

None was on show when they greeted me. Roel was older than I had expected him to be, with a full beard and a general look about him of someone who'd enjoyed the Sixties. Sander was in his early twenties and was unreasonably tall. Both were puffing on cigarettes.

'Tony, it's great to meet you,' said Roel, warmly.

I greeted them both and we made our way out to the car making small talk about the weather. To their credit, neither made any comment about my footwear, in spite of the awkward way in which I was being forced to walk. When we reached Roel's small hatchback I felt there was a slight tension between us which would only be lifted by providing them with an explanation for the circumstances which lay behind the footwear.

'We did wonder a little,' said Roel, when I'd completed my explanation and had begun to change back into my sensible shoes. 'But of course we knew that you are crazy because we have read your books.'

On the journey to The Hague, the conversation didn't exactly flow. Sander, who'd insisted on sitting in the back even though he must have been close to seven feet tall, was extremely quiet, maybe because his contorted body was causing him such pain. I was a little worried though, because here I was embarking on a project of such an outlandishly extrovert nature, and the person who was going to be my assistant seemed to be unduly shy and retiring. I reassured myself that perhaps he still hadn't quite recovered from the shoe thing and that there would be a way of coaxing him out of his shell.

'Ours is not an interesting landscape,' said Roel poetically, as he noticed me looking out of the window with the air of an inquisitive child.

Anyone who paid any attention in Geography will remember that Holland is uncompromisingly flat, largely because the Dutch reclaimed a good proportion of it from the sea. This, of course, was a most civilised thing to do. When they wanted more land, instead of invading a neighbouring country, the Dutch simply tipped some mud into the ocean and created a bit more territory that way. If only Hitler had adopted a similar policy, I mused.

I wasn't expecting The Hague to have the same vibrancy as other capital cities, and as we entered its outskirts it did have more of the feel of a mid-sized suburban town. Amsterdam is Holland's wild teenager – getting the sex, drugs and canals, whilst The Hague is the patrician elderly relative which soberly presides over the seat of government, the European Court of Human Rights and the official residence of the Royal Family.

In short, it is dull.

'Would you like to have dinner with some other people from the office and discuss some ideas on how we can help?' asked Roel as we pulled into what felt like a more central area.

'That sounds great,' I replied, looking out of the window and noticing how bare the streets were. 'There aren't many people about, are there?'

'The Hague is very quiet at night. People come to the centre only to work, then they go home. That's just the way it is. What kind of food do you like?'

'I'm easy really. I eat fish but not meat.'

'I have booked a traditional Flemish restaurant. Are you happy to go there?'

'Of course.'

~

The interior of the restaurant was most unassuming and seemed to make little effort to look traditionally Flemish, although the menu more than compensated by listing every dish in totally incomprehensible gobbledygook. I didn't know whether it was Flemish, Dutch or Martian. Like most non-Dutch speakers making a visit to Holland I'd made little effort to browse through Dutch phrase-books. What was the point when they all spoke such good English? I remembered what my friend Ben had told me about this country. A decade previously he'd come to Holland to work for a five-year stint and had taken weekly Dutch lessons. However, every time he started to speak the language to someone they would hear him struggling and immediately say, 'You're English, right? No problem, I speak English.' The annoying thing is that the Dutch speak English a good deal better than many Brits, albeit with a mildly irritating American twang to their accent. The problem is that they watch too much American television, when they should obviously be listening to BBC Radio 4.

'I'll have the fish,' I announced once Sander's translation had established that this was one dish which wasn't largely constituted of dead mammal.

We'd been joined by two of Roel's female colleagues, Maartje and Vonne, who were both eager to find out more about my reasons for paying them a visit. I decided to give it to them straight.

'I'm going to have a hit record in your country,' I said, unwaveringly, 'dressed as, and singing about, a pixie.'

'I understand,' said Maartje, offering an expression which suggested that this had been anything but the case.

'What is a pixie?' asked Vonne, displaying her ignorance.

'You must know what a pixie is,' I replied. 'Pixie – small green man. Pointy shoes and all that stuff.'

'Is it like a kabouter?' asked Maartje.

'What's a kabouter?' I returned, beginning to regret not having done my research properly.

It was becoming clear that no-one around the table knew what a pixie was. This could severely hamper my progress.

'It's a small fat man who does good deeds,' she said jovially. 'They make the beds and they live in mushrooms – or under the ground.'

The author, aged 17.
A promising start to a
musical career...

Where did it all go wrong?
Morris Minor and the Majors
top the charts in 1988.

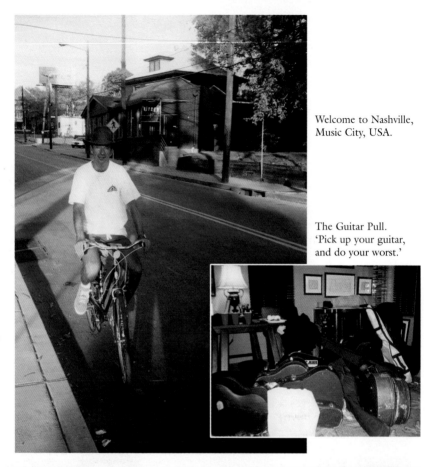

Welcome to Nashville, Music City, USA.

The Guitar Pull. 'Pick up your guitar, and do your worst.'

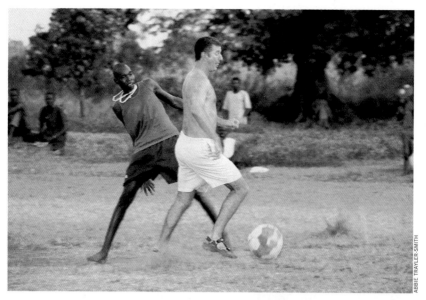

In Sudan, my footballing and musical skills provoked the same reaction – hysterical laughter from all around me.

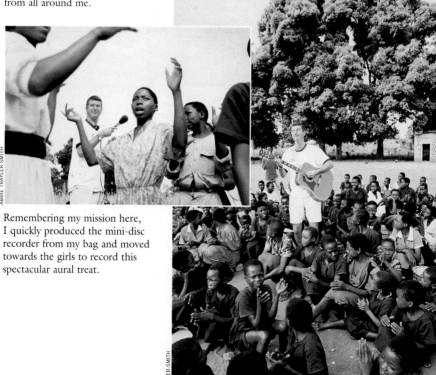

Remembering my mission here, I quickly produced the mini-disc recorder from my bag and moved towards the girls to record this spectacular aural treat.

The Pixie outfit. 'I'm going to Holland to be a pop star, and this is how I'm going to do it.'

Mark King of Level 42, being a good bloke, agreed to lay down some bass for us.

MONIKA AGGRELIUS

Tony Hawks and chart-topping beauty Paula Seling take the Romanian media by storm.

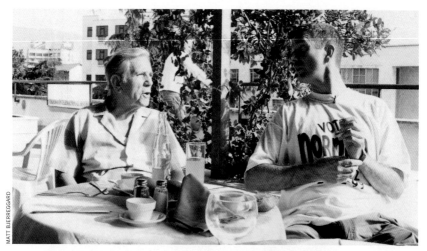

'Push me in the face.'
'You want me to push you in the face?'
'Yes. It'll be funnier.'

However hard he tried to learn them, Norman could never get the words quite right.

The crowds confirmed that Norman was indeed, Big In Albania.

Norman Wisdom and the Pitkins had extraordinarily broad appeal. Success was inevitable.

Pitkin! Suddenly Norman was surrounded by Albanian footballers.

Sir Tim Rice on (toy) saxophone. I bet things were never like this when he worked with Andrew Lloyd Webber.

The supergroup looking good and sounding great on Albania's biggest TV show.

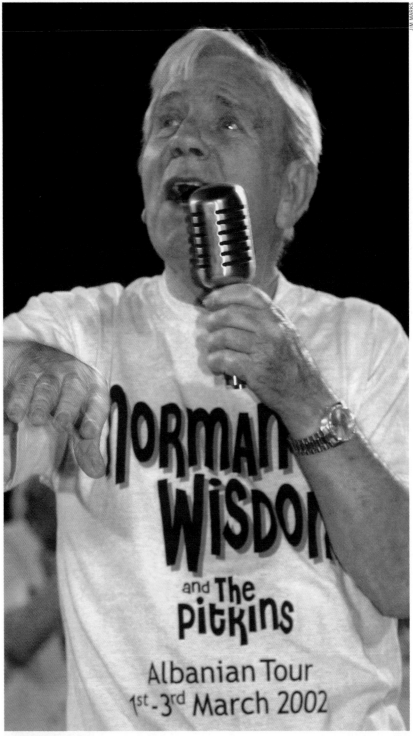

'I love Albania back – ooh I dooooo…'

'That's the kind of thing, except that I don't think a pixie is necessarily fat.'

'Well then a pixie isn't a kabouter,' concluded Vonne, emphatically. 'Kabouters are fat little fellows.'

'Is it a dwerg?' asked Roel.

Perhaps I shouldn't have written the song in forty-five minutes. Perhaps I should have been a little more scientific in my approach.

'Er ... what's a dwerg?' I asked, fully aware of what an odd conversation this was becoming.

'A dwerg,' explained Roel, 'is, I suppose, what you might call a midget.'

'No I don't think a pixie is necessarily a midget – although they're usually pretty small, I think.'

'Is it a dwarf?' enquired Sander.

'Isn't a dwarf the same as a midget?'

'I don't know. I don't think so.'

'Now come to think of it, I'm not sure either.'

It is an appalling indictment of the education systems of our respective countries that nobody at the table could confirm whether a midget or a dwarf are one and the same thing. A string of questions followed about the nature of pixies.

'Does a pixie act nicely?'

'Are they trolls?'

'Do they do good deeds?'

'Are they dwarves?'

'Are they magicians?'

'Are they like smurfs?'

'Do they have green faces?'

I answered all the questions, and with each 'don't know' it became more painfully apparent, as I sat at this dinner table with some of the cream of Holland's publishing community, that I didn't really know what a pixie was. It was weird, but it had just been something which I'd just assumed that I knew, but when it came down to it, I had no idea at all. My approach to this whole project had been completely half-arsed.

Maartje then dropped another bombshell. It seemed that I had competition.

'The Kabouters have already had a hit record over here,' she said. 'They appear on a children's programme and their song sold a lot of copies.'

'What was their record called?'

'"Kabouter Plop".'

Suddenly I felt confident that at least I was in the right country. Any place where a song called 'Kabouter Plop' could make the charts was surely ripe for my particular brand of nonsense.

'Anyway, whatever a pixie is,' said Roel, attempting to haul the conversation back to something more worthy of a group of educated adults, 'you are going to dress as one when you perform this song?'

'Yes. And I may dress up like it and try and talk to people, just to see what reaction it gets. I may film this and it may form part of the video which will eventually accompany the song.'

'You should know that our culture is different to yours. People here in Holland are not that light-hearted.'

'Really?'

'Really.'

'But what about "Kabouter Plop"?'

Roel was silent for a moment, before producing a most unsatisfactory answer.

'That was different.'

That night I returned to my room and wrote out a list of tasks which I wanted to achieve the following day. The plan was to get Sander on the phone all morning setting up meetings in Hilversum, while I went to the local dance school to see if I could recruit some dancers who might like to perform in my showcase with me. I'd decided that I would feel less of a prat if I wasn't jumping around as a pixie totally on my own and, given that I was intending to perform three songs, I was aware that the showcase could become exceedingly dull if I didn't find some way to spice the performance up a little. Years of watching *Top of the Pops* had taught me that many a drab performance can be rescued by a couple of sexy dancers gyrating alongside a lacklustre and unsensational singer. All I had to do was find two of my own, and then try and tempt them along by waving a wad of guilders in their direction.

Also on the list, was trying to find a mobile phone shop where maybe a member of staff could tell me why my phone wouldn't bloody work. It was supposed to have a thing called 'roaming', which meant that whatever country you turned it on in, it would immediately search for a network and supply you with instant communication forthwith. However thus far, each time I had turned mine on, it had simply supplied me with the message 'No networks found', and I'd done all I could to make it work, including shouting at it, but even that had failed.

I lay on my bed in my hotel bedroom feeling a bit like a travelling salesman. I suppose in a way I was. It was just that the product I was going to be selling was a little unusual. The pixie shoes sticking out of the top of my bag served as a reminder of that. I began to consider what the next day might bring, but then decided that I'd probably sleep better if I thought about something else. Suddenly I was stirred by a noise from the bathroom as something fell from a shelf and into the sink, which I'd failed to empty of water after the final wash of the day.

Plop!

OK, it hadn't been 'Kabouter Plop!' but I still took it as a sign.

CHAPTER 11 **PHONES, HAIL AND SEX FOR SALE**

After a hotel breakfast notable only for a dining-room atmosphere of silent tension better suited to that of an examination
hall, I began strolling into the centre of The Hague. As I drew
closer to the pedestrianised area where I'd been told that the
city's mobile phone outlets were to be found, I noticed that
nearly all shops had chosen to give themselves English names.
One, called 'The Last Minute Shop', had just closed down.
Evidently, restricting itself only to trading between 5.29 and
5.30 every day had proved to be commercial suicide. A retail
outlet going by the name of the 'Free Record Shop' caught my
eye next. Surely bargains to be had here, I thought. However,
upon browsing I discovered that the records weren't free at all,
and it turned out that the impudent proprietors expected you to
swap money for the items on sale. Clearly Holland is in need of
some kind of Trades Descriptions Act.

By accident I stumbled upon an area of governmental buildings and I wandered around aimlessly for a while. I found the
architecture practical and unexciting, much as I'd found the
Dutch to be themselves, thus far. But perhaps that view would
change in the coming days.

'It should just search for a network when you turn it on,' said
the helpful young man in the mobile phone shop I'd eventually
stumbled upon – in better English than a lot of shop assistants
can manage in Britain.

'Yes, but it doesn't, and I don't know why,' I replied.

My youthful assistant pressed a few more buttons on the
phone, frowned and handed it back.

'There must be a problem with the network,' he said resignedly. 'You will have to chase up your network provider.'

'That will be fun,' I replied.

Every time I'd called my network provider before, I'd been kept hanging on the phone for twenty minutes listening to jangly electronic music. This had only occasionally been interrupted by the recorded voice of a woman telling me just how important I was to them. It's an odd way of treating someone important – leaving them waiting on the end of the line, at their expense, listening to synthesised muzak. What did they do to unimportant people, I wondered?

Given that I was unfortunately incommunicado, I resolved to take advantage of the phones at the offices of my Dutch publishers. I arrived at the building and was ushered up to the second floor and into the bright but rather stark room where Sander had spent the morning making phone calls on my behalf. He had some news which was rather sobering.

'Most of the record companies I have called say that they can only make an appointment to see you in a fortnight from now,' he said, looking a little jaded. 'Sony Music even said that they would not be able to see you for a year.'

'A *year*?'

'That's what they told me.'

'But that's absurd!'

'I think so too, but that is what they said.'

Obviously Sony reckoned that saying they could see you in twelve months' time was more polite than simply telling you to piss off and stop bothering them, but it amounted to the same thing though, surely.

'Maybe you'll get lucky in a minute,' I said to Sander, hoping that he wouldn't lose heart. 'Try a few more calls, and if no one bites we'll have to think of a new approach.'

'What will you do now?'

'I have to call my mobile phone people back in England – so that should keep me occupied for a while.'

An hour later, I had achieved very little other than having considerably reduced my Dutch publishers' profit margin for the year. I'd been kept holding for ages on an international call, only for some bright spark in England eventually to tell me that there was a fault with the roaming network in Holland and that there was absolutely nothing I could do about it. Technology. It enables us to do all sorts of incredible things but the problem is that when it decides not to work, it leaves us utterly powerless. How one longs for the simplicity of the bicycle. If you get a puncture, then you get out your repair kit and begin to solve the problem (or at least look like you're going to until someone more practical comes along and does the job for you). But with modern technology all you can do is hope, because everything is so darned sophisticated that only 1 per cent of the population has any idea how anything works. How many people do you know who take the back off their computer and have a good rummage around every time it crashes? (If the answer to that question is four, I suggest that you implement a thorough review your social scene.)

'I'm going to wander round to the dance school you mentioned,' I said to Sander, in a desperate attempt to cheer myself up. 'I want to see if I can recruit any dancers for my showcase. You take yourself a well-deserved long lunch.'

When I saw the sign on the dance school door saying that it was closed for a fortnight's holiday, it suddenly dawned on me that The Hague was probably not the centre of Europe's entertainment industry. This probably wasn't the best place to have chosen as my base. It would have been a pretty good spot if I'd wanted to indict an international war criminal or sue a government over some human rights issue, but I had to face up to the fact that it just wasn't looking good for a dancing pixie.

'I think I need to go to Amsterdam,' I said to Maartje and Sander, on my return to the office.

'But what about me?' said Sander, looking more than a little hurt. 'Does that mean that you don't want me any more?'

'If I need to do any filming, you can still do it. How long is it to Amsterdam on the train from here?'

'The fast train is about forty minutes.'

'Well, there you are then, you can come and join me if I need you, and I'll pay you for your time.'

'Where will you stay?' asked Maartje.

'A hotel.'

'You may find everywhere is full. The Germans take their

holidays in the two weeks following Easter, and Amsterdam usually gets overbooked.'

Half an hour of phone calls later, Maartje's words were being borne out. Everywhere was full. Not for the first time, I cursed that I hadn't done more research.

I sat on the top deck of the train, thinking what a great idea these double-decker trains were. We could have them in England if we'd built higher bridges 150 years ago. No foresight, the Victorians. Amsterdam, Holland's capital, was now only ten minutes away and I was heading straight for the bawdy part of town. It wasn't out of choice, honest, it was just that the only vacancy that Maartje had managed to find me was a rather down-market travellers' hostel right in the heart of the city's world-renowned Red Light District.

I'd said my goodbyes to the people in The Hague who had done their best to help me, but I knew that theirs was an expertise in an entirely different field, and that their continued involvement in my project was actually more likely to hamper than enhance. Sander, I was sorry to admit, was just too reserved for the job in hand. I really needed someone who was as outgoing and daft as I was, who'd be able to *celebrate* being dressed as a pixie, rather than *tolerate* it.

'So, what do you want me to do now?' asked Sander, passing me my bag as I boarded the fast train to Amsterdam.

'Nothing at the moment,' I replied. 'I'll give you a call when I get to Amsterdam and I decide what the next course of action should be.'

Of course, what I should have said was: 'Do nothing. I no longer need your help. Good luck and thank you.'

I needed to get better at straight-talking.

I was still reading about the Centraal Station in my guide book, when the train drew alongside the waters of Amsterdam harbour and began to cut its speed before pulling into the station concourse. Apparently the station had been built on three artificial islands, and on 8,600 wooden piles. How lucky we British have been over the centuries in the way we have been able to approach the construction of buildings:

'Cedric, shall we build it over there on that bit of land, or shall we insert a load of wooden piles and build it on the water?'

'On the land I think, don't you?'

'Yeah, you're right Cedric. Land it is.'

The short walk to my hostel reminded me of two things. What a beautiful city Amsterdam is, and how unseasonably nippy it was for this time of the year. A bitterly cold wind forced itself between the tall gabled buildings which lined the city's elegant canals, and caused me to shiver in my light summer clothes, worn as a result of ill-judged meteorological expectations. It was the kind of bitter cold which makes you mutter out loud as you shiver.

'Christ, it's freezing!' I said, clearly loud enough to be heard by a passing cyclist, who nodded in agreement.

It was Easter for God's sake. What was wrong with this country?

The hostel was extremely shabby and my room didn't offer me the luxury of unpacking a few things, fixing myself a drink and running a nice hot bath. Its facilities stretched as far as ... well ... curtains, and even they looked like they would fall down if you did anything so bold as try to draw them. I sat on the bed. My bottom slowly seeped into the saggy mattress. I sighed. There might as well have been the slam of the cell door and a jailer shouting abuse at me. The only difference between this room and a prison cell was that I was paying for it. I figured that Dutch penitentiaries were almost certainly nicer than this, and I considered going straight out and finding the 'Free Record Shop' and taking its name literally, in order to land myself superior accommodation at a more favourable rate. Maybe I'd start with a walk, and then see how my mood took me.

It was an interesting stroll, because soon I noticed that where any normal city would have a grocers or a tobacconists, this place had a shop which purported to sell sex. Confectionery of a totally different nature. The tourist who was in the area to exercise more than just his walking muscles could browse shelf after shelf of dirty mags, videos, and diverse accessories designed for insertion into almost any orifice which might become available. Then, having thoroughly researched the subject, he could go outside and begin the search for a recipient of his newly acquired knowledge.

Professionals are available for this purpose, and they await their clients in various states of undress in the windows of beautiful canal-side residences, originally built for wealthy merchants who would have been a little shocked to find what was now being traded in their front rooms. A red light adorns each of these establishments, a handy sign which lets the passer-by know that the scantily clad person who is the subject of their perusal is actually available for hire, and they're not just relaxing in their undies after a hard day at the office, having completely forgotten to draw the curtains. It strikes me that the 'red light' seems to be an odd choice of light for advertising sex, given that in our car-dominated culture we have come to associate the red light with being told to stop. But let's face it, 'stopping' is exactly what the prostitute doesn't get you to do, unless of course your money runs out. It is precisely because the punter is *not* going to hear the words 'Stop, I'm not that kind of girl', that he's there in the first place. As far as he's concerned it's the 'Green Light District', and very grateful he is for it too.

I found myself window shopping, although I had absolutely no intention of making a purchase. I wasn't alone in that regard. I was surrounded by swarms of onlookers, both young and old, and of both sexes, all united by a sense of intrigue in an alien, forbidden world which is normally concealed from them by prudish authorities. Hats off to the Dutch, I thought, for being honest enough to admit that it goes on. It just seemed a shame that they'd chosen such a historic and graceful part of their capital city to host this bizarre flesh market. I couldn't help feeling that the magnificent buildings around me had been built with such a sense of pride, by a nation at the height of its prosperity, almost as a symbol of what can be achieved by endeavour and human ingenuity. And now it was reduced to being a place where people wander around looking at tits and arses; a tourist trap which reminds us that the tide of human spirit can just as easily ebb as flow.

A large group of lads, quite possibly a stag party, began to leer, letch and shout remarks towards a window display which had taken their fancy. I watched closely as the merchandise on show did her best to remain unflustered by this sudden burst of boisterous attention. She was good. Her expression hardly altered. Maybe because she was experienced. Maybe because she was bored. Maybe because she was drugged up to the eyeballs. But most likely a combination of all three.

'She's goooorgeous!' bellowed one of the lads. 'What the hell is she doing *this* for?'

I could only guess that in his present high spirits he had just asked a question to which he didn't really want to hear an answer. I wondered if he'd appreciate a social worker sitting him down on bench by the canal and really telling him.

'Actually she's doing this because she's been the victim of abuse as a child and a spectacular absence of love has driven her to drugs, and then onwards into the hands of those who see her as little more than rich pickings for material exploitation.'

'Yeah yeah yeah, mate, I guessed all that,' he might have replied. 'But how much is a shag, do you think?'

Suddenly, I was hit by the strong whiff of marijuana emanating from a nearby 'coffee house'. A pleasant, soothing smell, and ten times nicer than the odour created by cigarettes. It reminded me that it wasn't just prostitution which was on the receiving end of the liberal approach of Amsterdam's decision-makers. In this city, you could buy your dope and smoke it just as easily as you could hire a hooker and .... well you get my point. I watched as some customers of a 'coffee house' (I wonder how much coffee they sell?) emerged smiling and giggling, and I felt confident they weren't about to cause any trouble. In my opinion mari-juana should be handed out free to English football supporters when they travel overseas. Frankly, they need help in seeing the funny side.

A particularly icy gust of wind suddenly made me shiver. A shiver of both cold, and of realisation. I mean, what was I doing aimlessly ambling along these narrow streets of disrepute? I had work to do. I had record company executives to win over. I had to start making things happen fast and I needed to get myself into the right frame of mind. There was business to be done, and not of the sort that was currently on offer.

What I really needed was exactly what I'd left behind in The Hague. An office. Yes, I had a small sheet of paper containing the phone numbers of the music-biz contacts of Willie's manager

Andy, but the only place I could call them was from a public call box, and the only ones I could find were extremely uncivilised. They weren't actually boxes at all, because boxes have sides. The ones I kept finding were just exposed booths – a glorified version of a phone on the end of a stick.

I stopped at one and dialled my first number, as the icy wind howled and whistled about me.

'April! It's bloody April,' I said to myself as I heard the new sound of Dutch ringing tone in my receiver, followed by an answerphone.

'Hello Jep, this is Tony,' I said, responding to the outgoing message and trying to sound as upbeat as I could. 'I think Andy told you I was coming over. He said that you'd be prepared to stage my showcase at your studio. Unfortunately I'm not very contactable at the moment for one reason or another, so I'll call again later.'

I then dialled another number marked with an asterisk on the sheet of contacts that Andy had given me. The asterisk meant 'good guy, bound to help'. This time a real person answered instead of a machine, so progress was being made.

'Hello, could I speak to Menno please?' I asked.

'Yes, of course – who is it calling?'

'Tony Hawks.'

'From which company are you calling?'

'Er ... just say that I'm a friend of Andy.'

'Andy who?'

'Er ...' I struggled to retrieve the required information, but the cold had caused the recall section of my brain to freeze up. 'I'm sorry, I can't remember his name. Andy the manager. Menno knows him well.'

'Hold the line please.'

I held the line.

A minute passed.

A cold, windy, and not altogether pleasant minute. Then the small screen on the phone's control panel instructed me to insert more coins. I went through my pockets and deposited all my available change, and I waited for Menno.

I waited and I waited.

After what seemed like a very long time, and which certainly took its toll on my supply of loose change, I heard a voice on the end of the line.

'Hello, Tony?' asked a female voice. Strange, I'd expected Menno to be a man.

'Yes.'

'It's the receptionist again. I'm afraid that Menno isn't here. At least, he's not answering his phone.'

'Oh.'

'Maybe try again in half an hour.'

'Right. Yes. Thanks.'

I hung up the phone, but let my head hang down. As the spiteful hail began to pound me once again, I couldn't help but mumble a rhetorical question to myself.

'Did Sting ever have to go through this?'

CHAPTER 12 WHAT A NICE MAN

After a visit to a bank, my pockets positively bulging with coins compatible with Dutch call boxes, I tried my best to ignore the fact that God had taken the decision to fire hail-stones down from the sky. Showing great fortitude, I didn't allow myself to wince as the wicked little icy pellets bounced off my face and onto the all-too-familiar telecommunications apparatus before me. Having left two more messages on Jep's answerphone, I dialled the number for Menno again.

'Hello, could I speak to Menno please?' I asked, as tourists dashed past me heading for the havens of their lovely warm hotel rooms.

'Is that Tony?' came the reply.

I'd been calling so much that the receptionist recognised my voice.

'Yes, perhaps you could try him again,' I said.

'I think he's back at his desk now. Hold the line.'

'Yes, but before you do that can you just check—'

Too late. I was on hold, and I was listening to the music with which I'd become all too familiar. Menno's record company were obviously promoting one of their new artists by foisting their latest single on to losers like me who'd been left on hold. I'd now heard this song so many times that it was beginning to feel like I was undergoing some sophisticated form of torture. I will never forget its unmusical and yet mesmeric refrain:

'I'm gonna get you baby, and I'm gonna get you now!'

Yes, but never mind about getting *me* baby, how about getting *Menno*? These regular sojourns 'on hold' were crippling me

163

financially. I was beginning to wonder if anyone had ever spent so much money getting to know a song which they'd hated from the first few bars of the first hearing. Especially while standing outside in the cold with hailstones smashing into their increasingly tender forehead.

'Ouch!' I blurted, as a particularly large one bounced off my nose.

'Hello?' came the familiar voice of the receptionist, cutting off the music and reminding me that humans were available at the other end of the line.

'Ah, it's you again, now there's a surprise,' I said, with a sarcastic tone born of frustration. 'You're not by any strange twist of fate going to tell me that Menno can actually speak to me, are you?'

'Sorry, Tony. He really normally isn't this hard to—'

I can only presume that she went on to finish the sentence, but I was not party to it – having momentarily let my concentration dip and failed to insert the requisite number of coins to keep the line open. As the line went dead, I let out a huge and heartfelt sigh, which didn't feel unjustified. I mean, all I had to show for my efforts to communicate with Menno were empty pockets and storm damage in the form of little red pockmarks all over my face.

I imagined that Menno, if I finally established contact with him, was going to be the saviour of the situation. He was a senior executive at a big label and he knew and liked Andy. He was guaranteed to grant me a meeting (well, certainly within twelve months anyway, unlike those sloths at Sony), and I did have a gut feeling that he'd be exactly the kind of guy to see the potential of 'What Does A Pixie Do?' Then again, he might hate the track and just fob me off with some line about it not being what they were looking for right now. It would just be nice to know one way or the other, that's all.

I drew on my dwindling stocks of positive energy and resolved to track down the 'Dans School' that was listed in my guide to Amsterdam. If I could establish the 'team' that were going to perform as 'Shhh!' in the showcase then at least it would feel like this project had made a start. However, after forty-five minutes of walking and map reading, all I had established was that the 'Dans School' no longer existed at the address listed in my guide book. Time for another sigh, followed by another tactical rethink.

Having narrowly rejected the 'go into a coffee shop and get completely off my face' option, I found myself boarding a tram for the outer reaches of Amsterdam. The brief I'd given myself was simple enough – find a hotel with a vacancy for a room with a telephone in it, and then book myself in.

After a fifteen-minute ride, I appeared to arrive in an area which had more than its fair share of small guest houses, and so I alighted the tram and began my search. The streets were busy, and it felt good to be around people who genuinely *lived* in this city, and who weren't just trawling the streets looking for titillation or some form of relief. For me, this was a relief, and the kind that came cheaply and guilt-free. I began to feel the faint tingle of returning optimism as I climbed the steps to the first hotel.

An hour later, such feelings had been well and truly vanquished, after I'd been given the same story over and over again – 'Sorry, but we're booked up for at least the next four days.' I'd just begun to look around for a bar, hoping that a beer might provide some temporary respite from all things grim, when I passed a building which bore a plaque announcing itself as the BUURTCENTRUM LYDIA. I didn't know what it was, but it appeared to be some kind of community centre. Thinking that community centres have bars more often than not, I elected to go in and see if I could find some refreshment.

Inside, I found a large room with a dozen or so drinkers dotted around, and a stage at the far end where six musicians were setting up. A drummer, a bass player, a pianist, a trumpeter and two sax players. I ordered a beer at the bar, half expecting to be asked to leave, but there seemed to be no objection to my presence, so I took a seat at a table and waited for the show to begin. What began, in fact, was not a show but a rehearsal. A few minutes after I'd sat down, a bearded man appeared and began handing out sheet music among the musicians. I use the word 'musicians', but it turns out that is only really an accurate description of these people while they were standing around holding their instruments in readiness to play. Once they had begun, the word 'musician' seemed a little over-generous, because what emerged from their instruments was a farrago of seemingly random notes, presented in the form of strangled screeches, whines and reverberations, all held vaguely together by the frantic thuds and fluctuating rhythms of the over-zealous drummer. The bearded man, who I assumed must be some kind of music teacher, held his hand aloft authoritatively and one by one the 'players of the instruments' relented, and the sweet sound of silence returned to soothe the fraying nerves of the room's drinkers. The teacher then said something in Dutch, which I could only assume meant something like: 'I do this job because I love music, but when I listen to you, I never, ever hear any. I took you all on thinking I could help you. I cannot. I shall leave you now and go to a dark place where I will take my own life. Do not worry, I will not suffer – I will make sure I'm out of earshot of you lot.'

Whatever he did say, his pupils nodded keenly and then resumed with equal disregard for musical convention. Perhaps they were playing free jazz. Certainly the sound they were producing was not anything anyone would pay to hear. I sipped my beer, at a slightly quicker pace than I'd originally planned, and tried not to grimace in case one of the players saw me and became disheartened. I didn't want to spoil things by putting one of them off and causing them to hit a right note.

Whatever their shortcomings though, I began to warm to the sounds that I was hearing. They weren't pleasant to the ear, in fact they hurt a bit, but they still had a strangely comforting quality about them. First of all, they made me feel good about my own musicianship, but they also reminded me that excellence, or even basic technical competence, weren't essentials for enjoyment.

I looked at the faces of the participants, all of them, deep in concentration – lost in the mire of notes that were dotted on the pages before them. The troubles of the office or their relationships weren't on their minds now. They were unwinding, they were relaxing, they were de-stressing. Isn't this what it should be all about? A little healing for the soul.

I left the novices to their devices (which in the hands of the more gifted, would have been called instruments) and began walking back towards the tram stop which would take me back into the centre of Amsterdam. While I realised that the sextet that I'd just left behind were getting more pleasure from their 'music' than many others with twenty times their ability, I also knew that it was quite a wise move not to be around to hear the results of that pleasure. It was non-transferable.

On the tram back to the *centrum*, I looked out of the window and wondered whether I'd taken on the wrong bet this time around. The problem was that to win this bet I had to compete in the commercial marketplace, and that seemed to take the fun out of things. And anyway, didn't I have to face up to the fact that I was too old, too unfashionable, and rather too content for all this?

And then there was the question of whether I was sexy enough.

Even dressed as a pixie.

It was difficult to see it. In spite of my well-honed powers of self-delusion, it was hard to look at myself in the mirror and see a sex god.

Of course, right now, having alighted from the tram and begun the short walk back to my luxurious lodgings, I was in a place where you didn't need to be a sex god to get any action. All that was required was a fat wallet, and low self esteem. I was back in the theme park 'Sleaze-World', but I didn't find it remotely tempting. All the prostitutes seemed so bored. Most were making mobile phone calls, and one was even sat on a stool eating a Kentucky Fried Chicken takeaway. In such a loveless world, making love was the furthest thing from my mind.

Sleep, however, was quite appealing. It felt like I'd walked a hundred miles during the day and as my head hit the pillow, I felt as worn out as my room. I closed my eyes and imagined that I was in a luxury hotel, and that tomorrow was packed full of important meetings. It was so much better than thinking about how little I'd really achieved.

With each new day comes new hope (unless you live in Slough), and I awoke with a new game plan.

'Sod the phone,' I said to myself. 'Why don't I just *go* there.'

And that was exactly what I did.

The train pulled into Hilversum station at 11.07 a.m., exactly on schedule, leaving me almost an entire day in the town which

the Dutch had made the centre for their record, TV and entertainment industry. In the station newsagents I bought a very
impressive map of the town before proceeding to the nearby
Hotel de Waag to take a coffee. The first glimpse of the sur-
roundings made no suggestion that I was in a place which had
any connection with the glitzy world of showbiz. Hilversum
looked like a stereotypical sleepy suburb where excitement was
kept to a minimum and, when it occurred, took place behind
closed doors. Not unlike Music Row in Nashville, in fact. Just as
I sat down to my coffee and opened my map, it started to hail
outside. Heavy, hard, hectoring hail. As precipitation goes, hail
doesn't have much to offer. A walk in the rain can be engagingly
bracing, sometimes even a rather sensuous experience. Falling
snow is a beautiful sight, gently tumbling from the sky and reju-
venating the old and grubby with its pristine whiteness. But hail.
It just hurts. It's spiteful and horrid, and frankly I'd seen enough
of it in the last two days to last a lifetime.

I located Jep's studio on the map and was delighted to note
that it was within walking distance, and so I set off just as soon
as lumps of ice stopped falling from the sky.

'Jep's studio would be a good place to do your showcase,'
Andy had said, 'I've sent him the Pixie song and he likes it.'

Jep, although not as important a figure in the hierarchy of
the music business as the unreachable Menno, was now crucial
to me. I needed his enthusiasm, and access to his contacts.
Most of all, I needed him to be in. I'd left three messages for
him on his answerphone but I'd heard nothing back. This, I
hoped, had more to do with the fact that I'd been unable to
leave him any numbers he could actually call, rather than any
conscious desire on his part to ignore the crazy Englishman.
Yes, I was chancing it a bit by just turning up, but there didn't
seem to be much choice.

In less than ten minutes, I found myself outside the address
that I'd been given. At first I thought that I must have the wrong
place. It just looked like a private house with a shed on the side,
but closer inspection revealed that the shed had a plaque on one
of its walls announcing that it was in fact a studio. My first
thought was that it seemed a magnificently unimpressive place to
launch the career of Shhh!

I rang the bell and waited.

No answer.

I rang again and waited longer. Still no answer. I rang once more, this time leaving my finger on the bell long enough to annoy anyone who might happen to be inside.

No answer. Damn.

That was it then, probably the last chance of making anything happen on this trip had gone. I was just heading back up the path towards the gate when I heard a voice behind me.

'Hello?'

I spun round to see an immaculately dressed grey-haired man smiling at me.

'Are you Jep?' I asked.

'Yes.'

'Oh hi, I'm Andy's friend – Tony.'

'Goodness, I wasn't expecting you yet. You had better come in.'

Jep ran his own studio and had his own record label. I'd been impressed when Andy had first told me this, but here on the ground, I was discovering that things often sound better than they look. The premises which housed Jep's business empire gave too much away. I surveyed the recording equipment which was on show in the cramped control room and, even with my limited knowledge, I could see that it was at least twenty years old. A few record covers (not CDs) were hanging on the wall – all conspicuously unframed, unknown and unembossed with the words 'To Jep, commemorating sales of over 250,000 copies'. The smell of success was not in the air.

'Excuse me a minute Tony,' said Jep, 'while I tell Betty to take a break. I didn't know you were coming so I am in the middle of a session with her.'

'I can come back later if you want,' I offered.

'No, it's OK,' he replied.

Jep hit a button on the recording desk and suddenly we could hear what was happening in the studio's live room. Betty appeared to be singing along with some kind of Karaoke backing tape – the legendary 'I Will Survive'. Hers didn't seem to be as passionate a rendition as those I've seen in pubs from groups of inebriated females singing along with the jukebox. I've seen them pour their heart and soul into this anthem which demonstrates the injustices that women suffer at the hands of men.

They bellow the words, which demand that their man gets the hell out of their life because, frankly, he isn't welcome anymore. I always like to think that as soon as the song finishes, one of the girls then says to the others: 'I'd better get home now otherwise Barry'll kill me.'

'Take a ten minute break, Betty,' said Jep, using the microphone which linked him to the other room, 'and come and meet Tony.'

As Betty made her way through to join us for tea, Jep explained the nature of their relationship.

'Betty is a protégé of mine,' he said. 'We are making an album together, but first we are getting her confidence up by making her sing along with stuff in the studio. She needs to get used to hearing her own voice.'

'I see,' I said, a little puzzled.

I'd noticed, with some ease, that Betty was not in the first flush of youth, and it was difficult to imagine how she'd failed to become familiar with the sound of her own voice, given the generous amount of years that had been available to her in which to do so. I also wondered who would buy her album when she had eventually plucked up enough courage to sing on it. Should she secure a recording deal, it was hard to imagine her gaining much of a teen following, and in my experience, the more mature music lover tends to buy the CDs of artists whose pedigree is such that they don't need to sing along with 'I Will Survive' in order to feel good about how they sound. Jep explained to me that Betty was looking for new songs to record and wondered if perhaps I would like to write for her. I made a few mumbly noises which were intended to be polite, and changed the subject.

'Perhaps I could see where I might perform the showcase?' I asked.

'Of course, through here.'

Jep then showed me the 'live' area of the studio, which was spacious for recording purposes but very small for anyone who was considering hosting a showcase.

'Is it big enough?' I enquired.

'Yes. We have done it before,' he replied assuredly. 'We can get twenty or thirty people in to watch you – no problem.'

'Andy said that you would be able to get an audience of music people in to see me as early as next week.'

'Yes, but I'm not sure about that now. I've just come back from holiday and I have not spoken to anybody yet. It might be better if you come back in three weeks.'

I looked around me and considered everything that was on show here – the ageing equipment, the tiny room to perform in, and the calibre of the artists who worked here, and I really began to wonder if this was a place to which you'd make a special journey.

'I have important business in London,' I said, using the word 'important' in its loosest sense. 'It will have to be next week or not at all.'

'Hmm, it will be difficult.'

'Would you like to hear the CD of the song?'

'I have heard the Pixie song already,' he replied. 'Andy sent it to me. I like it, but I'm not sure that it is right for the Dutch market.'

'We've done two other songs as well. I'd value your opinion on them.'

We returned to the control room where Jep and Betty passed their judgement on the entire repertoire of Shhh! Jep liked the stuff but felt that two of the three tracks might be more 'English' than 'European'.

Betty seemed thrilled with it all.

'Will you write a song for me?' she asked me, with a charm which almost masked the underlying desperation.

'If I have time, yes,' I said.

I needed to get better at straight talking.

'What do you want to do about the showcase?' asked Jep.

'Well, I think we should try and go ahead with it – maybe on Tuesday?'

'Let me make some phone calls. Call me later today.'

'OK,' I said, trying not to look glum at the prospect of more hail-battered Dutch callboxes. 'And thanks for the tea.'

Jep led me to the door and gave me a warm hand-shake.

'It's nice to meet you Tony,' he said genuinely. 'Andy has told me a lot about you. I hope we can make something happen.'

'Me too.'

'Call me later,' he said, as he slowly closed the door on me. 'And good luck!'

'What a nice man,' I said to myself, as I retraced my steps to the Hotel Waag, where I planned on taking lunch.

The sky above was blue, providing a brief respite from the heavens' icy onslaught. It occurred to me that my situation seemed to mirror the weather conditions – mostly hail with occasional bright spells. I needed to find some way of securing a period of bright sunshine, and I was far from sure that I was going about it in the right way. I was a little concerned that furthering my association with Jep might lead to a sustained period of cloud and drizzle.

I'd already used the four words which summed up the problem with Jep. 'What a nice man.' Unwittingly I'd damned him with faint praise. The music business seemed to be one where being 'nice' didn't help much, certainly not unless it was backed up by a steely determination and a thick skin. Jep struck me as a gentle man, and I wasn't sure if that was going to be much use to me right now. It was true that in life I generally wanted to surround myself with 'nice' people, but it was also the case that in the music world I had to move forward. In the grubby waters of the music biz, Jep was treading water and handing out inflatable armbands to struggling swimmers. Just for the moment, I needed someone who'd give me a ride in their powerboat.

I made my way to a callbox only to spend more money establishing that once again, Menno was not at his desk. I decided that either he hated his desk and went to enormous lengths to avoid being at it, or he was deliberately avoiding me. So what should I do now? Hilversum, as far as the naked eye could see, had little in terms of entertainment for the out-of-towner with a few hours to kill, if indeed a few hours would provide enough time for Menno to pitch up at his desk. After a further few seconds of deliberation I concluded, and I doubt that I was the first in this, that Hilversum had failed to capture my heart. To my knowledge, nobody has written a song about this town, and I'm pretty confident of that remaining the case. Almost involuntarily my legs began to lead me back to the station, and on to the platform for trains back to the city.

On the train I reminded myself that you learn something from every experience, but as I stared out of the train window, vaguely focusing on the dull flat expanses of Dutch countryside, the only lesson I seemed able to draw from my two hours in Hilversum was that you only really wanted to spend half that time there. My meeting with Jep had begun to make me ponder the very nature of my quest and the way in which I was going about it. I couldn't just turn up in places and expect busy people to fit in with my plans, but this was what I'd done first in Nashville and now Holland. I was expecting too much. The important people who might be able to help were always going to be leading busy lives and wouldn't necessarily be available exactly when I needed them. I was trying to rush something which couldn't be rushed.

As we entered the final approaches to Centraal station I looked north across Amsterdam's harbour in the direction of England, and I really began to wonder if I wouldn't be far better doing what I was doing back in the UK. There were a number of advantages. At home I wouldn't have to sleep in a grubby little hotel room. At home I had contacts and my mobile phone worked, and at home I just might be able to generate some general interest in the project. It was difficult to imagine where the Dutch were going to find any real enthusiasm for this venture. There was no getting away from it – the pixie thing had more impact when you actually knew what the word pixie meant.

This whole thing needed a serious rethink.

PART IV
WHEN ALL IS
SAID AND DONE

We've shed a tear or two
And now it's me and you
And so we've learned a lot
To cherish what we've got

And now the day is at an end
What need is there to pretend?
Cos you're the special one
When all is said and done

The things we've done before
Don't matter any more
We'll trust ourselves to this
A look, a smile, a kiss

And now the day is at an end
What need is there to pretend?
Cos you're the special one
When all is said and done

I've lived a lie, pretended I
Was something I was not
But now we've found out what was wrong
What took the both of us so long?

There's been some lessons learned
And pages duly turned
And now it seems the signs
All point to better times

And now the day is at an end
What need is there to pretend?
Cos you're the special one
When all is said and done

CHAPTER 13 **TOO UGLY**

I returned to London with firm objectives. I would haul myself around the capital's record companies until someone saw the potential of the great work I was doing. I would write new songs and start fresh collaborations. I would do my darnedest to exploit the modicum of fame that I enjoyed in the UK. I would stop at nothing until my bet was won. At least that was the intention.

The reality was, however, that I forgot all about it.

The main problem was that the incentive had gone. The initial impulse to strive for pop stardom had, rather shamefully, been a sexual one. I had fancied Victoria. Victoria, however, had moved to New York, and with her had gone the prospect of intimate evenings discussing the current state of the bet's progress. Admittedly I was still left with the challenge of trying to prove myself once again in an arena where I'd once achieved greatness,* but things just hadn't been enough fun. All that seemed to be coming my way was rejection, and the truth was that I just couldn't handle it. I'd tried to kid myself to the contrary, but if I was candid I had to admit that the Holland trip had drained my resilience.

I was close to being a beaten man.

So it was that for one spring, and one summer, I resumed my erstwhile and considerably more successful career as a comic raconteur and all-round media tart. I presented radio programmes, guested on the odd TV panel show, acted in a play at

---

* *Well, of sorts.*

the Belgrade Theatre, Coventry and gave after-dinner speeches. My bank balance grew, but at the expense of my dreams.

It was Steve, my initial songwriting partner on the 'Bird's Egg' song, who tempted me back into the musical foray.

'Why don't you talk to some of the guys I know in the music biz?' he suggested, when he'd heard that I'd put the whole project on the back burner. 'Maybe one of them will be able to think of some ways of kick-starting the project.'

'Like who?'

'Well, you could talk to my mate Mark Fox.'

'Who's he?'

'He used to be the percussionist in Haircut 100, but now he's a successful A&R man* at BMG. He's the man responsible for "discovering" Natalie Imbruglia.'

'He could "discover" me.'

'Well, he could certainly offer some advice.'

Maybe I was beyond discovery. Perhaps instead I would have to rely on being found and handed in.

'I'll set up a meeting with Mark,' said Steve.

'Thanks,' I said.

Well, maybe it was worth one last try.

'Singles just don't make money any more,' said Mark.

It was a cold wintry morning, but my host was warm enough though, seated behind a chic designer desk in an office with walls overcrowded with gold discs, mainly connected with Haircut 100 and Natalie Imbruglia. This was not a business where you kept quiet about your achievements. Reputation is everything.

'A single,' he continued, 'is more or less used as a marketing tool to promote an album. And your problem, Tony, is that you don't have an album.'

Well, he was right there.

'You see the business has changed since "Stutter Rap" made the charts,' he said, leaning back in his chair. 'You had a hit with that record, if I remember rightly, largely on the back of a funny video.'

---

* An A&R man is the person charged by the record company to plan and shape an artist's career; however, most of the artists I know blame them for ruining theirs.

'Yes, that was pretty much the case,' I replied. 'We got virtually no radio play.'

'Exactly, radio won't touch novelty records.'

'That's why I was planning on making a video for a track called "What Does A Pixie Do?"'

'Yes, but the trouble is that you'd need to do more than that. At the time of "Stutter Rap", most of the kids who were buying records were watching either *Top of the Pops* or *The Chart Show* – or both. Now they are watching hundreds of different programmes on cable – or pissing about on the Web.'

'I see,' I said, rather disappointed. 'So I probably need to do a bit of a rethink.'

'I'd recommend it, if you want to win the bet.'

'So, what would be your advice to me?' I asked.

Mark shrugged.

'I don't really know. Maybe you'd be best concentrating on a dance track for the club scene. You might be able to break in that way. Or you could go and talk to Simon upstairs.'

'Simon Upstairs?'

'Not "Simon Upstairs" as in "Simon Upstairs" is his name. Simon – upstairs.'

I was disappointed. Simon Upstairs had a splendid ring to it. In fact, I decided there and then that if I did make a dance track I'd release it under that name.

'He's called Simon Cowell. Go chat to him and get his advice,' suggested Mark, with something of a twinkle in his eye. 'He's another A&R man. He discovered Westlife.'

Goodness. These guys made more discoveries than Columbus in a good month.

Simon Cowell's appearance suggested that his mirror was well used. He looked affluent too, and I thought, slightly camp. His office, like Mark's, trumpeted his success in the form of gold discs and awards. There was little to suggest, however, that in six months' time this man would become a household name in Britain. He would acquire that status as a result of becoming the 'nasty' judge in the hit TV show *Pop Idol*. What I didn't know then, and I can only guess that this had been the reason for the twinkle in Mark's eye, is that he already had something of a reputation for straight-talking.

'Tony, if you want to have a hit,' he said, this immaculately groomed man in his singularly tidy office, 'you have to know that you can't be the artist.'

'Why not?' I protested, gently.

'You're too ugly,' he said, without any change of expression.

This was Olympic standard straight-talking. He went on to suggest that I became a kind of producer figure who found a young good-looking artist and got them to rework an old song which had already charted years before. This, he reckoned, was the easiest way to get a hit. Unfortunately, this suggestion, apart from being an invitation into a world of formulaic mundanity, would not enable me to win my bet.

'Aren't you being somewhat narrow-minded?' I complained. 'I mean, you're ruling me out as the artist before you've heard a note of what I do. I might be quite extraordinary.'

'Look, Tony,' he stated firmly, 'it doesn't matter how extraordinary you are. You just don't look like a pop star.'

'And what does a pop star look like?'

'Not like you.'

I wasn't warming to this bloke.

'Pop stars are younger, better looking and easy to market. And young teenage girls will like them,' said Simon, clearly taking some pleasure in stating the rules as he saw them.

Although he was almost certainly right, I felt that I had to protest.

'So if after today I go on to become a bit of a sex symbol, you'd be wrong.'

'I'd be surprised and happy.'

'Have you been wrong before?'

'Of course I have. The first time I saw Gary Barlow in Take That, I said to their manager "Ditch the fat one."'

God, this guy was all heart.

'Look,' I said, foolishly allowing myself to become visibly riled, 'what you're basically saying is that I've got no chance of winning my bet because I don't fit some stereotypical view of what a pop star looks like?'

'I'm not saying "no chance", because anything is possible, but I'm saying that I don't think you'll do it.'

'And are you confident enough to be prepared to do something if I were to prove you wrong?'

'What do you mean – *do something*?'

'Well, for instance, would you eat your hat?'

'I wouldn't actually *eat* a hat. No.'

'What about if I made a very big cake which was hat-shaped? Would you eat that?'

Simon thought for a moment.

'Yes, I would,' he said with a smile which suggested he was enjoying the increasingly competitive atmosphere.

'But you'd have to eat *all* the cake.'

'OK.'

'And it would be a big one.'

'Fair enough. I accept.'

We shook hands.

The afternoon had been spent seeking constructive advice. All I'd succeeded in acquiring was a new antagonist.

But as it turned out, that was exactly what I needed.

The meeting with Simon Cowell had a positive effect at just the right time. Exactly at the point where I was becoming seriously disheartened, his obnoxiousness provided me with the spur I needed to see this thing through. I had some real motivation again. I wanted to make Simon Cowell eat his words, as well as a huge hat-shaped cake. OK, not much of a prize, I know, but the real desire was to wipe that smug smile off his face.

In the following weeks, I realised what an idiot I had been by not spending more time trying to exploit the Sudan-inspired 'We Are Happy' track. Hadn't I been told that with the right remix it would have a good chance of becoming a club hit? However, the fact remained that for a second consecutive summer I had left it too late to attempt to get some sort of finished dance track ready in time for the Ibiza market.

So, instead, I spent time working with Willie on a track called 'I Want You For Your Mind' which we felt could be something which I might be able to get Tom Jones to cover. Then, a couple of friends suggested that I try to get a hit in Ireland, given that this was a territory where you didn't need to shift a huge quantity of singles to make the chart. Also they pointed out that

I already had a ready-made ally in Gerry Ryan, the popular broadcaster and DJ who had supported me in my hitch-hiking journey around Ireland with a fridge.

I started to throw all my energies into this new initiative. I became rather taken with a traditional old Irish song called Whistlin' Phil McHugh, which had been written over a hundred years ago by a well-loved troubadour called Percy French. I found that by reworking his original tune, and adding new lyrics and a rhythmic drum loop, I was beginning to produce something rather promising.

However, my ever-vacillating attention was distracted from this project when a friend introduced me to a man called David Stark at my favourite London music venue the Kashmir Klub. David told me he was involved with various song competitions throughout the world.

'Could something like that be of benefit to me?' I asked, keen to grab at anything which might provide some momentum to my quest.

'Well, winning an international song competition won't guarantee you a hit,' he replied thoughtfully, 'but if your song gets to the finals you'll meet songwriters and producers from all around the world – and who knows what that could lead to?'

Certainly Abba's involvement with Eurovision hadn't done them any harm, even if that was twenty odd years ago.

'Are there any competitions coming up soon?' I asked.

'Well, it's a shame actually because you've just missed one – there's an international song competition in Bucharest. The entries close this Saturday.'

'But it's only Thursday now, that gives me bags of time,' I said playfully.

'Well, entering this one would be a little more time-consuming than just digging out an old song and sending in a cassette.'

'Why?'

'Because it's an International Song Competition for children.'

I understood now what David meant by time-consuming. The prosthetics needed for me to pass myself off as a child would be difficult to organise within the available forty-eight hours.

'The child doesn't have to write the song,' he added, somehow gauging my thought process from my expression, 'but the singer has to be fourteen or under.'

'I see. Well, I don't actually know any child singers so it'll be a little difficult to find one, teach them a song, and then get a CD off to Bucharest by Saturday.'

David looked pensive for a moment.

'If you're serious about this,' he said presently, 'I might be able to persuade the organisers to allow an extension on your entry.'

An extension on my entry, eh? I wasn't sure if I wanted one of those. It sounded a little painful.

'That would be brilliant,' I said.

'Keep your fingers crossed then,' said David, as I rose to leave.

'I certainly will.'

The answer came as early as the next day when I received an email from David telling me that the organisers had extended the deadline for my entry by one week, and were looking forward to receiving and listening to my song.

Ireland would have to go on hold. I had more pressing business to attend to.

Meeting the deadline was still a fairly tall order, especially since I had to write a song which would wow the judges, and with lyrics which would be appropriate for a child to sing. A difficult task since most children haven't yet embarked on the trauma of romantic love – the area which provides the material for most popular songs. 'Love' in its more general and unromantic sense seemed to provide the only real lyrical opportunity. The child would have to sing about how the world would be a better place if we all learned to love each other. It was corny as hell but I just couldn't see much mileage in them singing about bullying, homework or how crap their parents are, although I did have the germ of a lyric:

My parents are shit
They married in a hurry
All they're fit to bring up
Is curry.

It was good but it wouldn't win any prizes. Even in Romania.

Fortunately a few hours of more diligent work, largely spent rewriting a song that I'd already composed many years before called 'We Came So Near', provided me with the song entitled 'We've Got Love On Our Side'. Basically I'd added a big rousing chorus to what had previously been a rather gentle ballad. It hadn't necessarily been an improvement but it had certainly nudged the song in the direction of the type usually favoured by our European brethren. I felt that my chances of making the final would be good, provided I could find a child to sing it.

Having filled a piece of paper with all the people I knew who had young children, and then subsequently having dismissed their progeny as all being 'rubbish singers', I realised that auditions would be the only way. I called a couple of stage schools and they promised to organise a dozen or so kids for me to see. It was as easy as that.

So one bright, frosty, weekday morning I turned up at the Ravenscourt Park School for budding young stars. Kids in green uniforms bounced around the corridors, singing show songs and generally looking showbizzy. The sound of tap-dancing feet and vamping pianos filled the air, leaving me feeling like I was in a scene from the film *Fame*.

A teacher showed me through to a room which had been set aside for the auditions, explaining that the kids knew what everything was all about and that their parents had been consulted and had given their consent for their child to fly out to Romania if selected. It was all so well organised. I was impressed.

I shuffled restlessly on my chair behind a desk, waiting for the first child to be shown in. I felt uncomfortable. Soon I would be exposed to young people who were filled with expectation, ambition and dreams, and for all of them except one I would be the bastard who would dash them. I knew only too well what they would be feeling, having attended enough auditions myself in my early career when I'd struggled to find work as an actor. I recalled only too well the miserable nature of the whole tedious procedure. It didn't require a huge leap of the imagination to be back at one of those auditions surrounded by nervous fellow actors and actresses who either sat silently offering a rigid smile, or gushed and gabbled unbearably, possessed as they were by a feral nervous energy. Then the call came.

'Tony Hawks, would you like to come through?'

God, it was like a visit to the doctors, except you were the one who was going to administer the medicine. Your audition piece. As you were led through you had one last chance for an anxious cough before it was time to strut your stuff in front of two or three strangers who beamed enthusiastically in a vain attempt to deaden the awful pain of the whole experience. Then the relief of it all being over, followed by the dreadful realisation that you could have done it *so* much better.

Then the wait.

Then the phone call of rejection.

Then the month waiting for another audition.

Then the repetition of the same hideous process.

Oh, the glamour of the actor's life. It's no wonder most of them are potty.

I felt a little better when the accompanist at the piano assured me that these stage-school kids can attend as many as four or five auditions a week. Auditioning felt as natural to them as stealing bikes, smoking fags and discussing spot cream was to normal adolescents. It seemed that for them, attending an audition was something to look forward to, not least because it got you out of the first half hour of double geography.

The first auditionee was called in, a pretty girl neatly attired in the school's green uniform, and she seemed confident enough.

'Hello there, I'm Tony,' I said. 'How old are you?'

'Thirteen,' she replied eagerly.

'Good,' I said with a smile designed to set her at her ease.

Clearly I was the one who needed to relax. The problem, and I'm going to tell it straight here, was that I felt like a bit of a pervert. I couldn't help thinking that saying 'good' and smiling when a little girl tells you that she is thirteen is probably against the law. Move on, as quickly as possible, I thought to myself.

'And what are you going to sing?' I enquired.

'I'm going to sing "Whistle Down The Wind".'

'Excellent. That's from a musical, isn't it?'

'Yes.'

'Which one?'

'*Whistle Down The Wind*.'

'Yes, "Whistle Down The Wind", but which musical is it from?'

'*Whistle Down The Wind*. It's from the musical *Whistle Down The Wind*.'

'Of course, how silly of me. Sorry.'

Move on, as quickly as possible, I thought to myself.

'Off you go then.'

And off she went.

A fine performance ensued in which a thirteen-year-old girl sang her little heart out, occasionally unnerving her auditioner by fixing him in the eye and smiling rather too resolutely. The accompanist hit the final chord and the auditioner applauded enthusiastically.

'Excellent. Well done,' I said, trying not to sound patronising (but not succeeeding).

Seconds later she was gone. It was an odd thing, but there she was, this girl who'd just given me a personal and heartfelt rendition of a song, and yet I realised that I'd probably never see her again in my life. Unless, of course, I picked her for the job. And she was certainly good enough.

Nearly all the kids I saw that day were good enough. It seems that both the Ravenscourt and Sylvia Young Theatre Schools are overflowing with talented youngsters. However, one girl, a bubbly little redhead called Linzie, had stood out from the rest. It was difficult to put my finger on what it was that she had over the others, but her voice was terrific and she just oozed enthusiasm and energy, maybe because she'd just finished a long run in a touring production of the musical *Annie*. Whatever it was, she was just perfect for the project. I called the theatre school at the end of the day and they put me on the phone to her.

'Hello, Linzie. Guess what?' I teased.

'What?' came a nervous voice.

'I want you to sing my song for the Golden Star Song Competition, Bucharest.'

Screams of joy.

Well, at least one person was happy, even though twenty others would go to bed thoroughly pissed off.

Still, that's showbusiness.

A week later, after Linzie had recorded the song in the studio of the long-suffering Willie, it was my turn to get the uplifting phone call.

'Hello, Tony,' came a distant voice. 'It is Miruna here, from the Golden Star Song Festival in Bucharest.'

'Yes?' I said, fearing the worst.

'Congratulations, your song "Love On Our Side", sung by Linzie Cooper, has made it into the finals.'

I was thrilled. Even though I'd thought both the song and Linzie's performance were good enough, I'd geared myself up for impending rejection.

'Wow, that's great news. Thank you.'

Finally I was on my way. Bucharest was calling, and my master plan to dominate the European pop scene had at last been revived.

CHAPTER 14 TOO HANDSOME

As I boarded the plane in London, I was in bouyant mood. I wondered if the events that had conspired to put me on this aircraft were a sign that something significant was destined to happen. I was aware, however, that even if Linzie was to win the song competition with my song, it was still no guarantee that my bet would be won, since only the prestigious Eurovision Song Contest is ever likely to provide a spin-off hit for its winning songwriters. However, this didn't matter because I had another agenda. I'd discovered while perusing literature about the Golden Star Competition that the joint organisers were an outfit called the Phoenix Foundation who seemed to represent many of Romania's top recording artists. My plan was to ingratiate myself with these people and try to get involved in some kind of collaboration with a local pop star which could result in me catapulting up the Romanian charts, either as a writer or – better still – as a dueting artist. It was an enterprising plan, and one that had been largely scoffed at by friends and colleagues in London. My intention was to make them scoff on the other side of their faces. (An interesting sight, I would imagine.)

Bucharest used to be known as the 'Paris of The East', and as the taxi sped me through the city centre towards my two-star hotel, I could see the ornate and stylish buildings which bore the French influence. The trouble was, most of them were butted up against the ugly, monolithic architecture of the communist era. Bucharest, it seemed was a city of extremes. Freezing in winter, stiflingly hot in summer. Beautiful and ugly. Rich and poor.

All the trademarks of Eastern Europe were on show too. The leather jackets, the shabby cars and the hardened expressions on the faces of the people. Cheap fast food outlets had replaced state-run shops and canteens, and much of the city's youth were sitting outside them at plastic tables indulging in what appeared to be the Romanians' national pastime – smoking. Everyone seemed to have a fag on the go. I knew that cigarettes were only about 40p for twenty, but in a country where the average monthly income was 100 US dollars, that didn't necessarily make them cheap. Perhaps, following the social and economic upheaval caused by the collapse of communism, nobody had yet got round to pointing out that they weren't terribly good for you.

Linzie was already in Bucharest, having travelled out with a chaperone for rehearsals two days earlier. By the time I arrived at the hotel which was housing all the contestants, I was relieved to find a happy little bunny.

'Are you having fun?' I enquired after we'd shared a customary showbusiness 'luvvie' hug.

'Yes it's great,' she replied, ebulliently. 'Everyone is so nice.'

She went on to tell me how she'd made lots of new friends and enjoyed the many events and tours which had been laid on for the children by the festival organisers. But all the time she was talking to me I felt that I was preventing her from being where she wanted to be – with her new chums.

'What's the best thing that's happened so far?' I asked, desperately trying to elongate a conversation which had never really taken off.

'Meeting the Romanian president,' she said, without hesitation. 'He came to greet us when we went on a special trip to the parliament building.'

'And what was he like?'

'Oh he was really nice.'

'Yes, you say that, but did you ask him how he intends to deal with Romania's national debt and what he's going to do about the inherent corruption within the parliamentary system?'

'No.'

I reverted to a more sensible line of questioning.

'He was nice, you say?'

'Yes, very nice.'

And with those words she was gone. I guess I felt a little disappointed that I hadn't felt any special bond between the two of us – the artist and songwriter who would put Britain back on the European map. The conversation had been stilted and perhaps it would always remain so. Maybe she'd never be able to relax fully with the man who'd once been her auditioner. It wasn't that Linzie didn't like me. She just had better, more fun places to be, and that's where she'd gone now – back to her fellow competitors, who seemed a most relaxed and uncompetitive lot – dancing, singing and generally being jolly in the large hotel foyer.

The good news was that Linzie was happy. This meant I could leave her to her own devices and devote my time in Bucharest to a more important goal. Finding myself a pop star.

This process began when I met Mr Nanca at dinner. He was one of the producers of the whole event and the main man behind the Phoenix Foundation. It looked like he was in his late forties and not at all like your average Western pop music guru; in fact he resembled an old-fashioned tailor, in his formal dark suit and with glasses hanging on a cord around his neck. I felt like he was going to produce a tape measure at any moment and size me up for a dinner jacket.

In the course of our conversation it became clear, much to my delight, that Mr Nanca had already begun to suspect I could be extremely useful in introducing his acts to a wider audience. And why not think that? After all, I had accidentally mentioned that I'd had been a Top Five recording artist in the UK.

'There is one of my singers who you must hear,' began Mr Nanca. 'Paula Seling. I will give you some of her CDs – she is wonderful. She is beautiful, talented and she has a magnificent voice.'

'Is she very famous here?' I enquired.

'She is a star. Soon the national TV channel are making an hour-long special about her life in music.'

'I have to say, Paula sounds great.'

'In two nights' time,' continued the now ebullient Mr Nanca, 'Paula will be singing in a jazz club for a special invited audience. Would you like to come to that?'

'Of course, it sounds wonderful.'

'Paula is more than wonderful – and she has that extra something special.'

It was becoming clear that either Paula was a veritable star, or that Mr Nanca, despite his appearance, was just like a Western pop guru after all.[*] For now anyway, I was prepared to believe the former to be the case.

After a pleasant meal and a lot of small talk about the song competition Mr Nanca proposed that I meet with Paula the following day for lunch, an assignation which I readily agreed to, especially when I saw from the CD covers which were being handed to me, that Mr Nanca had not been exaggerating about Paula's beauty.

'What will you do with the rest of your evening?' asked my new friend.

'I have to do an interview on a radio station.'

'What? But you have only just arrived. Which station?'

'I think it's called Radio 21.'

'Ah, this should be fun. What time are you on?'

'They told me midnight.'

'In that case I will listen. Good luck.'

I guess it must have seemed impressive to Mr Nanca that after only a few hours in the country, I was appearing on a top radio station. It seemed unusual to me too, but it was just the way that things had worked out. Back in England some months earlier I had received an email from Alina, a Romanian woman living in London who had read the book on my Moldovan exploits, and she had offered to help me with contacts and advice should I ever decide to go to Bucharest. A meeting over coffee one afternoon in London had provided me with a number of very useful media contacts, and a further afternoon phoning them all had led to a bizarre offer from an extremely friendly man called Bogdan Moldovan.

'You can come on our midnight show and talk with Nik about what you are doing,' he had said. 'Nik is a crazy guy and you sound perfect for him.'

Now, as I made my way to the radio studios which were nestled on the corner of one of Bucharest's busy squares, I tried not to think about what 'being perfect for Nik' might involve. All I knew was that it was something of a coup to have landed exposure on the Romanian media this early in my trip. I prepared myself for what

---

[*] *i.e. full of bullshit.*

Nik might be like. Was the Romanian version of a DJ who was a 'crazy guy' exactly like the British one? In other words, someone who wasn't crazy at all but who just said some wacky things on air from time to time? In my experience these 'crazy guys' have wives, families, financial advisers and big mortgages. They like to think they are living *close to the edge*, when really they're just *close to the hedge* in their vast back gardens most of the time.

It was difficult to fathom quite how this interview was going to work as a piece of radio, given that my Romanian was limited to a handful of words, the pronunciation of which meant that few managed to convey their intended meaning. I'd been told that a translator was going to be supplied, but I still felt it likely that the listeners would tire of a broadcast which would end up sounding like a session at the United Nations. I decided that I would have to enter the studio equipped with a few Romanian sentences which would brighten the interview and potentially disarm the 'crazy' Nik. I enlisted the help of Daniel, the particularly friendly young driver who'd been supplied by the Song Festival to ferry the contestants and songwriters from A to B during our stay in Bucharest. He was delighted by my request, and chuckled as he supplied each nugget of vocabulary during the short drive from the hotel to Radio 21.

At the radio station I was greeted by Bogdan Moldovan, who turned out to be younger than I imagined, and certainly keener. He seemed genuinely pleased to meet me.

'We are so pleased that you have agreed to come on the show *La Strada* with Nik.'

'My pleasure.'

'I hope that you will be OK. Nik is crazy. He is wild – you never know what he will do.'

'I think I'll manage.'

'Are you nervous?'

'Not really.'

'Good. I guess that you are very experienced.'

The absence of nerves actually had much more to do with the fact that I didn't really care. This whole episode had begun to feel faintly unreal to me, maybe because that very morning I'd woken up in my bed in London and now, just hours later, I was about to be broadcast across the airwaves in Romania. I was shown through to the studio where, sure enough, Nik turned out to be distinctly 'uncrazy'. If anything he seemed a little nervous. He wanted to know what we would discuss and I suggested that we talk about my quest and the likelihood of my achieving any success here in Romania. I handed him a CD of the songs which I'd recorded to date, and he said that he would probably play them during the interview.

The interview kicked off. Well, I say 'interview' but it wasn't really. I was there, ready to be questioned, but Nik just rambled on for what seemed like a full five minutes. When he finally came to me, he asked me why I thought I could have a hit record in Romania.

'Well, Nik,' I replied as slowly as I could, hoping that a good percentage of the young audience would have a smattering of English and wouldn't need to rely on the translation. 'It's quite simple really. I suppose I believe that I will be a success here because I am so handsome.'

Silence from Nik.

I continued.

'It is a shame that this is radio. If it was TV then people would be able to see just how lovely looking I am, and in the morning they'd rush out and buy my records.'

Nik paused, searching for something to say.

'And what kind of music do you do?' he finally managed.

'All kinds. You will see from the CD I gave you.'

'Well, let's hear some.'

Nik then began to play my CD, the first track of which was, rather unfortunately, 'What Does A Pixie Do?'

Nik looked shocked.

'And you have entered *this* in a song competition?' he asked incredulously as he faded the music.

'Er, no. Not this one. Another song.'

I figured it was time to throw in my first Romanian sentence. '*Ai un par frumos.*'

In what was now becoming a bit of a common occurrence in this interview, Nik was silent again. He had been thrown by my remark. I don't know why – it seemed reasonable enough. I'd simply told him that he had smashing hair.

Nik played in some adverts and tried to gather himself for the next section of this truly awful interview. I found it difficult to believe that anyone would still be listening. He passed me a small glass containing some kind of spirit and urged me to drink it.

'It's Tuica,' he said, 'drink it. It's beautiful.'

I drank it down in one. It was very strong. I think you are supposed to sip it. Nik looked shocked, but he poured me another, in keeping with Romanian hospitality.

'I believe that you are known a little in your country, Great Britain,' he began when we went back on air. 'What do your people like about you?'

'A few things I suppose. I write a bit and I'm on the radio quite a lot but I suppose that what they like most of all is that I'm so handsome. I really am very lovely looking. Perhaps you could explain my beauty to your listeners.'

Nik was beginning to look sick.

I took another swig of my Tuica as a flushed Nik gave a further song from my CD a spin – the uptempo track 'I Want You For Your Mind', that I'd written for someone like Tom Jones. Nik tapped his foot and looked to be more approving of it than he had been of 'Pixie'. Maybe he was just relieved that when the music was playing then it meant that I wasn't talking.

I finished my second Tuica and felt even more mischievous than I had before. I cannot remember what Nik asked me next, but I know I replied with a further pre-prepared Romanian sentence. In this one I simply asked Nik what he was doing up so late, and was he not worried that late nights would affect his looks? Instead of answering he played another one of my tracks. This was good, the cheekier I was, then the more of my music got played. At this moment Bogdan appeared alongside me in the studio. He tapped me on the shoulder and urged me to take off my headphones.

'Tony, do not fight with Nik,' he said firmly.

'What?'

'He is not a good guy to make a fight with.'

'I'm not making a fight.'

'I think it is best if you just answer his questions. Maybe not to make the remarks about it being late or about his hair.'

'But it's smashing.'

'Tony, please.'

Nik was supposed to be the wild man yet he had to be protected by his producer from my gentle ribbing. Mind you, with two Tuicas in me I was pretty much prepared to say or do anything. Perhaps this hadn't escaped Bogdan's attention.

The interview concluded as messily as it had begun and the warm handshakes which followed it probably had more to do with Romanian good manners than any genuine affection for this idiot who'd come on air and been a pain in the arse.

Daniel the driver seemed amused though as he explained as we drove back to the hotel.

'It was funny,' he said, 'I never heard that guy lost for words before.'

'I hope I wasn't a disgrace.'

'Not a disgrace, no. Tell me Tony, what is a pixie?'

'I'll tell you tomorrow.'

As I made my way into the hotel I wondered if Mr Nanca had listened to the interview. I hoped not. I didn't want the lunch with Paula to be cancelled.

One of the major disadvantages of staying in a hotel which is full of children who are competing in a song competition is that at 9.00 a.m. they start practising their songs. I was woken by the sound of the girl in the next room relentlessly singing the refrain of a song which could only have been called 'Good Thing' – judging by the number of times she felt the need to sing those two words at the top of her voice. For me this was not a good thing, in fact it was unquestionably a very bad thing. I was tired and wanted further sleep, but it was proving impossible. The efforts from the neighbouring room only served as a reminder to the other competitors that their vocal chords also required immediate exercise, and soon the hotel was filled with the sound of warbling teenagers.

After a short but unsuccessful battle against this din, in which I attempted to use pillows over my ears in self-defence, I conceded defeat.

'All right you arseholes – you win – I'm getting up!' I cried, warmly recognising the need to rise and share in the joys of a new day.

Actually I did feel quite optimistic about the day ahead, not least because I had a lunch arranged with Mr Nanca and Paula

Seling. I struggled down to a breakfast room which was full of the children who weren't currently singing in their rooms. They were either accompanied by their parents, the composer of their song, or some kind of chaperone figure. I sat down and observed. A loud American lady seemed to be dominating proceedings, reacting to contributions which were coming in broken English from diverse European accents, ranging from Dutch to Turkish. I noted that many of the men had rock'n'roll hair – the kind that all old rockers have – long and overly-coiffured, and usually a sign that its bearer is refusing to accept that he is fifty and no longer deeply desirable.

'So how are you feeling this morning?' I asked Linzie, after I'd spotted her and wandered over to her busy table, packed as it was with her international friends. 'More rehearsals today and then the big night tomorrow, is that right?'

'That's right,' she said, before leaning towards me and adding confidentially, 'I'm feeling just fine, and I'm going to do my best to win this competition you know.'

'Good for you,' I replied, 'but remember it doesn't matter whether you win or not. The most important thing is that you enjoy yourself.'

After breakfast I returned to my room and started to sort through the pile of CDs and cassettes which Mr Nanca had left with me. It seemed that I had been given Paula Seling's entire back catalogue. I was impressed by what I heard. Yes, some of the production seemed a little dated and suffered from being smothered by lavish synthesiser string parts, but Paula's voice was excellent, and her most recent CD would have been just the sort of thing I'd like to listen to in my car, but for the incomprehensible Romanian lyrics. I was pleased that when I saw Mr Nanca I wouldn't have to indulge in the old showbusiness tradition of telling somebody you liked something when in truth you thought it was shite.[*] I picked up my guitar and began trying to come up with ideas for songs that Paula and I could perform together. For a while I'd contemplated following Simon Cowell's advice and opting for an

---

[*] *Noël Coward used to have a good trick for this one. Whenever he saw an inferior play or performance he would kick off the back-stage banter with the winningly ambiguous 'Darling, you've done it again!'*

established song which was already a tried and tested hit, but this felt like a cop out, and besides I wanted to feel that glow of excitement which would come from creating a hit from nothing.

After a decidedly uninventive half hour I elected to trawl through my own back catalogue of songs, and I was particularly pleased when I remembered a ballad I'd written some ten years previously. It was a duet called 'When All Is Said And Done', and had originally been written for a musical comedy which had been staged at the Edinburgh Festival. It felt perfect for the job in hand, although the version which I quickly recorded on to a cassette clearly left room for considerable improvement.

'Well that's the song,' I said to myself as I put down the guitar beside the bed. 'All I've got to do now is meet the girl and persuade her to sing it with me.'

As I made my way to the restaurant where we had arranged to meet for lunch, I began to wonder what Mr Nanca had told Paula about me. Not a good deal, I wouldn't have thought, given that he didn't know much. Perhaps he'd just said something along the lines of 'be nice to this guy and he can get you exposure in Britain'. I arrived at the Burebista restaurant five minutes early and began to survey the rather brutal and somewhat disturbing decor. Burebista's speciality food was 'game' and as a consequence the proprietors had felt the need to have as many stuffed animals hanging from the walls as the building's foundations could support. Pigs, wild boar, deer, several hares, rabbits, miscellaneous wildfowl, and even a forlorn-looking bear looked down at me through their lifeless glass eyes. It was all a touch disconcerting for someone who'd often struggled with the morality of killing animals for meat.

The restaurant offered an English translation of the menu:

File de urs 'Sarmisegetuzza' cartofi taranesti
Bear fillet 'Sarmisegetuzza' with country style potatoes

Tocanita de urs cu ciuperci de padure si mamaliguta
Bear ragout with wild mushrooms and polenta

It was all too fancy. If there'd been something as simple as bear and chips then I might have been tempted.

I began to concern myself with the business in hand, which was to impress a young and beautiful Romanian pop star and persuade her to perform a duet with a washed-up old has-been from Britain. Naturally, I wouldn't be presenting the proposition using exactly those words. I'd have to slip in a few euphemisms like experienced, seasoned and well-versed, and hope she wouldn't interpret them as washed-up, old and has-been respectively.

I was just making last-minute adjustments to my hair and considering the opening conversational gambits when I noticed Mr Nanca enter the restaurant. Alone.

'Tony, I am sorry,' he said as he reached my table. 'But Paula has had some bad news.'

'Oh dear.'

'I am afraid that her father has had a heart attack and she has rushed off to be at his bedside.'

'Oh dear.'

'They think that he will be OK, but naturally she is concerned. Since he lives over 650 kms away from Bucharest this means that she will not be able to do the show at the jazz club tomorrow night.'

Oh dear.

In the space of thirty seconds the wheels of my trip had well and truly come off. I found myself momentarily lapsing into a moment of self-pity, but then I remembered Paula and her father's predicament, and I quickly put it all back into perspective. 'Will Paula be back in Bucharest before I leave for London?'

'Yes, I think so, but for now she will remain with her father.'

'Oh well, I guess we will get to meet.'

'You will. I'm sure of it.'

This meant that there wouldn't be much time to implement my master plan in which Paula would record a duet with me, and the man now seated opposite me would be charged with getting it into the Romanian charts. Mr Nanca, as yet unaware of his expected role, picked up the menu.

'Are you going to try the bear?' he asked. 'I'm told that it is good here.'

'I'm sure it is but I think I'll have the mushroom soup, all the same,' I replied wimpishly, before remembering that I had something important to hand over. 'Mr Nanca, could you give this to

Paula?' I added, producing a cassette from my pocket.

'What is it?'

I drew a deep breath. I felt a little apprehensive about making this next suggestion.

'It's a song called "When All Is Said And Done" which I want Paula to listen to. If she likes it I thought we might record it together as a duet.'

'I will see that she listens to it,' said Mr Nanca, without giving much away.

Having spent the afternoon discovering that Bucharest is not Europe's top city for shopping, I returned to the hotel to find one of the Song Contest's mullet-haired songwriters leading the kids in a sing-song in the hotel lounge area. This normally would have been the kind of thing that I would have got involved in, but I was hungry and more in the mood for edible pie, rather than the version of 'American Pie' which would almost inevitably be sung shortly. I smiled politely to the vocalising throng and made my way into the hotel dining room. After a while I noted that the sing-song in the lobby had become something of a solo concert by the long-haired guitarist, and I could hear him begin a song which the Romanian contingent seemed to recognise.

'This was his big hit,' said the waitress as she finished taking my order.

'So what is the name of the guy doing all the singing?'

'His name is Laurentiu Cazan, and this song is called "Say Something". He is famous for this song. Do you like it?'

'I guess so, it sounds quite catchy.'

When I heard the enthusiastic response which the conclusion of the song prompted in the lobby, I began to feel a little envious of the singer just outside the door. What a great feeling to be able to sing your hit song to a group of appreciative young people. I remembered the tingle of excitement everyone had felt at the Guitar Pull in Nashville when Randy Goodrum's hit 'You Needed Me' was recognised. Maybe that was the real reason I'd taken on this bet. Maybe that was why I was going to all this absurd effort. Wasn't that what a hit record meant? Recognition.

The big question was whether or not the song competition could deliver it.

CHAPTER 15 WHEN ALL IS SAID AND DONE

I was woken again by children singing. Normally this would have been a joyous and uplifting sound which I would have cherished, but coming as it was before nine o'clock for the second morning in a row, it was having a less beneficial effect right now. I lay in bed wondering if murdering the perpetrators would be frowned upon by the competition judges, and perhaps lead to disqualification. After a few minutes' deliberation I chose the pillow over the ears option, given that ultimately I didn't want to let Linzie down in front of her friends.

With most of the day free, I persuaded Daniel to whizz me round Bucharest on a tour of the city. I soon found it to be a place which has been painfully stamped with the identity of Nicolae Ceausescu. Even by the normal standards of totalitarian dictatorship, this bloke went too far. The best example of his wanton extravagance is the Palace of Parliament, an absolutely massive edifice built on three tiers, which Ceausescu intended to be, in terms of surface area, the largest building in the world.*
Daniel told me, between drags on almost continuous cigarettes, how one-sixth of Bucharest, including twelve churches, three monasteries, two synagogues and 7,000 homes, was bulldozed to make way for this shrine to Ceausescu's growing megalomania. Apparently in the Eighties, when the building was lit, it took only four hours for it to consume the equivalent of a day's supply of electricity for the rest of the city.

'It's no wonder the people went off him a bit,' I said to Daniel with a wry smile.

---

* *He just missed out to the Pentagon in Washington.*

He smiled back, being young enough not to bear the scars which would have prevented such a relaxed response.

'Tony, what do you do in London?' asked Daniel, somewhat out of the blue.

'Oh, I write books and I do some comedy too,' I replied, rather coyly.

'And is life good there?'

'Yes. For me, it is, yes.'

Daniel, as well as being knowledgeable about Bucharest's history, seemed to be genuinely interested about life in Britain. He didn't seem a typical driver at all. We'd not been together long, but I already knew that I liked him.

'Thank you for taking me on this tour,' I said.

'It is my pleasure,' he said, taking a cigarette out of the now almost empty packet, 'but it is not over. I have more to show you.'

And see more we did. Daniel showed me the railway station which had been specially built for the use of the Ceausescus and their cronies, and the concrete apartment blocks which had risen from the rubble of the beautiful old houses – demolished because they did not fit in with the dictator's vision of the great city. At the Piata Revolutiei we saw the balcony from which Ceausescu made his fateful speech shortly before his rapid and unsavoury removal from office. Finally, we drove past the eyesore of a National TV station which in the late Eighties had only provided two hours' airtime a day – one of which was devoted to presidential activities. You can imagine how the show might have run:

'Hi there and welcome to the Nicolae Ceausescu Show, with me, your host, Nicolae Ceausescu! (*Audience applause*) On today's show, we're going to be taking you on a little tour of the forty-one houses around the country that my good lady wife and I have acquired for our own personal use. (*More applause*) Then I'll have my first special guest – yes you've guessed it – it'll be my beautiful wife Elena, and she's going to show you the diamond-studded shoes she's just had made for her! (*Cheers*) Then we'll have our Round Robin Forum in which politicians will pay tribute to my policies of banning abortions and insisting that every healthy woman in the country under forty years of age must have at least five children. (*Screams of delight*) Then the show will be over I'm afraid folks (*boos*), and you'll be able to leave your TV sets and get back to your daily activities of queuing for food, accompanied by random interrogations by the Securitate.' (*Standing ovation*)

It really is no wonder the people went off him a bit.

The big night arrived.

As I made my way to my seat in the 'Children's Theatre', Linzie was backstage, almost certainly pacing up and down and giving herself last-minute pep talks. She would have a long wait ahead of her since hers was going to be the penultimate performance of the evening. An excited audience waited for the curtain to rise while TV cameramen hovered in readiness. I began to wonder how my effort would stand up against the other twenty songs, and I looked around me to see if the audience were a sturdy enough bunch to withstand the imminent aural bombardment which awaited them. They looked up to it. Most of the adults had withstood years and years under Ceausescu, so for them a children's song contest was going to be a breeze.

The first entrant was an eleven-year-old Romanian girl who was wearing a smile which barely concealed her nerves. The song, according to the translation in my programme, was entitled 'I Will Always Sing'. A noble enough sentiment I suppose, but I couldn't help feeling that a lot of these kids needed to be taught precisely when *not* to sing – e.g. before 10 a.m. in hotels where I was staying. The Romanian girl finished a competent performance of an unremarkable song and the audience responded with generous applause. The atmosphere was warm and supportive.

She was followed by a rotund little fellow from Finland who jigged about with confidence to a jolly ditty called 'Nikolas', with lyrics half in Finnish and half in English. By the end of the song I was still a little confused as to how 'Nikolas' was worthy of being lauded so vociferously, given the only lyric I'd properly understood was one explaining how Nikolas was 'satisfied when his dog was by his side'. He didn't sound so deep.

'A Message For Love And Peace' would have meant more to me if it hadn't been sung in Egyptian, but I took a fair guess that the song was encouraging us to be nice to our fellow man, rather than urging us to nick stuff from shops and stamp on each other's toes. The Egyptian singer, who seemed a little moody, was the first female entrant whose physical appearance suggested that she was fully familiar with the workings of a bra. Others were to follow, one girl in the second half causing an almost audible inhalation of breath from the audience as she plodded on to the stage.

The highlight of the first half had absolutely no breasts at all. Not something to worry about though since he was a nine-year-old boy from Croatia. His performance belied his tender years and was a quite extraordinary sight. It was like watching Rod Stewart, Cliff Richard and Mick Jagger all rolled into one tiny little body. He strutted, leaned forward, leaned back, posed, spun, danced, clapped and waved his arms above his head in the song's lively finale. His performance was highly entertaining, being as brave as it was accomplished, but it was also very funny. He won the audience over as one, with his rendition of an extremely catchy song called 'Emily'. We cheered him unreservedly when he finished. We couldn't stop ourselves. As he left the stage clutching a bouquet of flowers that had been tossed to him, I couldn't help worrying that Dino Jelusic had peaked too early. That he might burn out by the time he reaches sixteen.

The second half lacked some of the energy of the first, maybe because the audience was getting tired, or perhaps the songs weren't as strong, but either way this didn't stop the tension building for me as Linzie's performance drew ever closer. Before her, a Moldovan girl sang beautifully, her performance only marred by the creative decision to sing the middle section of the song to a stuffed dog which she'd brought on to the stage with her. It was somewhat baffling, especially to those of us who had no idea what she was singing about – and the image of a small girl serenading what looked like a deceased dog did little to complement the pretty melody. I kept imagining an irate parent shouting to her from the side of the stage.

'Dearest, will you stop singing to the dog! How many times have I got to tell you – it's dead.'

Then Linzie, pleasingly dogless, wandered on to the stage in an evening gown. The audience applauded and I let out a little cheer. She was tiny compared to some of the other girls who'd appeared earlier, but given that this was a children's song competition I felt that her youthful appearance could be a boon. Her backing tape began and Willie's keyboard introduction filled the theatre. For a moment I was back in his studio, discussing with him the implausibility of this moment ever arriving. But it was here, and Linzie was looking assured. She launched into the song with all the confidence of someone who'd spent the last twenty years in show business. Instead of being paralysed by the scale of the event, she was being lifted by it. She was delivering the best rendition of the song I'd ever heard from her. Unlike some of the previous performers who'd engaged in clearly choreographed moves which had no doubt been forced upon them by their adult mentors, Linzie's movement and gestures were her own and they seemed in tune with her interpretation of the song – and boy, was she making that sound good.

As the song progressed I began to be overtaken by a real sense of pride. I could see that there was genuine joy behind Linzie's expression, a sense that she was doing what she really loved. I looked around me and saw the appreciative expressions of the audience and I realised that something was really being *achieved* here – perhaps for the first time since I'd taken on this bet. After more than a year's endeavours, finally one of my songs was receiving a public airing – in a rousing inspirational performance by an authentic young talent. And then there were all the kids all around me. All that youthful exuberance, and that innocent expectancy – as yet completely untarnished by the cynical world which they were about to enter. Before I knew what was happening, my heart underwent a sudden attack of soppiness, and unexpected tears began to well up in my eyes. My male, British, eyes.

I'd pulled myself together before the song's big finale, and that last note which Linzie had confessed to being worried about hitting. I took a deep breath on her behalf and crossed my fingers. With consummate professionalism Linzie moved the microphone away from her mouth and blasted out the note. Perfect.

Absolutely perfect.

The audience didn't rise to their feet but I did, and Linzie was given a magnificent reception by all, and one which had only been surpassed by that for Dino, the nine-year-old Croatian phenomenon. Linzie beamed proudly, and then I remembered.

The flowers!

I quickly picked them up from where they'd been lain at my feet, and I dashed up to the side of the stage.

Unfortunately Linzie had started to exit the other way. I rushed on in an effort to reach her before she'd disappeared from the audience's view but I was too late and, in a rather unshowbizzy manner, the presentation ended up taking place in the wings.

'Linzie, you were fabulous,' I gushed, 'and I really really mean that.'

'Thank you Tony, I really enjoyed myself,' she replied, her face brimming with nervous energy.

'It showed.'

And then an odd silence. I couldn't think of what to say and neither could Linzie. Well, what *was* there to say? She was thirteen and excited and she needed to get back and share her joy in the dressing room with her new friends. I was the old, tall bloke who happened to have written the song she'd just sung, and I was just getting in the way.

'Well, off you go – go and celebrate!' I said, rather pathetically.

'OK,' she spinning round to go, almost in relief. 'And I hope we win.'

'It doesn't matter. You've already won with that performance.'

'So, how did you get on?' asked Willie from back in England, as I spoke to him on my mobile. I was walking back to the hotel, slightly tipsy after the post-contest party.

'Well we didn't win, but ...'

'But ... what?'

'Well, we came second!'

'You didn't!'

'We bloody did! Linzie was great – but of course it was your backing track which made all the difference. Can you believe it! Second place! And what's more we won 3,000 dollars!'

Willie laughed.

'I don't believe it, Hawks, you really are a most fortunate bastard. But I take my hat off to you.'

I felt pretty damn good, but so far Linzie had really done all the work. Mine began now. I had to persuade Paula Seling to perform a duet with me.

And that wasn't necessarily going to be easy.

It was mid-afternoon and I was seated alone at a table waiting to meet Paula, who'd just got back into town. Mr Nanca had arranged the meeting here, at the interestingly named 'Madhouse' café. Perhaps he'd picked this place because he felt this was where I, the instigator of the forthcoming liaison, belonged. I was a little nervous because I realised that if I didn't make a favourable impression now, then I'd have to accept that the whole Romanian excursion hadn't really nudged me any closer to winning my bet. If I cut an impressive figure the next hour or so, then I might just be able to capitalise on Paula's recent success. I reminded myself that I was a former Top Five recording artist, and recently, a prizewinning songwriter. Paula ought to be nervous of meeting me, I told myself – albeit not that convincingly.

I rose to my feet when Paula finally arrived. She was not, I was delighted to find, a disappointment in the beauty department. As she approached me across the café floor, there seemed to be an atmosphere of restrained excitement among the other coffee drinkers. Even if Paula hadn't been a well-known pop star, I still think that her looks alone would have been enough to have caused most heads to turn. She greeted me cordially and I took her hand and kissed it. I was treading a fine line between polite and downright creepish, but I'd read in my Romanian guidebook that this was considered good manners and a mark of respect.

'*Sarut mina*,' I said, using the words which the book had told me should follow the gesture.

This meant 'I kiss your hand'. I wondered if Romanians were always this literal. For instance, did they say 'I smash your face in' after landing you a left hook in the eye?

'Ah, I see that you are a gentleman,' said a smiling Paula.

Excellent. Things had got off to a good start. Mr Nanca, whom I'd barely noticed was accompanying Paula, ushered us both to sit down and we began talking business. I loosely explained about my bet, and I hinted at the possibility of indulging in some form of musical collaboration with a

Romanian artist.

'It would certainly be interesting,' she said, somewhat cagily.

'Would you like to make it big in England and maybe America?' I enquired.

'What do *you* think?'

'I think that you would.'

'Well, you are right. This is my dream.'

'I was hoping, Paula,' I said, plucking up my courage, 'that we might be able to work together in some way.'

'I hope so. Mr Nanca has told me that you like my music.'

'Yes. Very much.'

I was tickled by the formal way she referred to her manager as Mr Nanca. Back in London, all the pop managers were called things like 'Wizz', 'Bonzo' or 'Jed'. It appeared that the Romanian music business hadn't yet fully emerged from the formality of the communist years, when permits had to be granted by government officials for every live performance by an artist, and when every song lyric needed to be passed by a panel of censors. In a society where homosexuality was rewarded with a prison sentence and the Securitate was said to have infiltrated one in three families, there had simply been no room for the Wizzes and Bonzos of this world. (Which ultimately, I suppose, proves that there's an upside to everything.)

'So Tony, I heard your song which came second in the song competition,' offered Paula. 'I liked it very much.'

'Thank you.'

She hadn't mentioned the duet 'When All Is Said And Done'. Did this mean she didn't like it – or just that she hadn't got round to listening to it yet? There followed a slightly awkward pause in which neither of us quite knew how to move things forward. Some more small talk was clearly required before I dived in with more on the subject of our possible duet.

'Have you eaten bear in a restaurant?' I enquired, clumsily breaking the silence, and fiddling with the menu.

'I'm sorry?' said Paula, looking a little taken aback.

'Have you ever eaten bear in a restaurant?'

'Er, no,' she replied, looking almost a little piqued by my question. 'If you will excuse me for a moment, I must go to the bathroom.'

'Yes, of course.'

As Paula got up to leave the table I tried to fathom what it was that could have caused this sudden change in her mood. Then I realised.

And it wasn't good.

Yes, it may have been the case that I had asked the perfectly innocent question 'Have you eaten bear in a restaurant?' – but it now occurred to me that what she had heard was something entirely different – 'Have you eaten *bare* in a restaurant?' Obviously not the most polite thing I could have said to a successful pop star and renowned Romanian beauty.

Before I could explain what I'd really meant, Paula was already making her way across the café floor towards the bathroom. I considered calling her back, but too many people were watching her already, and besides I didn't want to make things worse. I just remained seated at the table like a lemon and watched her walk away from me. Oh well, that was it, my hopes were going with her – the collaboration was over. I had killed it stone dead with my unwittingly lascivious enquiry.

Paula seemed to be gone an age, and the wait was almost unbearable; however, when she did return she looked decidedly more good humoured.

'When you met with Mr Nanca, did you meet him at the Burebista restaurant?' she asked.

'Yes.'

Paula immediately began to giggle.

'I see now what you meant,' she said. 'You wanted to know if I have ever eaten bear – the animal.'

'Yes.'

'That is much better than what I thought you asked.'

I let out a huge sigh of relief, and Paula some cathartic laughter. Then I joined in with the laughing. From this moment forth the ice was well and truly broken and Paula and I began to have some real fun together. We discussed life in our home cities and talked about the music and artists we liked best.

'When are you flying back to London?' she asked, as I drained the last drops from my second cup of coffee.

'Tomorrow afternoon.'

'Well, why don't we try to work on some ideas together in the morning?'

'Great. Did you get a chance to listen to my song, by the way?'

'Yes. I liked it. A lot. That is one of the things we should work on tomorrow.'

Things had turned around very quickly. Only a few minutes before Paula had thought of me as the pervert who wanted to know if she dined naked, but now I was being asked if I wanted to work with her.

'That would be great,' I replied, trying hard to conceal my delight. 'Are you sure you are free in the morning?'

'Most certainly.'

'In that case just tell me where and when and I will be there.'

We met at 10 a.m. in the dark basement of Casa Eliad, a cafe and folk club which Mr Nanca had arranged for us to use as a place to work until it opened for business at lunchtime.

When I arrived I kissed Paula's hand again.

'*Sarut mina,*' I said, hoping that this would still be construed as good manners rather than me coming on to her.

Actually, in this regard, there was no need to worry. The atmosphere between the two of us was relaxed and pleasingly without complications. While I respected and admired Paula's beauty, I was relieved to find that I wasn't overcome with a burning desire for her. As for Paula, well, she'd mentioned on the previous day that she had a boyfriend, and presumably her love for him was enough for her to be able to resist my generous good looks and charm. So, from a work perspective, the news was excellent. There was no complicated chemistry between us. In fact there was no physics, geography or maths between us either. Biology and PE weren't even on our timetables. We were just going to sit next to each other in class, giggle a bit, and then do surprisingly well in the end of term exams.

There was a knock at the door. Who could this be?

'That will be Daniel and Sorin,' explained Paula. 'My bass player and guitarist. They are going to learn your song, so that we can record it.'

I was more than a little surprised when Daniel turned out to be the same guy who'd been driving me around the city over the last few days.

'Daniel!' I said, shaking his hand. 'You never said you played bass for Paula.'

'You didn't ask.'

It was becoming clear that the music business was a completely different affair here in Romania. It would just never be that a band member of a top recording artist in one of the Western countries would need to have another job in order to subsidise their income.

'Shall we start singing?' asked Paula.

'Er … yes … why not?'

And sing we did; in fact for the rest of the morning we sang our hearts out. Paula and I soon worked out some harmonies, and we were delighted to find that our voices blended rather well together. I played rhythm guitar while Sorin provided some tasteful jazzy guitar licks, and all the time Daniel produced a refined and well-judged bass part, proving that he wasn't just accomplished at hill starts and three-point turns. To my delight, even after a couple of hours, and when we'd finished rehearsing the song, we all continued to make music together. Just as a joke, Sorin the guitarist began to play the song in a heavy rock style, and to his surprise, the rest of us followed suit. On completing this, we then launched into a jazz swing version, before discovering that there was great fun to be had with the reggae dub interpretation. We played this one four times in a row – it was such fun. It was just a shame that the café wasn't yet open for customers – surely they couldn't have failed to be charmed by the sight of four people sharing in such uncomplicated joy. This was music for purely recreational purposes – which, if you think about it, was all the Great Composer in the Sky probably ever intended for it in the first place.

'Do you think this song could work if it was released as a single in Romania?' I asked Paula, indelicately returning matters to business when we stopped for a well-earned coffee break.

'Maybe,' she replied. 'How about in Britain? Could we release it as a single there?'

'I hope so.'

It was clear that Paula and I both wanted something from each other. Superficially it may have seemed a little mercenary, but then wasn't this really the basis for all working relationships? Ours was just honest. I was hoping to exploit Paula's beauty, fame and talent to win my bet, and Paula wanted to use mine to get exposure in Britain.

One of us was clearly getting the better deal.

'Tony,' continued Paula, 'perhaps you could help with some of my songs?'

'What do you mean?'

'I wondered if maybe you could write some English lyrics for some of the tracks off my album.'

'OK, I don't see why not,' I replied assuredly.

'Do you think that I could have some success in your country? If I sing in English?'

'I see absolutely no reason why not,' I said. 'In fact, I think I can help you with this.'

'How?'

'Just trust me, I have some ideas.'

Of course, that's precisely the thing that any beautiful singer trying to make her way in the music business should not do. Never listen to some bloke who turns up with a load of vague promises and says 'Just trust me'. The only difference here was that I wasn't a complete bastard intent on ripping her off and treating her like a piece of product.

Honest.

'You must keep this collaboration going in spite of the distance between you,' said the newly arrived Mr Nanca, whilst taking some pictures of the two of us for 'publicity purposes'.

'Yes, I will work hard on Paula's song,' I replied. 'And we must find a way of recording the duet together.'

'Yes, maybe in London,' said Paula, as the owner of Casa Eliad announced that my taxi had arrived to take me to the airport. Paula proffered her hand for my now routine kiss. 'I have never been to London.'

'Tony,' said Daniel, who had now dispensed with his bass, freeing himself for handshaking duties in the small parting ceremony which seemed to be developing. 'Don't forget – keep up the writing.'

'Don't worry, I will,' I replied. 'My intention is to try and write a book about all of this.'

'No, I don't mean the books,' he said, warmly shaking me by the hand. 'Keep writing the songs. You can really do it, you know.'

'Thanks,' I said, genuinely chuffed. 'In fact, thanks to all of you. I've really enjoyed my time here.' I turned to Paula. 'The next time I see you, it will be for something really special.'

'Like what?'

'I'm not sure yet, but do trust me.'

I didn't know it yet, but much to my surprise, I was actually going to deliver on this one.

PART V
BIG IN ALBANIA

From Scutari to Koritsa, from Gjirokastra to Berat
From Valona to Tirana, I'm really where it's at
From the mountains to the Adriatic shore,
I give my all and still they cry for more.

I've made my name in many places
A thousand falls, a thousand faces
But nowhere's more devoted than Albania —
Cos they've got Norman-mania
(They've got Norman-mania — he's Big in Albania)
I may be way off track but I love Albania back.

On the hillsides, in the valleys, in the forests, on the lakes
All Albania cries out Norman — 'Hey you got what it takes!'
As I wander down each fine Albanian street
The crowd's affection sweeps me off my feet.

I've made my name in many places
A thousand falls, a thousand faces
But nowhere's more devoted than Albania —
Cos they've got Norman-mania
(They've got Norman-mania — he's Big in Albania)
I may be way off track but I love Albania back.

And when the leaders saw his films they told the nation
Wise up to Norman 'wisdom', proletarian salvation
Don't pan him, don't can him, don't criticise or ban him
His struggle with the boss will be the workers' inspiration

They've got Norman-mania
(They've got Norman-mania — he's Big in Albania)
(They've got Norman-mania — he's Big in Albania)
I may be way off track but I love Albania back
(Big in Albania) I love Albania back
(Big in Albania) I love Albania back

CHAPTER 16 **WISDOM**

Parkinson is a clever bloke. His law, Parkinson's Law, was particularly relevant to me right now, because it states that 'work expands so as to fill the time for its completion'. In other words, if like me, you had two years in which to do something, it's unlikely that you'll work like a dog to complete it by the end of the first month. Not when there are other pressing matters which require attention – like attending parties, watching TV, or lounging in the sun whenever it happens to come out. You need the deadline to draw a little closer before you truly apply yourself. It's human nature. Or so Parkinson reckons, and who am I to disagree with him? I mean, he's met Muhammed Ali, and Rod Hull and Emu.

So it was, that on a late September morning, I realised that I was officially *running out of time*. A few weeks before, the world had witnessed the tragic events of 11 September. Initially, like everyone else, I was in shock but soon afterwards I started to notice a new phenomenon. Whenever businesses suffered a dip in trading, they would blame '9/11'. At first this didn't seem that unreasonable since it was obvious that airlines, the tourism industry, and the share markets would have to endure a downturn. However, the trend spread and I began to notice that the destruction of the twin towers had been allowed to become a universal scapegoat. Once you begin hearing it used as an excuse for shoe shops closing down, or for a worldwide drop in the sale of frisbees, then you know that things have gone too far.

But then again, if everyone else was doing it, why shouldn't I?

'Have you had your hit yet, Tony?'

'Not yet. This whole September 11th thing has really put a dampener on things.'

Actually there was a certain amount of veracity to my claim. For a while, the magnitude of the events of that extraordinary day seem to belittle everything else. When scenes from the ultimate disaster movie had just become an authentic news item, and when some kind of terrorist Armageddon seemed to be about to befall all of us, then the undertaking to make Simon Cowell eat a big hat-shaped cake lost some of its potency.

Things weren't in great shape anyway. My excitement about the Paula Seling/Tony Hawks collaboration had already begun to subside now that there were hundreds of miles between us, the Sudan dance track was on hold till the following summer, and the Ireland initiative had been dealt something of a blow when *The Gerry Ryan Show* had failed to return my calls. Eighteen months into my musical pilgrimage I'd lost my sense of direction for a second time, and I was in danger of losing faith.

A chance liaison was to change all that. The occasion was a routine meeting with my agent in a café in Covent Garden, in which we were discussing mundane matters of no great import. Before we were half through our café lattes, there was a commotion by the door, and we looked up to see an elderly gentleman indulging in some form of slapstick comedy in order to elicit laughs from the considerably younger woman who seemed to be accompanying him. It has to be said that he was having considerable success, and it wasn't just the young lady who was laughing either, because soon customers at nearby tables were joining in. From where I was sitting, the whole thing began to look like a rehearsed routine, being executed by a performer of some accomplishment. Suddenly the grey-haired old man in question grabbed the young lady and began waltzing her down the café towards us. Seconds later I could see the man's face and I instantly knew who it was.

'Charles, you'll never guess who that is,' I whispered. 'It's Norman Wisdom.'

'Yes,' replied Charles. 'And the thing is, I think he's here to see me.'

'Really? What makes you say that?'

'Because the girl he's with is my new assistant.'

'Blimey. Well, why would he want to see you? Do you know him?'

'Well I've never actually met him, but we've been corresponding for years. He wants to make a film based on a J.B. Priestley book which we handle the rights for. I guess he just wants to say hello.'

And that was exactly what happened. Upon arriving at our table Norman released his dancing partner and said 'hello' to Charles. A short conversation followed, I was briefly introduced, and that was it – the legendary British comedian and film star of the Fifties and Sixties grabbed his young partner and waltzed back out of our lives.

At least that was what I thought at the time, but later that same day I started to think of Norman Wisdom in an entirely different way. I began to consider him as someone who might be able to provide a winning resolution for me in my bet. From some distant recess in my mind I somehow recalled that, quite bizarrely, Norman enjoyed cult status in one of the more unlikely corners of the world. I returned home and researched the subject, to discover that Norman had become a hugely loved figure in Albania after the former communist dictator, Enver Hoxha, had banned nearly all Western films except his. Believing Norman Wisdom films to be both morally and politically acceptable to the doctrines of the regime, Hoxha ordered that they were shown at least once a week, and as a result the Albanian people had grown up idolising the British comic actor.

All of this only became relevant to me when I had my idea, which was as brilliant as it was simple. All I had to do was write a song for Norman Wisdom to record, and then release it in Albania. Surely his popularity would guarantee a hit. I only had two problems. First, Norman would need to be persuaded, and secondly, there was no song as such, for him to record. Still, these were minor hurdles that could be overcome.

I didn't have to wait long for progress to be made, and it came as a result of an appearance on the BBC Radio 4 panel game *Just A Minute*. One of my fellow panellists was the world-renowned lyricist Sir Tim Rice, whom I'd met on a couple of previous occasions and always found to be good company.

Before the recording, in the theatre's green room, Tim became genuinely interested as we discussed the details of my latest bet.

'And do you have to get the hit in the UK?' he asked.

'No, it could be anywhere in the world,' I replied.

'So you could bring a record out in some obscure country where you hardly have to sell any copies to get into the charts,' he observed.

'Yes, and I've had a bit of an idea on that front. Shall I run it by you?'

'By all means.'

I explained my foolhardy idea to Tim, and to my amazement he didn't laugh me out of court. In fact, he looked intrigued.

'Do you think it could work?' I asked.

'I don't see why not. If you get the right song, and if Norman's up for it.'

At this point in our conversation we were interrupted by the producer who reminded us that there was an audience waiting to be entertained, and would we mind having the good grace to join the others on stage. Being professionals through and through, we obliged.

As a consequence of having to engage my brain in the petty pedantry that was necessitated by the daft panel game which ensued, I didn't really have time to think any more about the Norman Wisdom/Albania idea. In fact, if truth be known, I forgot all about it. That was, until I was saying goodbye to Tim at the end of the evening. Maybe the two quick beers that I'd downed after the show had forced it back into my consciousness, but whatever it was, I found myself standing in front of Tim contemplating a preposterous proposal.

'You know the Norman Wisdom/Albania idea we talked about earlier?' I asked, just before Tim headed off for his waiting taxi.

'Yes?'

'Well, you don't fancy writing the song with me, do you?'

It was bold. It was brash. Quite possibly it was downright cheeky – but there was something about Tim which gave me the confidence to ask it. Tim stood for a moment, just looking at me, perhaps to gauge if my question was a sincere one.

'Do you write songs?' he enquired, not looking like he was going to opt for *instant* rejection.

'Yes, I've been writing them for years,' I replied eagerly. 'They haven't all done as well as yours though ... not yet anyway.'

Tim shuffled on his feet for a moment, then took a deep breath as if the air would help him make a decision.

'All right then,' he said, nonchalantly. 'Count me in. I'm on board.'

'Really?'

'Yes, why not? It could be fun. But we'll need to ask Norman if he's up for it.'

'Do you think he might be?'

'I don't see why not. What has he got to lose?'

Tim oozed confidence. Perhaps this had been one of the major contributory factors to his enormous success over the years.

'I've met Norman once before,' he continued, 'and we got along very well. I've got his number at home somewhere, so I'll give him a call and see what he says.'

As Tim left I shook my head in disbelief. Well there you go, it seemed that what I'd been told as a youth was true after all: 'If you don't ask, you don't get.' Mind you, I hadn't actually got anything yet.

There was still a lot of work to do.

Extraordinarily, less than a week later, I was in a car with Sir Tim Rice whizzing down to Epsom to meet Sir Norman Wisdom.

Tim told me that he'd put the idea to Norman, but that the response had been a confused one, so this meeting had been set up in order to explain our intentions more fully and discuss how to move things forward.

'When you spoke to Norman, did he have any idea who I was?' I asked Tim rather vainly, as we sped down the A3.

'Now, how can I put this?' replied Tim. 'Well, let's just say that if Norman was going to go on *Mastermind*, then he wouldn't pick Tony Hawks as his specialist subject.'

'I see.'

I sensed that we were both rather excited. Tim had met Norman years before at a cricket dinner, but in the course of our car journey I learned that Tim was something of a Norman Wisdom fan, fondly recounting visits to the cinema as a child.

'I remember queuing to see his latest films at the St Albans Gaumont,' he said nostalgically. 'Just as soon as they came out. I still get a tingle thinking about it.'

My appreciation of Norman's work was less subjective, being free of such sentimental reminiscences. Nevertheless I'd always admired his great comic skills and extraordinary ability to radiate warmth on screen. He had undoubtedly been a master of physical humour, understanding the simple rudiment of comedy – that falling over is funny. I felt thrilled at the prospect of this meeting, not only because I was going to meet the great man, but because I felt proud to have been the orchestrator of this bizarre collaboration. I was quite simply delighted that Sir Tim Rice, Sir Norman Wisdom, OBE, and the commoner Tony Hawks were about sit down and discuss a creative project together. Perhaps we could form a band – called 'Two knights and a prat'.

When we arrived at the flat we were greeted by Norman's assistant Sylvia, who showed us through to the simply decorated living room. And then Norman emerged.

He was smaller than I had imagined him to be and a little frail. Understandable I suppose. He was no longer the spritely, cheeky chappy of his black and white movie days. He was now an eighty-seven-year-old man.

'So, how can I help you gents?' he asked, with all his impish charm.

'Sir Norman,' I began rather formally, 'I understand that—'

'Don't call me Sir Norman,' he interrupted playfully. 'Call me Wizzie.'

'OK, er … Wizzie,' I said, a trifle uncomfortably, 'basically you know what all this is about, don't you?'

'No, I haven't the faintest idea,' he said, with a look of genuine bewilderment.

'Oh. I thought Tim explained on the phone?'

'Well he did. But it all sounded gobbledegook. Something about a bet or something. You'd better tell me again.'

Tim stepped in and did exactly that, and most eloquently.

'We were wondering if you'd mind,' he added, 'if we wrote a song for you to release as a single in Albania.'

‍‍‍‌‍‌‍‍‍‌‌‍

‌‍‌‍‌‍‌‍

'Yeah, I don't mind,' said Norman, still looking a little bemused by all our attention, 'I've been there before you know. I went to open a children's library.'

'Did you like it?' I asked.

'Yes. The people are really kind. They're a nice lot.'

The look on Norman's face suggested that he held genuine feelings of fondness for the Albanians. I guess it must be difficult not to warm to a nation of people who absolutely adore you. I'd certainly find it tough.

'I may go over to Albania soon to do some research,' I said, 'to find out whether what we're suggesting is a viable proposition. What advice would you offer me?'

'Take sandwiches,' he said, with a wry smile.

Eighty-seven or not, Norman hadn't lost his sense of humour.

'You do realise that we've got to write Norman a song now, don't you?' observed Tim, as we began the drive back to London.

'Yes.'

'The words aren't going to be in Albanian, are they? Because if they are then I'm not your man.'

'No, I think that the lyric should be Norman singing about how proud he is to be big in Albania.'

'And do you see this as a ballad? Because Norman's got a lovely voice you know. Way back, he had a big hit with his own song "Don't Laugh At Me Cos I'm A Fool".'

This had been a hit well before I was born, in 1954. Another hit was certainly long overdue.

'I don't see this song as being a ballad though,' I said. 'For some reason I think something more up-tempo is required.'

'Is this based on a detailed study of the Albanian charts, Hawks?'

'Not really, no.'

'Do we even know if they've got charts?'

'Yes. I had a look on the Web and they do have a Top Twenty.'

I explained that my research had revealed that their chart included only one Albanian artist, the rest being made up of The Spice Girls, Christina Aguilera, Robbie Williams et al.

'So you reckon we should just do our own thing and hope they like it?' asked Tim.

'Yes. Maybe something based around the title "Big In Albania"?' I said, feeling a little self-conscious about making suggestions to an Oscar-winning lyricist. 'Unless, of course, you come up with something more inspired.'

'All right, I'll give it some thought. Is there any hurry for this?'

'A little, yes. Time is running out for my bet.'

'Well, with any luck I'll be able to come up with a lyric on the plane to Sweden tomorrow.'

'Why are you going to Sweden?'

'I'm working with Benny and Bjorn from Abba.'

I tried not to gulp. I was in the big league now.

When the fax arrived, I tried to do everything I could in order not to panic. Tim's previous collaborations had famously been with Andrew Lloyd Webber, the Abba boys, and more recently Elton John. These were all composers who were internationally recognised as being quite good.

As I looked at Tim's words creeping out of the facsimile machine before me, I smiled at the thought of sending a fax straight back to Tim saying 'Call yourself a lyricist?' I decided against it. Maybe we didn't know each other well enough just yet to risk a gag like that.

The contents of the fax suggested that Tim had been adjacent to an atlas when he'd written the lyrics.

> From Scutari to Koritsa, from Gjirokastra to Berat
> From Valona to Tirana, I'm really where it's at
> From the mountains to the Adriatic shore,
> I give my all and still they cry for more
> I've made my name in many places
> A thousand falls, a thousand faces
> But nowhere's more devoted than Albania —
> Cos they've got Norman-mania

I smiled. The lyrics, as Tim's scribbled self-deprecating note at the end of the fax expressed, weren't the work of genius. But they were fun, and that was exactly what was required.

I picked up my guitar and began tentative strumming. It was ten o'clock at night and I was a little tired, but still I thought it might be useful to come up with a couple of musical ideas right now, and then devote a more concentrated effort to the cause in the morning. I sat poised with my guitar on my lap, trying to empty my head of the day's events and free a space for invention.

The process of musical composition still amazes me, requiring as it does a kind of faith, and trust. No melody existed yet for these words and somehow it would have to be created. From whence would it come? Is there a God of melodies? And if so, was He, She or It going to help tonight? Something unique needed to be fashioned from the mere twelve notes which the miserly universe has granted us, ideally before bedtime, but failing that, first thing in the morning.

Somewhat to my surprise, a tune began to emerge from the first tentative chords, and it seemed to fit the lyrics. It wasn't bad either. I continued composing for a further hour, the process filling me with a new energy and excitement. At around midnight I had something down on tape which I felt confident could be knocked into shape in the morning.

And so, I went to bed a contented man.

'Well Tony,' Tim said on the phone a week later, a few days after I'd sent my demo of the song over to him. 'It's a hit! It's definitely got something.'

I wasn't entirely sure if he'd been joking, but either way I was greatly relieved that the music had passed its first audition. It now meant that Tim was enthused enough to try and persuade Norman of the song's virtues, and, much to my relief, he succeeded.

The following weeks were quite extraordinary. Norman had now become rather keen on the whole project and had taken to calling me up on my mobile phone from time to time to see how things were progressing. It was never a routine conversation. The first occasion it happened I was at a supermarket checkout.

'Hello, is that Tony?' I heard a vaguely familiar voice ask.

'Who's that?'

'It's Joyce here.'

'Joyce?'

'Yes, Joyce. Do you remember me?'

'That's not Joyce. That's Norman. Isn't it?

'Yes. Hello. How's it all going? When do you want me to come and do the singing?'

I'd sent Norman a cassette of the song, with piano and my rough vocal, and now he was setting about learning it.

'Soon, Norman,' I replied. 'But Willie and I are still working on the backing track.'

'Righto. It's just that I'm not getting much time to learn the song as I keep having to travel to Manchester and back to do some filming.'

'Well, have you got a Walkman?'

'Yes, I've got one of those.'

'Well you could listen to it on that, as you travel.'

'I don't think it's got any batteries.'

'Well, you could get some.'

'Yes. Yes I suppose I could.'

'Then you'd be sorted.'

'Yes. Yes I would. Thank you Tony.'

'Goodbye Norman.'

The next couple of weeks were peppered with these odd, slightly surreal phone calls from Norman, until the day arrived when I was once again with him in the flesh – standing alongside him in the vocal booth of a west London recording studio. Willie, who I'd roped in to produce the track at the usual gratis rate, looked on from the control room.

'I hope I'm going to sing it OK for you,' said Norman as he hovered behind the microphone, looking a little uncomfortable in the large headphones he'd been given. 'I don't really like pop. I prefer the old standards.'

'Norman, you'll be fine,' I said, with an insouciance belying my genuine concerns.

We only had three hours of studio time booked and I had no idea whether Norman could still hold a tune or deliver what we required of him. He'd had trouble keeping time in the first run-throughs of the song and had specifically asked for me to stand beside him, so that I could conduct him, and mouth the words where necessary. I guess that the whole experience of being in an alien place surrounded by bewildering technology was somewhat unnerving for him, because when I'd offered to leave him on his own he'd immediately grabbed my arm.

'No, stay here,' he'd said. 'It gives me confidence.'

As it happened Norman's diligent efforts were better than could have been expected, even though on some of the takes Norman sang the song with only a fleeting nod towards the original words and melody. Had Eric Morecambe been watching proceedings from the great control room in the sky, no doubt he would have passed comment.

'Norman is singing all the right notes,' he'd have said, fore-finger pushing his glasses up the bridge of his nose, 'but not necessarily in the right order.'

However, in the course of the twenty or so versions that we taped, it became clear that Norman had provided us with the complete song, albeit in jigsaw form. Willie, who would later be charged with piecing it all together while I looked on supportively, felt confident enough to declare that we had what we wanted.

'That's it, Norman,' he announced from the control room. 'We've got everything we need.'

'No,' said Norman. 'I want to do it again. I can do it better.'

Norman had worked for over two hours, refusing a tea break and turning down even a glass of water. If he was tired, he was doing a fantastic job of disguising it. He reminded me of a Jack Russell terrier who would keep playing 'fetch' until his legs gave way from under him. If Norman had learnt a lot of things in his long life, then knowing when to stop hadn't been one of them.

He sang the song once more and then immediately asked if he could do it again. Through my headphones I could hear Norman's assistant Sylvia voicing her concerns that Norman would overdo it, and I began to feel concerned for his health.

'Norman, we've got what we need,' I said.

'Oh can't I have another go,' he pleaded. 'Please.'

I looked across to the control room and I saw Sylvia shaking her head.

'No, Norman,' I said as firmly as I could. 'We've run out of studio time.'

I hoped that Norman didn't look up at the clock. He might

have been able to take an intelligent guess that most people don't book studios from 10 a.m. until 12.40 p.m.

'All right,' he said begrudgingly, remaining oblivious to the clock. 'As long as you're happy.'

I was happy all right. We were about to have a hit in Albania. All I had to do now, was go there and warn the locals.

CHAPTER 17 HOLES AND BUNKERS

For some reason or other Albania has failed to establish itself as any kind of tourist destination, and consequently there are no flights from London to its capital, Tirana. Of the various ways to get there I plumped for the one which required switching planes in Milan and taking a much smaller one onwards from there. It was only during this second leg of the journey that I began to experience a genuine feeling of excitement, albeit tempered by a good measure of apprehension. I was a little concerned that in spite of the enormous amount of energy I'd put into this project, people on the ground would still show very little interest. Why should they? Albania was the second poorest country in Europe,* with its people doing their best to eek out some kind of living. Even if they did love Norman as much as I'd been led to believe, why should they have any time for our song?

And there was another concern. The previous week I'd learned from the Albanian embassy in London that the prime minister had resigned amidst something of a constitutional crisis. I had been assured that the situation wasn't about to lead to civil unrest, and since my reconnaissance mission meant that I'd be in and out within a few days, I figured I'd be safe enough. Nevertheless I was a little concerned that the people whom I needed to help me would be preoccupied with domestic politics and have little time for a stranger peddling his rather odd CD.

My background reading on the country hadn't offered me

It had been at number one for a long time but had recently been knocked off the top spot by Moldova.

much reassurance either. I'd failed to uncover an Albanian guidebook in any bookshop, and so was relying on a publication written in 1994 which I'd found in my local library. It painted something of a bleak picture of Albania, reminding the reader at almost every opportunity that they needed to 'be careful'. According to the book, the Albanian tradition of banditry had not been completely eradicated: gypsy children could be a menace, and corrupt police and officials colluded in scams designed to fleece the naive traveller. It did indeed sound like I would have to be careful, and this didn't appeal. I was prepared to avoid being care*less*, but experience had always taught me that being care*ful* can limit one's potential. Maybe I'd just have to ignore the guide book's advice.

I closed my book, told myself I'd be fine, and glanced out of the window of the plane which had now almost completed the Milan–Tirana flight. Below me I could make out little farms nestled in the craggy mountainous terrain, farms which had been collectivised in the postwar communist regime, but had now been returned to their prewar owners. Soon I would be setting foot in a country which for half a century had been closed to the world. Even its initial allies the Soviet Union had eventually been dismissed as being 'bad communists' by this little country, which had chosen to go it alone. Well, to be more accurate, its leader Enver Hoxha had. In keeping with most communist countries of the time, the people hadn't been given much of a say in the matter. Prevented from leaving the country or being visited by anyone from anywhere else in the outside world, they'd learned to rely on the odd Norman Wisdom film to lift them from the routine task of grinning and bearing it.

My guidebook had suggested that the plane might be required to circle a few times whilst 'wandering livestock were removed from the runway', but thankfully our flight suffered no such indignity. Things had evidently moved on since '94, but nonetheless it was interesting to note that not so long ago this had been a country where an international flight could be delayed by obstinate sheep.

I was accosted by an enthusiastic taxi driver before I'd even come through passport control. Rather impressively he'd somehow managed to get himself 'airside' in order to solicit clients.

'You want taxi?' he asked.

'Yes,' I replied. 'But let's just see if they let me into the country first.'

He looked confused by my response but as I queued for passport control he continued to hover by my side, presumably in the belief that the fact I'd said anything to him at all was a good sign.

Eventually I rewarded him for his persistence and he beamed as he loaded my bags into his beaten-up Mercedes. We set off and I discovered that he wasn't going to let the trivial matter of driving a car prevent him from eagerly showing me a team photo of Manchester United. I would have preferred his attention to have remained on the weather-beaten and uneven road which was stretching before us.

'David Beckham,' he said proudly, in a thick accent. 'He very good.'

'Yes, but I prefer Michael Owen,' I replied, contentiously.

'Ah he good – but he play Liverpool. Liverpool no good.'

An unexpected first conversation and one, when the opportunity arose, I chose to take in another direction. As the car drew to a halt at a junction I produced one of the photos of Norman which I'd brought along with me. I held it before the driver.

'Who is this man?' I asked.

The driver studied the photo for a moment and then his face widened into a smile even broader than the one he'd produced when I'd first hired him.

'This is Pitkin!' he exclaimed.

Exactly the response I'd been hoping for and expecting. I'd been told by Norman that most Albanians refer to him by the name of the character he played in most of his films – Norman Pitkin.

'Mr Norman!' continued the excited driver. 'You know him?'

'Yes, I know him.'

'Pitkin. He great actor. Wow! Pitkin. Mr Norman. Wow!'

'Is he better than David Beckham?' I enquired playfully.

The driver laughed.

'Pitkin good. David Beckham good. Liverpool no good.'

I sensed than any conversation with this man was going to be circular in nature and always end with a derogatory comment about Liverpool. We didn't talk for the rest of the journey though, the driver being content just to turn to me, smiling and winking at regular intervals, something which under any other circumstances would have been most disconcerting.

'Have good day!' he said as he dropped me at the hotel.

'Thank you. I will.'

I'd met my first Albanian and I liked him.

I found myself standing on the corner of Skanderbeg Square, so called after the great national hero George Kastioti Skanderbeg who resisted the Turkish Forces for a good proportion of the fifteenth century. Despite his efforts Albania had eventually succumbed to the Turks, becoming a satellite state of the Ottoman empire for nigh on half a millennium, until a true Albanian nation state emerged after the First World War. The subsequent history is complex to say the least, but regrettably it unfolded in such a way as to create the all too recent horrific conflict in the Serbian region of Kosovo, an area which had once been part of a Greater Albania.

As dusk fell I looked out across the bustling square, which somehow seemed to represent the different periods of this country's turbulent history. At its southern end there stood a group of ornate government buildings, built in Italianate style in the 1930s by the slightly daft-named and self-proclaimed monarch of the time, King Zog. Most of the rest of the square appeared to be the product of prosaic post-war Soviet architects, most notably the Palace of Culture and the National Library, which were embellished with vast social realist mosaics depicting beefy square-jawed workers who looked like they could weld, farm or fight, but never be great company at a drinks party. The eclectic mix of the square was rounded off by the presence of an Islamic mosque, complete with minaret and nearby Ottoman clock-tower. All that was needed as a finishing touch to the cultural amalgam was a Macdonald's, and I fear we won't have to wait too long for that situation to be rectified.

The second Albanian I met was pleasing in an entirely different way to the first. She was beautiful. She smiled politely as she greeted me behind the reception of the modern hotel which I'd booked into for my first night. Partly as continued research, and partly in a pathetic attempt to impress, I produced the photo of Norman once again.

'Do you know who this man is?' I asked as I leant towards her, attempting a flirtatious twinkle in my eye.

'Of course. It is Mr Norman. Everyone knows who he is,' she replied, disappointlingly with no recognisable reciprocation on the flirtation front.

'Do you like him?'

'Of course I like him. Everybody likes him,' she declared as she handed me my key.

Since I couldn't think of anything else to say other than try and elicit her view on the merits of the Liverpool team, I headed off to my room to rest after the long journey. As I lay on the slightly hard bed in my unluxurious quarters, I felt a great sense of relief. I hadn't been robbed by bandits and Norman really was, to quote the recently written song, *Big in Albania*. All I had to do now was get him into the charts.

That night I had dinner with Bilal, who had come recommended by the Albanian embassy in London as someone who could translate for me and generally be of assistance where necessary. He was a confident young man who worked as a lawyer in the Ministry of Justice. We ate in an area of the city known as 'The Block' which, despite the lack of street lights, seemed to be surprisingly well endowed with bars and restaurants.

'We have this electricity crisis,' explained Bilal, 'which means that we have power cuts during the day and no street lights at night, but foreigners who come here are always surprised that things are better than they were expecting.'

'Yes, there seem to be a lot of people going out, and quite a lot of nice places to go,' I commented.

'It's amazing, but the average Albanian wage is very low, but people still manage to find money for eating out or buying cars and such like. I don't know how they do it. Just look around you.'

We were eating in a restaurant which could have been anywhere in the Western world. Well decorated, light, and full of customers deep in animated conversation.

'This is nothing like what I have seen when I was in Moldova,' I said as I tucked into my delightfully tasty fish. 'They don't really have a restaurant culture. Do you think it's like this here because of the Italian influence?'

'Well, I don't know. It's true that the Italians invaded and ruled Albania in the past and I guess they have quite a strong influence in the post-communist era, but I like to think that it is our own Albanian culture,' replied Bilal, as he tucked into a pizza. 'But this country has many problems too. You will see that the rest of the country is not all like "The Block".'

'Of course. Tell me Bilal, why is this area of the city called "The Block"?'

'Because this was the place where the party leaders and members of the Politburo used to live. Until 1991 this area was heavily guarded and the people of Tirana could not enter it. It was their block.'

'And now it is yours again.'

'Yes, not before time.'

'It seems that communism was designed for the people but ended up excluding them.'

'This is what happens.'

We both looked up as the waiter arrived with some Albanian wine.

'Bilal,' I said, changing the subject, 'could you tell me where this restaurant is exactly so that I can come here again. I really like it.'

'Well, I don't know the name of the street. I'll ask the waiter.'

After a burst of Albanian between the two men, during which the waiter did a lot of shrugging, Bilal explained that the fellow didn't know the name of the street either.

'But he works here, he must know,' I protested.

'Yes, but he says that if he needs to tell people where he works then he just explains which buildings it is near and then people know.'

'But that's ridiculous.'

'Not really. Albanians don't really use street names. During the communist regime Mr Hoxha decided that not putting up any street names would cause confusion for foreign invaders.'

'Really?'

'Yes, he was a really paranoid guy. You have much to learn about him.'

So much to learn. And so little time.

As Bilal dropped me back at my hotel he told me that he'd

arranged to take me on a trip to a place called Berati in a couple of days' time.

'Do you know anything about this town?' he asked.

'Only that it gets a mention in our song.'

Bilal laughed.

'How can you write about a place which you have never seen?'

'The world's a big place,' I offered with a shrug. 'Sometimes you've just got to bluff it a bit.'

'Much of life is about bluffing,' said Bilal, as I lifted myself from his car.

I thought for a moment, scratching my head.

'Yes, but how do I know you really mean that?' enquired the pedant in me.

'What?'

'Nothing.'

'OK,' said Bilal, happy not to pursue this query any further. 'Goodnight then.'

'Goodnight.'

It was raining. Tirana's streets were muddy and the city was shrouded in darkness. But I liked the place.

Before breakfast I took an early morning walk around Skanderbeg Square, now overladen with circulating traffic coughing toxic fumes into the already heavily polluted air. Tirana is not a clean city. I raised an eyebrow at the volume of cars, a surprising number of which were BMWs or Mercedes. I marvelled at how so many people could afford to buy and run them in such a poor country. It was only later in my trip that I was to learn that many of these cars had formerly been parked on the streets of countries like Switzerland, before being stolen and driven down to Albania by gangs of organised criminals. Evidently in this country if you wanted to buy a car you didn't visit a dealership – you just asked around.

Feeling adventurous, I elected to extend my walk and I began to head down the large avenue at the south of the square. Soon I drew level with a large hotel on my left, almost entirely concealed by big pine trees which shielded it from the hurly-burly of the street. I felt a tingle of excitement when I realised that this was the Hotel Dajti. I'd read a little about this hostelry and learnt that for years it had been Tirana's top hotel, having been a centre for collaborationist intrigue during the Second World War, before becoming the main establishment for accommodating visiting foreigners during the subsequent communist era. Apparently it had become a notorious location for activity by the Albanian secret police, the *Sigurimi*. I wondered whether this might be the kind of place which would be suited to the next dramatic moment in Albanian history: the arrival of Norman Wisdom. I went inside to take a look.

It was easy to tell that the Hotel Dajti hadn't yet been privatised. Instead of the pretty uniformed receptionist of my first night's stay, I was welcomed by one of two ladies dressed in overcoats, both of whom resembled someone's mum who was helping out while they were off sick. There was also a faint smell of cat in the reception area, which is something which most entrepreneurial hoteliers tend not to encourage. When I enquired as to the price of the rooms I was surprised to learn that they were cheaper than at my other hotel, and so I immediately decided to make this my new home in Tirana. Looking around me I could see that the Dajti was in disrepair and in need of an expensive facelift, as well as somehow managing to be considerably colder inside than out, but for me it still had a grandeur about it which can only be developed over time. When I asked the lady if they had any vacancies, she replied 'of course' in a tone which suggested that to anyone in the know, this was a given.

When I returned with my bags half an hour later I got several funny looks from more overcoated staff. Evidently seeing people check in here was something of a novelty. I made my way to the first floor and began to wonder if anyone else was staying here at all. Perhaps the place was haunted. Certainly if I was a ghost then this would have been exactly the kind of place I would have hung out in. Its crumbly walls, big echoey corridors, and history of intrigue would have made it most appealing to your average ghost, I would have thought. I dumped my bag in my spacious room, with its once quality but now shabby furnishings, and made my way to my first appointment of the day.

Elsona worked for the British Council, an organisation funded by the British Foreign Office to promote the British way of life and cultural interests overseas. I was rather hoping that they might throw their weight behind the whole venture and fork out for flights and hotel accommodation. Elsona was warm and helpful, but unable to provide a promise of any financial assistance. All she could offer was a list of TV and radio people with whom I should have meetings.

'We do get involved with promoting British Artists,' she explained. 'But these have to be what we call *cutting edge*.'

'And you're saying that Norman Wisdom *isn't* cutting edge?' Elsona laughed.

'Almost. I like what you are doing and it is a great idea but I'm not altogether sure that it falls within our remit.'

Over the years I'd come to discover that 'falling within remits' wasn't one of my strengths. I do seem to have this knack of being able to fall just outside them.

'Why don't you talk to the guys at Top Albania Radio? I think they will be able to help.'

'Really?'

'I think this is your best option,' she said with a smile. 'Then you will meet my friend Vjollca who works at State TV. I will call them all now and tell them to expect you.'

'Thank you.'

'It's a pleasure. And good luck.'

One of the things I was beginning to like about Tirana was that everything of importance seemed to be located within a couple of blocks of Skanderbeg Square. Consequently it was only a matter of minutes before I was approaching the extraordinary building which housed Top Albania Radio – a striking example of Albanian modernist architecture. The previous evening Bilal had called it 'the best building in Tirana' but looking at it now, I had to disagree. Basically it was a small pyramid and that was that. It caught your eye certainly, but aesthetically it was a let-down. It had been originally designed as a memorial to the life of Enver Hoxha, and opened on his eightieth birthday as a museum containing nearly everything he'd ever touched or used. I imagine that at one time ordinary Albanians could file through this museum looking at exhibits of their great leader's early underpants and favourite garden rakes. For some unfathomable reason the 1991 revolutionaries had decided that most of this stuff would look better in a skip, and so now the edifice was home to a national commercial radio and TV station instead.

'Are you Tony from London?' enquired a pleasant-faced young man.

'I am.'

'Hello. My name is Alban. Allow me to show you around the building.'

I'm not sure what message Alban had received, but for the next twenty minutes I was treated like a visiting dignitary and taken on a guided tour of the surprisingly well-equipped building.

'It's all very impressive,' I said to a proud Alban. 'But do you know why I am here?'

'Not really, no,' he replied.

I had begun to suspect as much.

Alban listened carefully and with a grave expression as I explained the nature of my business in his country, before ushering me through to a studio. He didn't seem terribly excited about Norman and I wondered if this had something to do with his tender years.

'Are you old enough to remember Norman Wisdom?' I enquired.

'Pitkin? But of course. His films are still shown now. Maybe one a month. He is a great comic actor. But now we hear your song.'

Alban pushed my CD into the machine and twiddled with nobs as the horn section intro chimed in. Through this top-quality equipment the track sounded good. Damn good. 'Big In Albania' was now a stomping track which benefited from the contributions of talented musicians rather than machines. It had real drums, real brass, real backing vocals and real inspiration. I was particularly pleased with the brass which had been added courtesy of my two Australian muso chums Jason and Jason, and the girlie backing vocals which Tim's daughter Eva and her friend Lucinda had provided. Bizarrely, given that Norman Wisdom was supplying the vocal, it had the feel of an old Stax or Motown track. All the work that Willie had done in the weeks between Norman's recording session and my departure for

Albania had paid off. At least those were my thoughts until Alban's reaction demanded their immediate revision.

'It is a very professional production,' he said as he removed the CD from its player, 'but maybe Norman should do something with a more ethnic Albanian feel.'

Alban reached for another CD. 'Listen to this,' he added.

I was now subjected to three minutes of fascinatingly odd sounds set against a modern drum beat. I liked it, but I knew someone who most definitely wouldn't.

'I'm not sure that it's Norman's cup of tea,' I suggested.

'Really?' said Alban with genuine surprise.

'Well, Norman had his last hit with an old-fashioned ballad in 1955. I'm not sure that even I can persuade him to go ethnic Albanian with his next effort.'

Alban looked more than a little disappointed. I tried a new tack.

'Alban, you have a pop chart here at Top Albania Radio, is that right?' I asked.

'Yes.'

'How is it calculated?'

'We do it according to air play and votes.'

'Don't sales count?'

'No. You must remember that ours is still a bootleg culture. Let me give you an example. The film *Titanic* was shown on Albanian TV before it was even released in the cinema in the UK.'

'How come?'

'Albania has signed no international copyright agreement, so it does what it likes.'

'So, for Norman to get into your chart he would need to get airplay and votes?'

'Of course.'

'And would you play the song?'

'I don't know that. It's not my decision.'

'Whose decision is it?'

'The director of radio along with a panel of DJs.'

'I see.' I reached into my bag and took out a dozen of Norman's CDs. 'Could you arrange for one of these to get to all the DJs and important people within the station?'

'Yes. I will do this.'

'And if they start to play it and the public like it, then we could make your charts?'

'Yes.'

This I liked. No need for a record deal and all that nonsense. No need for anyone to have to go out and buy anything. This was the perfect chart for my current requirements, which were simply to have a hit. Alban and I shook hands and he promised to do what he could to help. He was a nice guy and he seemed like he wanted to be of assistance, but I suspected that he may have been a lowly figure within the hierarchy of the station. Nevertheless, it seemed that he would do what he could.

I left Top Albania Radio feeling confident and took a coffee in a busy café over the road. It was something of a surreal experience – sipping espresso overlooking an Albanian pyramid with a CD of Sir Norman Wisdom on the table in front of me. The constant attention of children trying to sell me cigarettes and phonecards from shoeboxes hardly served as a reminder that I was a bona fide resident of the 'real world', however. After shaking my head and explaining to a child for the umpteenth time that I didn't smoke or need to use the phone, I got up and headed for the floodlights that I'd spotted in the distance during this short caffeine pit-stop. I'd had an idea.

The words 'Stadiumi Kombetar Qemal Stefa' greeted me as I looked up at the exterior of the Albanian national stadium. It was very small, probably smaller than the stadia of most Third Division clubs in English football, but that didn't matter because it was perfect for what I wanted. I noticed that a side gate was open and I surreptitiously slid inside and on to the turf itself. I stood in the centre circle and looked out at the empty stands. Not too dissimilar an experience to that of the average Albanian footballer who played here every Saturday, I shouldn't wonder. It was here that England had rather unimpressively scrambled a 3–1 victory in the World Cup qualifiers of 2002, a flattering scoreline which hadn't reflected the game. I remembered watching that match on TV, never for a moment believing that I was looking at the venue that would one day provide the backdrop for one of the greatest moments in my life.

At least that was the plan. Because by the time I was standing on that pitch I had formulated the idea of arranging a stadium gig for Norman. It just had to be done. I'd always dreamt of being a part of such an event and here was a wonderful opportunity. Norman would perform 'Big In Albania' to his adoring fans, and I would muscle in and crash the party with my stunning rendition of the rap section of the song. Standing in the centre circle I could visualise the scene. Doddery Norman, proud Tony, and Albanian crowd – excited and baffled in equal measure. My task, surely, was to make this a reality (although frankly it was beginning to feel like I'd lost my grip on that quite some time ago).

My final appointment of the day was with Vjollca, whom I met at the State TV station and who took me to a very nice café just around the corner from 'Sedili's Hole'. This is how the locals refer to a massive excavation created by a Kosovar investor who, soon after the collapse of communism, promised city planners that he was going to build the first Sheraton Hotel in Albania. Unfortunately, just after the builders had toiled to create this colossal hole in the heart of the city centre, the investor Sedili was arrested for embezzlement in Switzerland and promptly imprisoned. Tirana has now been rewarded with a huge orifice as a testament to what capitalism can achieve. One of the advantages of the communist system was that at least they finished building their eyesores.

Vjollca, a friendly and bubbly woman, ordered two coffees as I squinted in the bright Albanian sunshine, and we discussed what media exposure Norman could get when I brought him over. She seemed to think that most TV programmes would be delighted to have Norman on as their guest, but she reckoned that the best one to do would be *Telebingo*. This was the Albanian lottery show and it was extremely popular.

'Do you think the producers will have us on to perform our song?' I asked.

'I cannot see that they will say no to Norman,' she replied in excellent English. 'You have to remember that he is far more famous than any Hollywood film stars in our country. The young people might know who Brad Pitt is, but *everyone* – absolutely everyone – knows and loves Norman.'

'Well, it would be great if I could confirm a booking for that show while I am here.'

Vjollca laughed.

'We Albanians are not very good at confirming things,' she said. 'You will find that we are good at saying "yes" today and "no" tomorrow. But I am almost certain that I can organise for you to be on this show when you come back.'

'That is very kind of you,' I said, sipping my coffee and feeling rather confused as to where that actually left me. 'I've never been a promoter before, but so far it feels like I'm having quite a lot of success.'

'That is because you are promoting Norman Wisdom in Albania. This is easy.'

I knew my business. Norman Wisdom in Albania. Yes, I was no fool. As a promoter I would never have taken on Dana in Peru, or Marc Bolan in Mancuria.[*]

'What are you going to do tonight?' asked Vjollca.

'Oh I don't know. Do you recommend anything?'

'Not really,' she said with a shrug. 'Tonight will be quiet I think.'

'Maybe I'll just call in at a few hotels to try and arrange favourable rates for Norman when he comes over, then have dinner and go to bed. I have an early start for a big day trip tomorrow. I am going to Berati to see if it would be a good place to film Norman, in case we decide to do a video for the song.'

'Ah, Berati. You will enjoy this,' said Vjollca enigmatically.

At breakfast I dined alone for the second consecutive morning. I was seriously beginning to wonder if there was anyone else at all staying in the Hotel Dajti. Maybe the whole place was some kind of front for another activity. Well, if it was, then it wasn't something I needed to know about. I had things to do.

Before Bilal arrived to collect me I went to the hotel manager's office, a musty crumbly room, just behind reception where the underworked and overcoated ladies handled the keys. The manager was younger than I had expected and he greeted me warmly, a warmth which grew when he learned that I was the great entrepreneurial showman who was going to bring Norman Wisdom to their hotel.

---

[*] *Not least because Marc Bolan died in 1977.*

'Could he and his assistant have free accommodation here when he comes?' I asked, with a boldness borne of the man's great standing. I'd been offered some good rates the night before in posher hotels, but up until now I hadn't had the gall to ask for an out and out freebie.

'I think this will be possible,' answered the manager, a little to my surprise. 'But as you know, this hotel belongs to the State. We have a council which sits to make these kinds of decisions, but I will put this at the next meeting and I am sure that they will approve of this for Norman.'

'Thank you.'

I smiled. It was a great job this 'Promoting Norman in Albania' gig. A doddle.

The drive to Berati began with a crawl through Tirana's grubby and poverty-stricken suburbs, but soon Bilal's car gathered speed on the road which was leading us to the Adriatic coast and I began to notice concrete bunkers by the side of the road.

'What are these?' I asked Bilal.

'This is one of the crazy things that Enver Hoxha did because he had decided that Albania was going to be invaded,' he replied, a cynical tone creeping into his voice.

'Invaded? Who by?'

'The United States, Russia, Italy – anyone who had an army. He was paranoid.'

As we continued the drive I started to notice that these bunkers were all over the surrounding hills. It was extraordinary – they littered the countryside.

'How many of these bunkers are there?' I enquired.

'Not as many as there used to be. Most of them have been taken away. But before there were as many as 700,000.'

'You're joking.'

'No I am not,' he said with a laugh. 'Unfortunately this is just one of the crazy things which that government did.'

'But it must have cost a fortune.'

'Yes. Some engineers have estimated that the cost of building all these bunkers would have been enough to build an apartment for every Albanian.'

'And these things are totally useless?'

'They are now and they always have been. Actually they did serve a purpose and it is quite funny.'

'What purpose was that?'

'Well, young people who were still living at home with their parents used them to have sex in. They were perfect for this.'

There couldn't have been many better ways of expressing the sentiments of the old slogan 'Make love not war'. I wonder how many of these kids realised just how laden with meaning their first adolescent fumblings had been.

'If you do it in a bunker,' I asked Bilal, 'does that mean you still need to use protection?'

'I don't know man,' giggled Bilal. 'I haven't thought about that.'

As we neared the coast I began to realise that there were nearly as many half-built houses as bunkers, making much of the landscape resemble a huge building site. It seemed that Albanians didn't worry about having enough money to build a house, merely about whether they had enough to begin the process. Evidently once they had successfully constructed the ground floor, they moved in, hoping that the rest of the house would follow just as soon as economic circumstances would permit.

'In Albania, they build with Kismet,' said Bilal.

'What do you mean, Kismet?' I asked.

'It kind of means "with destiny, faith and trust".'

'I see. In England it is hard to find a building society who will lend you money on the strength of that.'

Bilal laughed.

'I don't think these guys are building these houses with borrowed money.'

Half an hour later we arrived at the beach, which was beautiful, provided you ignored the building site which surrounded it. It was as sandy as it was expansive, and the Adriatic sea looked inviting, even though it was early February. The only thing which I found slightly disconcerting was the way that cars appeared to be driving along the beach just like it was a road.

'Is nowhere sacred?' I asked Bilal. 'There must be somewhere where you can escape the dreaded motor car?'

'How about – in the sea?' came his suggestion, along with the now familiar and infectious laugh.

'All right. If that's what it takes,' I declared, taking off my shirt. 'Then I'm going in!'

'Are you crazy man?' asked a startled Bilal.

'As crazy as Enver Hoxha,' I replied with a grin.

'No one is that crazy,' he laughed.

'We'll see about that.'

I didn't really swim. I just ran into the sea, dived under the first wave, and then ran straight out again. It had been a success though because now I felt all tingly and very much alive, every sense ready to appreciate the day ahead.

It hadn't looked that far on the map from Tirana to Berati but it ended taking us about four hours to get there (or 1,700 bunkers, depending on how you measured it). One thing was sure though. It was worth it. It turned out to be a remarkably preserved Ottoman city surrounded by imposing mountains, at a point where the Osumit river had cut a huge gorge to form a gigantic castle-rock. Upon that rock a fine medieval citadel kept permanent vigil over the town which had been built on the layers of river terraces below it. Enver Hoxha had proclaimed it a 'Museum City' in 1961 – a considerably better decision than the one he'd taken about building the bunkers.

Bilal and I climbed the hill to the citadel and entered the courtyard which lay within the ancient gates. Instead of discovering ruins as we'd expected, we found ourselves inside a remarkably well-preserved hamlet where a couple of hundred people still dwelled. It was like walking back into a piece of history. A boy passed us, pulling a donkey behind him, and entered a whitewashed house with a wooden overhanging balcony with finely carved decorations. I felt the hint of a shiver at the timelessness of it all. Only the TV aerial gave any clue as to the century we were in.

Upon reaching the other end of the fortress we climbed the thick walls and perched ourselves in one of the defensive positions. This afforded us breathtakingly beautiful views back across the river valley below. There, in miniature, was the magnificent old town nestling beneath, and beyond it the twentieth-century sprawl of apartment blocks and factories which the Hoxha regime had produced as its incongruous addendum. The contrast couldn't have been more marked.

'This place is extraordinary,' I said to Bilal. 'Not just because it is so beautiful, but because we're the only visitors.'

'Yes, I have been to Berati before but I have never been inside this citadel,' he replied. 'It is amazing.'

'In some ways you are lucky in Albania,' I remarked pensively. 'If this was anywhere else in Europe it would be crawling with tourists.'

'Yes. That is one of the reasons why we is poor and you guys is so rich.'

I guess he had a point. Modernisation and progress come with a lot of unattractive baggage. Albania's leaders would have to decide which path its young country would have to take in order to feed all its children. Sometimes life's choices can be stark ones.

'So what do you think?' enquired Bilal. 'Will you bring Norman up to this citadel?'

'I would love to, but it's a long drive – and promoting the record will have to be our priority.'

'So when are going to come back with Norman?'

'Soon. Tomorrow I fly back for some business with a beautiful Romanian singer.'

'Is this some more business trying to get the hit record?'

'Yes.'

'You are a very resourceful guy.'

'Yes,' I said. 'Resourceful is the kind way to describe me.'

'How much time do you have left?'

'Two months.'

'Wow. You'd better hurry up.'

I looked at the spectacular panorama that stretched before me and for a moment I felt that anything was possible.

'Bilal, I think this hit will come one way or another.'

Bilal nodded approvingly, not knowing how fine the line is that divides resourcefulness and delusion.

CHAPTER 18 LEAVE IT WITH ME

'*Sarut mina*,' I said as I kissed Paula on the hand, in the lobby of her London hotel.

'Hello Tony,' she said. 'I see that you are still a gentleman.'

It had taken some doing but I'd pulled it off. Paula had arrived the previous night for a flying visit to London at my invitation. I had kept my promise of UK exposure for her and organised a TV debut for the international singing duo Paula and Tony. We were going to sing 'When All Is Said And Done' live on the afternoon show *Gloria Hunniford's Open House* on Channel 5 – regardless of the fact that we had never performed the song together in public before.

'Today is a big day. How do you feel?' I asked.

'Very nervous, but I am excited too.'

It was good to see Paula again. And Mr Nanca.

'Here, Tony,' he said, handing me a magazine. 'See how you have become famous in Romania.'

I opened the magazine to see a double-page spread all about my collaboration with Paula, including the pictures which Mr Nanca had taken at our Café Eliad rehearsal.

TONY HAWKS

UN PARIU NUMIT PAULA SELING

I didn't know what it meant, but I knew that it must be good.

'This magazine, *Pro TV*,' said Mr Nanca, 'it has a big readership. It is very popular.'

I suddenly began to consider the possibility that this

Anglo–Romanian partnership was really going to produce the hit that I required after all.

'The taxi is waiting to take you to the studio,' said the man behind the hotel reception desk, reminding us that we had pressing business in hand.

'You look so calm, Tony,' said Paula, reaching for her coat. 'Are you not nervous?'

'No. It'll be fun,' I replied. 'Just imagine that it doesn't really matter and then you'll be fine.'

It was easy for me. I'd been on Gloria Hunniford's show three times before and I knew the form. Paula had never even been in this country before, let alone performed live on one of its TV shows on her first full day, singing a song in a foreign language. I looked at her face and saw that the strain was showing.

'Relax, Paula, it will be fine,' I said, as soothingly as I could. 'We'll have plenty of time to rehearse when we get there.'

'I just don't want to let you down.'

'Paula,' I said, taking her hand. 'Just do your best and enjoy the moment. You can sing the wrong words or sing out of tune, but whatever you do, you won't let me down.'

We got into the taxi. In less than three hours' time we would be singing 'live' to the nation. Well, to be more precise, 'live' to the nation's old people, unemployed, and mums.

'Twenty seconds till the end of the commercial break,' announced the floor manager, as he stood before me and Paula, flanked by three cameras and with the studio audience beyond him. 'As soon as I give you the signal Tony – hit the first chord.'

'OK.'

'And good luck.'

Unexpectedly I felt myself tense up. I may have been 'Mr Relaxed' up until now, but I'd remained so at the expense of being mentally prepared for what was about to follow. I was just a few seconds away from playing guitar and singing live on TV – something I hadn't done since ... wait a minute, I suddenly realised that this was something that I'd *never* done. Morris Minor and The Majors had mimed live, but that was hardly the same, and my live TV performances as a comedian counted for little now that I had a guitar in my hand and a Romanian songstress by my side.

As the floor manager raised his hand to cue me, I wanted to say 'Stop! I'm not ready for this!' but it was too late. His arm dropped and so did mine, playing the first chord of the song as it did so. Thank goodness for the two-bar intro because it granted me valuable seconds to steady my unforeseen bout of nerves before any singing was required. By the time I'd strummed the downstroke on the eighth beat of the song, I'd relaxed again. Thank goodness for that. I hadn't been far from a short burst of complete panic which would have left me playing all the wrong chords and blanking on the words. I would have been humiliated before the viewing public, and become the laughing stock in the British OAP community. Never again would I have been able to hold my head high walking along the promenade at Eastbourne.

Paula, of course, was having her own little mental battle. However, since she'd been terrified pretty much most of the day, the start of the song acted as something of a release for her. OK, she was still scared during the performance, but I was the only one who knew it. She was experienced enough to know how to sing through the fear. She sang beautifully, just as I had been expecting. It was more of a surprise that my performance was competent, featuring as it did all the right chords and a vocal which hit nearly all the right notes.

Paula and I had been good, and the warm applause from the studio audience proved that they'd liked what they'd heard. For a moment I allowed myself to believe that I could be on the brink of something rather wonderful here. Move over Kylie and Jason, Donny and Marie, yes and even Renee and Renata, because the new kids Paula and Tony were in town. The prospects were good. Paula seemed to like both me and the song, and the chances of her releasing a single in Romania were looking promising. It was just a shame that we were promoting it in completely the wrong country. But then you can't have everything.

'It was great,' said Mr Nanca when he greeted us backstage afterwards.

This meant very little since I reckoned that saying 'It was great' was pretty much part of his job, but I was still relieved that he hadn't slapped me on the back and said 'Darling, you've done it again!'

Paula and I were both glowing, but it was difficult to know what we'd really achieved. Most guests go on Gloria's show to publicise some product which they are selling, be it a book, a film, a TV programme or a CD. Paula and I had none of these. All we'd plugged was the unusual liaison between Englishman and Romanian lady, which had only really been created for another marketplace – in far-off Eastern Europe. Paula couldn't have done herself any harm though. TV is a powerful medium, and who knows who could have been watching and spotted her potential? Simon Cowell himself may have just finished uttering the words 'She's great – but lose the ugly one'.

'We'll just have to wait and see if there is any reaction to this,' I said to Paula, as we reached our respective dressing rooms. 'Anything could happen. Meanwhile, you enjoy the rest of your stay here.'

'Thank you, Tony. I will.'

Paula worked pretty hard whilst she was in town, giving a concert for London's Romanian community and, on her last night, singing at a special party at the Romanian ambassador's official residence. I attended this latter event and was able to watch her perform solo for the first time. She looked great and sang beautifully. I was convinced that she had star quality, but the problem was how to market and package her in one of the most ruthless and competitive businesses on the planet. It was a tough one, and I was glad that it wasn't my job.

My job, as I had to keep reminding myself, was to have a Top Twenty hit anywhere in the world, and however promising things were starting to look with Paula, I had to accept the fact that I was up against the clock. My rigid adherence to the basic tenets of Parkinson's Law had left me little room for manoeuvre. Time was, unquestionably, running out. I had to be realistic and recognise that the efforts of Mr Nanca with me and Paula were unlikely to result in anything being released in Romania before the bet had expired.

With only a matter of weeks to go, there was really only one place left to turn.

'So what do you want it to say on the T-shirts?' said Paul.

'"Vote For Norman" on the front,' I said. 'And on the back "Norman Wisdom and The Pitkins, Albanian tour, March 2002".'

I was on the phone to Paul, whose job was to manufacture the merchandise for bands who were embarking on major world tours. Usually he took orders in the hundreds but he'd accepted my request for ten T-shirts because he was so amused by the nature of the project.

'So who exactly are The Pitkins?' he'd asked.

'Well, so far, they are me, Tim Rice and his son and daughter, and their friend Lucinda.'

'And you guys are actually a band?'

'Not exactly, no. The trip is more of a holiday for Tim, so he's just bringing whoever he wants to invite.'

'And because they're on the trip that means you then invite them to become part of the band?' asked an incredulous Paul.

'Well, it would be rude not to.'

All the great acts of show business have a look of spontaneity about them which masks, more often than not, hours of preparation and intense practice. Norman Wisdom and The Pitkins didn't really fall into this category. They had chosen to embark on their first tour without ever once having all been in the same room together, never mind having set any time aside for the indulgence of rehearsal. I began to wonder what our lead singer felt about this.

'How are you getting on with learning the lyrics?' I asked when I called him at his home on the Isle of Man.

'Cor blimey,' Norman replied. 'It's all funny words. It's all saur kraut. I can't remember hardly any of it.'

'Do you think a rehearsal would help?'

'Not 'alf.'

And that's why, on the eve of our departure, I found myself sitting in Norman's Epsom flat, sipping a nice cup of tea that his assistant Sylvia had just made me.

'He's been working terribly hard on it,' she said. 'But it just doesn't seem to be going in. He doesn't like to admit it but his memory isn't what it used to be.'

When Norman came into the room in his slacks and sports

jacket, he seemed genuinely pleased to see me. I felt rather touched.

'Hello, Tony!' he said at volume. 'Nice to see you again. Right, what are we going to do about this song?'

I explained that when we got to Albania we would only be miming and that I'd found an especially large microphone behind which he could hide every time he became unsure of the words.

'Well, that'll be the whole bloody song at the moment,' he said, looking more than a touch concerned.

'That's all right Norman, it won't matter. Just move in right behind the microphone for your singing and then mess around near it when you're not.'

'All right. Let's try it then, shall we?'

'OK, I'll put the mic on its stand and we'll give it a rehearsal.'

The extent to which Norman had failed to grasp Tim Rice's lyrics really became apparent in the following three minutes. He was all over the place, only managing to lip-sync with his own performance on the odd occasion (and then only by accident), but the main problem was that he was standing nowhere near the microphone. Sylvia and I kept signalling to him to get in close but I guess he'd been performing at a certain distance from the mic for the last sixty-five years, and old habits die hard. Things did improve a little in subsequent runthroughs and I found myself assuring Norman that we'd be fine.

'I don't want to let you down,' he said, rather sweetly, echoing the same sentiments Paula had expressed just weeks before.

'Norman, you won't let me down. Whatever you do, you can't let me down. Just enjoy it.'

'I just want to do a good job, that's all.'

'You will. You will.'

After we'd run through the song for the fifth time Norman suggested that I pushed him away from the microphone just before I took over to do my rap section of the song.

'It'll be funny, and I can do a bit of business,' he said.

'All right. You mean like this,' I said, giving him a gentle shove on the shoulder.

'No, not like that. Push me in the face.'

'What?'

'Push me in the face.'

'You want me to push you in the face?'

'Yes, it'll be funnier.'

I wasn't sure about this. It seemed unlikely that this gesture was going to make me a huge favourite with the Albanian audience.Wouldn't I get taken aside after the performance and quietly lynched? Norman was their hero, the man they'd watched hundreds of times, in some cases from infant to geriatric. Soon they were going to be confronted by some young upstart waltzing over and pushing him in the face. I tried to protest but Norman remained adamant that this was the funniest way to present our piece, and so I obliged in each subsequent run of the song.

'That's good,' he said, after the last rehearsal. 'But do it harder.'

This Albanian trip was going to be very interesting.

Never before had all The Pitkins been in the same place at the same time. The venue was Heathrow Airport, at the check-in desk for our international flight. It was the first time I'd ever even met one of the band, a splendid fellow called Donald, who'd made it into the line-up on the strength of being Tim Rice's son. Right now, he didn't even know which instrument was going to be alotted to him for future miming, and I wasn't about to tell him just yet. No need to spoil his flight.

As we stood in line waiting with our bags, I decided that Norman Wisdom and The Pitkins had an extraordinarily broad appeal. We had beauty and glamour in Eva and Lucinda, the gorgeous backing singers who'd be guaranteed to win over the male audience. In Donald we had a handsome and debonair matinée idol who'd make the perfect pin-up for the teenage girl's bedroom. I was perfect for the female 30–40-year-old 'once-divorced' market, Tim for the 'twice-divorced' and dear old Norman could take care of those who'd lost count. Success was inevitable.

We caused quite a stir in the airport. Well, Norman did. The Pitkins were comparatively well behaved. At every opportunity Norman played the fool. He climbed on to the scales with the baggage, he tried to duck under the desk at passport control, and he ran up the down escalator. It was a hilarious performance and, judging by the look of resignation on Norman's assistant

Sylvia's face, it was one that he did every time he got to an air-port. The real trouble came when he marched round the X-ray machines and started to head off down towards the gate. Most people had spotted that this was Norman Wisdom and were laughing accordingly, but not all the security staff were privy to this information. What they saw was a potential international ter-rorist, and in the post-11 September climate, that wasn't a good thing to be mistaken for. I looked around, hoping that an armed policeman wouldn't decide to gun him down, but thankfully none was on hand and Norman was intercepted by security per-sonnel just before he made it into Sock Shop. He'd been lucky. A few seconds later and he could have been shot dead, or worse still, bought some socks that he hadn't really needed.

The London to Milan leg of the journey was relatively normal (apart from Norman deliberately tripping up the air stewards and stewardesses every time they passed his aisle seat), but once we boarded our onward flight from Milan to Tirana, the adulation for Norman really began. A man standing next to me was pointing and whispering to his wife, and all around us I could feel the lev-els of excitement building in Albanian faces. However, nothing could have prepared us for what was waiting at Tirana airport. As we walked across the runway tarmac towards the antiquated build-ings which constituted Tirana airport, I could see that Norman had a twinkle in his eye. He'd been to this country before and he looked like he was ready for what was going to happen next.

It was a policeman who spotted him first.

'Mr Pitkin!' he cried at the top of his voice, waving frantically and momentarily forgetting that his sombre navy blue uniform and peaked cap was to supposed to mark him out as a figure of solemn respectability.

His face lit up as Norman offered a little wave back as he moved towards him.

'Hello mate, how are you?' said Norman chummily as he drew alongside his admirer.

As the policeman shook Norman's hand I could see his face become illuminated with a childlike joy. The stature and stand-ing of his position meant nothing right now. All that mattered was that he shook the hand of his hero in a moment that he would cherish for the rest of his life.

On seeing the source of their colleague's attention, other policemen rushed over. Tim and I looked over to see our lead singer mobbed by four uniformed officers. Someone who didn't know better might have assumed that Norman was an international criminal being apprehended by zealous law-keepers, but handshakes, not handcuffs, were the order of the day.

'It's incredible, isn't it?' remarked an amazed Tim.

'Quite extraordinary,' I agreed.

'Look at everyone's faces,' he said, pointing to the other airport officials who were just clocking Norman for the first time. 'They're so excited.'

'It's like the return of the Messiah or something.'

'Do you think Norman's going to be OK?' asked Tim, looking a little concerned.

'He'll be fine. Look at his face. He's loving it. He seems to feed off being the centre of attention.'

'Well, it looks like he's certainly going to be that over here.'

The Albanian official pointed out that my passport only had a few weeks before its expiry date. Just like my bet. It served as another reminder that *time was running out*. As the official stamped the entry visa into my worn-out passport, it dawned on me that I was entering yet another new territory. The fifth since I'd taken the whole thing on. I'd become involved in a kind of *real life* 'Jeux sans frontières'.

But this time I was playing my joker.

Norman.

There was no passport control for Norman. He was whisked straight through to the somewhat decrepit baggage carousel by his entourage of adoring policemen. Soon he was mobbed by a fresh wave of Albanians. Outside the terminal building a crowd had somehow developed from nowhere and Norman quickly became lost in it. I fought my way past enthusiastic men, women and children in an effort to ensure the safety of my would-be pop star.

'Are you all right, Norman?' I asked when I finally reached him.

'I'm fine, Tony,' he replied nonchalantly, almost as if this was the kind of reception that greeted him every day.

Then he was off. Quite suddenly and quite unexpectedly Norman shimmied to the left and freed himself from the grasps of his doting devotees and broke into a run, a comedy run, which took him towards the field of sheep which adjoined the airport runway. As one, the crowd burst into fits of laughter. It must have been the funniest thing they had seen in a long time. Norman, eighty-seven-year-old Norman, stopped after about thirty yards, turned, gave a little wave and then headed off in another direction. However, when he saw a new crowd coming towards him, he did a quick 180 and started back towards me, this time with some genuine motivation.

A chauffeur-driven car pulled up alongside us and a man in a peaked cap got out.

'Car for Mr Pitkin?' asked the man.

'Yes please, could you take us to the Dajti hotel?' I replied, a little surprised since we hadn't ordered a car and were expecting to have to queue for a taxi.

'Anything for Mr Pitkin.'

I was just about to climb into the rather grand, leather-seated vehicle along with Norman and Sylvia when I remembered my fellow Pitkins, who had been excluded from the 'star treatment'. They must have felt rather neglected as I'd left them to fend for themselves in the manic muddle that is Tirana International Airport. I looked up to see that they'd all crammed themselves into a rather shabby taxi.

'Tim,' I called over. 'You know where you're going don't you?'

'Yes, the Hotel Dajti, isn't it?'

'That's right. We'll meet you there.'

'There's just one problem.'

'What's that?' I asked.

'The taxi driver can't get the car to start,' replied a giggling Tim who, along with his fellow travellers, had clearly seen the funny side.

At that moment the taxi driver, who looked even more neg- lected than his car, threw open the bonnet and began looking at the engine pensively. I do a similar thing if any car I'm driving breaks down, even though I know nothing whatsoever about motor mechanics and all this can achieve is confirmation that the car does actually have an engine beneath the bonnet. I then check the oil, scratch my head and call the AA. This taxi driver was scratching his head, but it really didn't look like he was a member of any motoring organisation.

'We won't leave in our car until we see if he can get yours started,' I said to Tim, as the laughter continued unabated from the contingent inside the car.

Soon there was a big crowd around the open bonnet of the taxi. It seems to be a universal male thing to want to offer suggestions to the victim of a vehicle breakdown. It's like you gain credibility from your peers if you can offer a plausible theory. And so the Albanian equivalent of 'It must be the carburettor', 'What about the battery terminals?' and 'It's your starter motor mate', were bellowed by those who had pushed their way forward in order to stare rather impertinently into a stranger's engine.

Some kind of consensus was reached after a certain amount of poking and wire-wiggling, and the driver climbed back into his car and turned over the ignition. At first nothing, but then after an agonising few seconds, the engine roared into life, coughing and spluttering and generally announcing to the world that it wasn't very well.

'OK Tony, we'll see you there,' said Tim.

'I hope you make it,' I replied.

'Me too.'

More laughter from inside the car. The Pitkins seemed a rather relaxed bunch.

Everything about the demeanour of our driver suggested that this was the proudest day of his life. By now Norman looked very tired, but to his credit he attempted to make conversation as we headed into the capital.

'Blimey, there's a lot of new buildings being built isn't there?' he said, as he looked out of the front window.

The driver smiled a smile which suggested that he had understood nothing. Norman tried again.

'Do you live in Tirana?'

The driver kept smiling, but shrugged. He was clearly finding communication with Pitkin harder than watching him on the telly. He'd been used to subtitles appearing every time Norman opened his mouth.

'Is it far to the centre of Tirana?' asked Norman, having one last try.

This time the driver made no attempt to reply but simply reached forward and took out a case from the glove compartment. He opened it up and showed us all what was inside. A pistol.

Bloody hell, it was a gun!

Beaming a big smile he then took something out of his pocket and waved it in the air. Handcuffs.

What was going on here? This wasn't normal behaviour. I concluded that the fellow must either be a policeman or some kind of bondage-loving gangster. I knew which one of the two I'd prefer to have as an escort into Tirana city centre.

'Are you a policeman?' I asked.

The man nodded and produced a peaked cap which Norman then took from him and placed on his own head. This appeared to be the funniest thing that our driver had ever seen and he nearly careered off the road as he descended into fits of giggles.

'Don't be too funny, Norman,' I said. 'It's dangerous.'

Upon reaching the hotel we were all rather surprised to find that Tim and his party had got there first. I had predicted a further breakdown and ensuing hilarity, but they were laughing anyway when we joined them in reception.

'What's happened?' I asked.

'Well,' started Tim, 'the sight of four people arriving to check in at the same time seems to have thrown the receptionist and her friends into a complete panic. The keys to our rooms are in a drawer which is locked shut. At the moment they are trying to force it open with a knife.'

Behind reception a group of Albanians were huddled round the locked drawer much like they had been with Tim's taxi, the only difference being that no one was making suggestions regarding the carburettor or the starter motor.

'The hotel smells a bit of cats, doesn't it?' said Tim, turning away from the scenes of key confusion for a moment.

'Yes, did I not mention that when I told you about it?'

'No, I believe you omitted that information.'

'Yes. Well there's a much nicer hotel just down the road if you want. I suppose I'm a bit eccentric and I like this one because it's got character.'

'It's got plenty of that,' said Tim with another chuckle, looking over to the staff who were making jabbing motions behind the counter with assorted kitchen cutlery in order to try and provide room keys. 'Maybe we'll take a look at the rooms before we fully commit.'

'Do that. Actually it does look a little more run-down than I remember it.'

It had been less than a month since I'd last been at The Dajti but as I peered around the lobby I could see evidence of a rapid deterioration. The walls were crumbling, more bulbs had gone, and the whiff in the air suggested that the cat had taken up permanent residence.

'Do you think Norman will be all right here?' enquired Tim.

'Well, Sylvia said that Norman's not a prima donna. As long as the rooms are warm she says he'll be happy.'

I approached reception and said 'hello again' to a slightly nervous woman who I remembered from my first visit. She looked like this was the worst day of her life. She and her chums behind the counter had become used to passing the time by chatting, reading the paper or playing cards, and now they were faced with a genuine 'hotel situation'. Real customers too, not just friends of the communist party. Overseas guests, one of whom was the most popular and famous man in Albania.

'Do you have the two rooms for Norman and his assisant?' I enquired, honestly believing that the question would be enough to make the woman burst into tears.

'Yes. Here,' she replied, offering me two keys.

'Oh. Thank you,' I said, somewhat surprised.

Star treatment in this hotel obviously meant that they didn't lock your keys in a drawer and then throw away the key.

'Also,' I continued, watching the fear in the woman's eyes visibly grow. 'Could I have a key to any room just to show my friends here what they're like?'

'Yes,' she said, immediately returning to the drawer-forcing fiasco behind her.

Minutes later, The Pitkins let out a huge cheer as the drawer was finally opened and a key handed to us for room inspection.

~

Walking down the bleak corridor of decay to room 112, I knew that I'd made a mistake booking us all in to this place. Opening the door only provided confirmation. This hotel really wasn't suitable. It had sufficed for my last trip but this time it was different. This time it was rock'n'roll. And there would be no point in smashing up these hotel rooms because they looked like somebody else had already done it for you.

'Well, Tony,' said a most urbane Tim, 'I do take your point about the character of this place, but would you think it snobbish if us lot did check in to the other place that you were talking about? It's just that this is more of a holiday for us than it is for you.'

'Of course.'

'You won't be offended?'

'Not at all. I don't blame you. It's much worse than I'd recalled. And cold too. I hope they've remembered to put the electric fires into Norman's room as I'd requested.'

I returned reception and explained to the 'nervously breaking-down' woman that Tim and his party would be staying somewhere else after all. This came as something of a blow since their keys had only just been successfully laid out on the counter seconds earlier. I put the Pitkins in a cab, arranged to pick them up later for dinner and then took myself up to the second floor to check on the state of the suite that Norman had been promised.

There was no suite. Just a bog standard room which was cold. A room that had clearly not had a heater in it for months and had retained in its walls the bitter chill of the long Albanian winter nights.

'Norman, don't unpack,' I said firmly. 'I'm going to get you somewhere warmer than this. Let's go.'

'Oh I don't mind,' said Norman, rather sweetly.

'Yes you do. It's too cold.'

'Well, it is a bit cold.'

'Come on. Let's go.'

'I'm afraid Norman and his assistant are going to stay somewhere else,' I said to the now slightly deranged-looking receptionist.

'Really?'

'Yes, well we were promised a suite and I'm afraid his room is too cold.'

The woman shrugged, took back the key and mentally added another paragraph to her 'boy, what a day I had at work' speech.

Another thrilled cab driver took us to the Hotel Tirana where on my previous trip they'd offered an extremely favourable rate for Norman and where, frankly, I should have booked all of us in the first place. The improvement in quality was dramatic. It was quite plush, extremely warm, and ironically enough, all the things at which I'd turned my nose up on my previous trip on the grounds that it could have been a hotel absolutely anywhere in the world.

Norman and Sylvia liked their rooms and retired for well-earned naps before dinner. I wasn't so lucky I had to return to the crumbling icebox into which I'd booked myself. Or did I? As I was leaving the hotel I was struck by the absurdity of the situation over which I'd just presided. Norman Wisdom and The Pitkins were now staying in three different hotels in Tirana. Wasn't this the kind of thing that happened when your band had been together for five years and couldn't stand each other? It all seemed a little premature, especially since we hadn't even had a rehearsal yet.

'Excuse me,' I asked the attractive uniformed receptionist. 'I am with Mr Pitkin and I was wondering if you had another room vacant at the same rate which you have offered him?'

'Of course sir, that will be no problem. When do you want it it?'

'Tonight.'

'This is fine.'

'Thank you. See you in half an hour.'

Back at the Dajti the receptionist looked a broken woman. She must have been able to tell exactly what I was going to do from the look on my face, and from my recent track record, because when I reached her she just put out her hand to take my key. No words needed to be exchanged.

In the space of one and a half hours the hotel had gone from being busier than they had ever been, to empty.

Well, that's capitalism for you.

~

At dinner that night I gave the troops a military-style briefing on what we hoped to achieve and how we hoped to achieve it. Also I gave out the Norman Wisdom and The Pitkins tour T-shirts which had an important phone number printed on the front.

'As you know, men', I announced, 'the Albanian chart is calculated by a combination of radio airplay and votes. While we are here we need to encourage as many Albanians as we can to 'Vote Norman', so that we can get ourselves into the chart. So don't forget to point to the number on your T-shirt during performances. Any questions?'

'Yes Tony, about these performances,' said Tim drily. 'What exactly will we be doing?'

'Good question, Rice. Norman will be miming the lead vocal. I shall be nearby with a guitar ready to take over when the rap section begins. Eva and Lucinda will be doing choreographed moves and miming to the backing vocals which they have already so ably recorded. And you and Donald ...'

I hesitated. Even posing as I was as a rather daft English army officer, I was still rather embarrassed about what I was going to say next.

'You and Donald will mime playing these,' I said reaching for a plastic bag beneath the table.

I produced a toy trumpet and a toy saxophone, both still wrapped and bearing the words 'Suitable for age three and over'. Tim and Donald did what they'd been doing for most of this trip so far, and descended into fits of giggles.

'I thought they were very suitable,' I said. 'Since there's a lot of brass on the track, and both of you are aged over three.'

'Who's going to play what?' asked Donald.

'I have no preference. Just sort it out between you.'

I clapped my hands to get the attention of the rest of the party who, in a rather ill-disciplined manner, had begun sniggering among themselves.

'Rehearsals will begin in the morning at ten hundred hours sharp in the Hotel Tirana. Enjoy your dinner.'

At 5 a.m. in my hotel room I was woken by Norman wailing. Well, at least that was what it sounded like. It turned out to be the call to prayer from the mosque outside in Skanderbeg

Square, but bizarrely the voice emanating from the speakers happened to sound distinctly like Norman wailing. Not that I'd heard him wail, or indeed ever wanted to, but lying in my bed and still only semi-conscious, I felt pretty confident that were Norman ever to attempt a bit of wailing, then what I was hearing now would be precisely the sound that would be produced. The call to prayer continued long enough for me to feel the need to obey it, and I did so by praying that it wouldn't last too much longer so I could promptly fall back to sleep.

Actually I was a little surprised to discover that the mosque was functioning at all. Enver Hoxha had done his best to extinguish religion in a country which, at the time of his accession to power, had been mostly Muslim with large Catholic and Orthodox minorities. In the Seventies most of the 1,500 mosques and 400 churches were either destroyed or used for other purposes, sometimes in a manner which was clearly meant to ridicule – the Catholic cathedral in the northern town of Skhodra even being used to host volleyball matches.

Five hours after my early morning prayer, rehearsals were ready to begin. We were all gathered on the terrace of the Hotel Tirana, the ghetto blaster poised ready to play the track for the first time. The Pitkins were basking in the sunshine of a fine Albanian day, while Norman was pacing around still grappling with the lyrics. To Norman's credit, he still seemed concerned about the quality of his miming.

'The words just won't go in,' he said with a concerned grimace.

'It doesn't matter. Just hide behind the microphone,' I reminded him for the umpteenth time.

It was rather an exotic location for a first rehearsal, resembling the settings of The Beatles' and U2's famous rooftop gigs. There were fewer roadies, but the autograph hunters were there. The hotel's waiters were standing around just waiting for the moment when they could get Norman to sign something to take back and show to their families.

I hit play on the ghetto blaster and the band prepared itself for its maiden voyage into the three minutes twenty-one seconds of 'Big In Albania'.

There was an immediate problem. The music was nowhere

near loud enough. The sound of the traffic from the nearby square was almost drowning out the efforts of the sound system.

'Tony, we need bigger speakers,' said Eva.

'Yes, I think you're right, but this is all we've got.'

'We'll have to try and borrow something when we do it for real,' said Donald.

'Maybe, but remember we're on a roof by a very noisy square here.'

The trouble was that my ghetto-blaster didn't live up to its name. At full volume back home in my front room it had seemed capable of blasting a ghetto, but now it was becoming clear that it wouldn't even raise an eyebrow in such a place, let alone blast it. It might cause enough of a disturbance to merit an abrupt 'shhh!' in a sedate English village, but that was all.

In spite of the distinctly distant sound of the playback, Norman Wisdom and The Pitkins gave it their all in the two run-throughs that time would permit. Norman stood proudly at the front, with me hovering just behind occasionally urging him into the microphone and counting him in for the two parts of the song which he consistently forgot. The Pitkins strutted their stuff with a surprising vigour and passion as the hotel waiters looked on, amused but not noticeably impressed.

'How was I on that last one?' asked Norman as he turned around to face Tim behind him, flushed from his performance on toy sax.

'Norman, from where I was standing, you mimed it perfectly.'

We split up after the rehearsals. Not in the 'musical differences' sense, but in the 'doing different things with the rest of the morning' connotation. Tim and his party went off to explore Tirana, while I dragged Norman around State TV and Top Albania Radio to try and drum up some kind of media campaign to bolster our efforts. We didn't have a lot of luck. Given the many emails that I'd sent from England, the head of State Television displayed a somewhat alarming ignorance of why we were there in his office.

'We are greatly honoured to receive Mr Norman, your great comic actor,' he said as he sat behind the desk of his rather drab office. 'But this is the first knowledge that I have that he is in our country.'

'So you haven't arranged for us to be on *Telebingo* on Sunday?'

'No. Because I did not know you were coming.'

Well now. How could that have happened? Something of a major blow.

'But is it too late for you to get us on to that show?' I asked, imploringly.

'I don't think so. Leave it with me and I will see what I can arrange.'

From what I'd gleaned thus far, the expression 'Leave it with me' was another way for an Albanian to say 'Let me erase all knowledge of that from my memory'. But I had no choice, and so I left it with him.

As we departed the building Norman was immediately mobbed by a group of locals who spotted him and came running over. Soon he was surrounded by a crowd of adoring fans who wanted to shake his hand and thank him for the years of joy he had given them. I got out my camera to take the photograph which somehow bore out the lyrics to our song. There was no doubting it. Anyone looking at this scene would have to concede that Norman was indeed 'Big In Albania'. I wandered up the road a little further to get some shots which would capture the whole scene but soon I felt a hand on my shoulder and I spun round to see a policeman with his hand out, demanding my camera.

In the following minutes I was to discover that, rather unfortunately, one of the buildings which had been included in my photograph was none other than the American Embassy. It seemed that in the post-11 September atmosphere of paranoia, a pretty dim view was taken of types who hung around photographing American military and diplomatic establishments. The policeman, who had now been joined by several colleagues, was demanding the film from my camera and all my refusals and explanations were falling on deaf ears. My frantic pointing towards Norman was having little effect since the man himself was hidden behind a big crowd of fans. To the police my behaviour was making them even more convinced that I was a possible unhinged terrorist type, since all I was saying to them was 'Look I'm with Pitkin', over and over again. Let's face it, it's the kind of behaviour that would get you locked up in most countries.

To my relief, just when one of the policemen was about to remove the film from my camera, I saw Norman emerge from the crowd and start looking around for me. I bellowed to him to come over and help, and he immediately launched into his famous walk. Immediately the expressions changed on the faces of the policemen. Their jaws dropped. They melted. In a matter of seconds Norman had turned them into pussycats. The policeman, who moments before had been on the point of becoming aggressive, shook my hand and passed me my camera.

'Have a good day,' he said.

That was precisely my intention, and had been all along.

Upon his arrival at Top Albania Radio, Norman was given the star treatment and he was clearly delighted by the interest he received from the pretty receptionists. However, there still seemed to be an element of surprise that he was in the country at all. We were greeted by Alban and others who'd been around on my previous trip, but this time heads of departments were summoned, mainly so they could pay homage to Norman. After a lot of hand-shaking and adulation, we all sat down to discuss the situation. Confusion still reined as to why we were actually there. For what was probably the fifth time, I spelt it all out again.

'We need to get Norman into your chart otherwise we will lose a very important bet,' I explained.

'Ah yes. Your song. "Big In Albania",' said a man in a suit who I hadn't seen on my previous trip. 'We have been playing this song and I believe it is becoming quite popular.'

'Really?' I said, genuinely surprised.

This was great news. At least something was going to plan.

'We are in your country to do a short tour promoting it and urging people to vote for it,' I explained, pointing to my T-shirt. 'Look we have the phone number right here.'

'I see.'

'Do you think that we have a chance of making it into your Top Twenty?' I asked.

'Yes, I think so. In fact I think that it may be at Number 18 in the next chart that we publish on Tuesday,' he said routinely.

'*Really?*' I said, visibly astonished.

If this was true, then it really was quite stunning news. Surely I must have misheard or misunderstood.

'You say,' I enunciated slowly and clearly, 'that we will be Number 18 in the chart on Tuesday?'

'I think so,' he said in a rather deadpan manner, oblivious to what potentially momentous news this was.

I *think* so. Why did he *think* so? Why didn't he *know* so?

'Well if this is true,' I said, trying to control the adrenalin rush which I was now feeling, 'then that means I have won my bet. How can I find this out for sure?'

'I will ask my colleague.'

'Where is he?'

'He is not in today.'

'When is he in?'

'Tomorrow. I think.'

God! Why did he *think*? Why did he not *know*?

'Can you ask him tomorrow then?' I asked, only just managing to fight off a begging tone of voice.

'Leave it with me.'

This was as frustrating as it was exciting. On this unimportant little trinket of information hung the entire outcome of endeavours that had consumed me for the past two years. And if what the man was saying was true then Norman may well have just become a world record holder, being the oldest person to have a Top Twenty hit. Surely he'd be as excited as me? I looked across to where he was sitting to see how he'd taken the news.

And I saw.

He'd fallen asleep.

CHAPTER 19 A PALACE, AND THEN A MISSING CROWN

I tried to put the news of a possible chart entry out of my mind. If the man at Top Albania Radio had got things wrong then the disappointment would be too hard to bear. I decided not to pass the news on to the other members of the band just yet. The best thing was to carry on with the original plan as if nothing had happened. Besides what harm could it do us? If we were already at Number 18 then all our efforts on this trip would only serve to push the record higher up the chart. Perhaps even to Number One? A Number One in Albania. Every schoolboy's dream.

So, immediately after siestas had been taken at our respective hotels, it was time to kick off the tour, and Durres was, quite literally, the first port of call. This coastal city was about a forty-minute drive from Tirana and had once been the capital of Albania. Indeed its strategic position on the coast, with a bay offering one of the best anchorages in the Adriatic, had meant that over the years it had become a sought-after prize for invaders. Since the year 1000 it had changed hands no fewer than 33 times.

The trip enabled me to renew my acquaintance with Bilal whom we'd hired to be our tour guide. He looked pleased to see me again but there was real joy on his face when he saw Norman for the first time.

'Norman,' he said as he shook his hero's hand. 'It is a real pleasure to meet you. I can tell you that I have seen each of your films maybe three or four times. Just as it is for all Albanians I have grown up with your work. Thank you so much.'

'Oh that's all right,' replied Norman, with a mixture of embarrassment and nonchalance. 'What's this place Doris like?'

'You mean Durres.'

'That's what I said – Doris. What's it like?'

'Oh well, I don't think that it is anything special but it has the Roman remains of an amphitheatre and also it has the former Palace of King Zog.'

'Oh yes, old Zoggy. I remember him. Good name.'

Most of the drive to Durres was pretty unattractive, but it was fascinating for most of the Albania virgins in the minibus, who marvelled at the number of half-built houses and the ludicrously excessive bunkers which dotted the roadside and surrounding hills.

'These are Enver Hoxha's bonkers bunkers,' I said, rather lyrically, and showing great local knowledge.

When we arrived at the amphitheatre we found that it wasn't exactly one of the Seven Wonders of the World. Maybe it would have come in at 1,942nd in the Wonder charts, just after the King Alfred swimming baths in Hove. Actually, that's a little unfair. The problem was that this place really was just the *remains* of something special. To an archaeologist it would have been a treasure, but to Norman Wisdom and The Pitkins, it was just a hole with significance. I guess that over the years the Albanians hadn't developed a culture which had shown a great deal of interest in preserving the past, and consequently it had only been relatively recently that excavation had taken place on this ancient site.

Next on our sightseeing tour was the Palace of King Zog, perched as it was on top of a hill overlooking the busy port of Durres below. Zog had possibly been the first great Albanian politician to harness nationalism and help create a nation state, although he fell rather heavily under the influence of the Italians and was later overthrown by them. In fact the palace, which was built in the 1930s, looked very much like Mussolini might have built for himself.

'Shall we go into the city centre before it gets dark?' I asked Bilal. 'I think we should do some leafleting and let Durres know that Norman is in town.'

'This is a good idea. It is traditional to take a stroll at dusk and there will be a lot of people on the streets. Here I think you will see – to quote your song – a lot of Normanmania.'

'More than in Tirana?'

'Oh yes. I think that the people in Tirana are less excitable than in the provinces. You will see.'

Bilal was not wrong.

As soon as we parked the minibus near what seemed to be the city's main thoroughfare, a group of men saw Norman and started waving excitedly.

'OK team,' I said, assuming the army officer role for the second time. 'Here's the plan. Norman does a bit of a royal-style walkabout, and we all hand out leaflets urging people to phone up the radio station and vote for our song.'

'Tony, you should stay close to Norman,' whispered Bilal, 'just in case things get out of hand.'

I really believed that Bilal was being overly cautious, but as soon as Norman stepped out of the van people started rushing towards him.

'Pitkin! Pitkin!' they shouted.

At first Norman smiled and laughed with the people, much as he had done at the airport and outside the TV and radio studios in Tirana, but when he saw the crowd growing in size, I could see a look of apprehension creep cross his face.

We were getting rather hemmed in on the pavement, and so I suggested to Norman that we cross the congested road and move to a more open space where he could meet and greet more easily and where the others could hand out leaflets.

'Blimey,' said Norman. 'Busy, isn't it?'

It was about to get busier. We'd only made it half way across the road when a woman, who was holding the hand of her young daughter, intercepted us and started demanding that Norman pose for a picture with her child. Cars were passing us on either side, but this did not deter the woman. I tried to usher her away but there was something akin to a look of hysteria in her eyes. She grabbed her daughter and forced her next to Norman. A pedestrian traffic cop appeared from nowhere and tried to move the woman on, seeing that she was holding up traffic. Drivers angrily tooted their horns but she refused to move. Her camera was out and was poised for the picture and nothing was going to stop her, not even the shouts of the irate motorists and the blaring car horns. Just when I thought that the traffic cop was about to take some decisive action, he stopped dead in his tracks when he recognised the subject of the intended photograph, and a huge grin appeared on his face.

'Pitkin!' he bellowed, drawing even more attention to poor old Norman.

People in the log jam of cars looked and waved. Some started to get out of their vehicles. Norman grabbed my arm and looked up at me.

'I don't like this, Tony. Come on, let's get out of here.'

I could see that he wasn't joking. There was a look of genuine fear in his eyes, and with good reason. The kind of hysteria which is normally reserved for boy bands and teenage film stars was being unleashed on a five foot five, eighty-seven-year-old man.

'Don't worry, we'll leave right now,' I said, as calmly as I could.

I spun Norman around and we tried to head back to the minibus, but we were prevented from moving by the crazed woman photographer whose camera seemed to have jammed. She'd evidently decided that she wasn't going to let Norman out of her sights until her child was in that snap. I looked to the policeman for help but he was handing Norman a pen and paper and demanding an autograph, so I put a protective arm around Norman and assumed the role of bodyguard.

Then an opportunity arose. The small lorry which had been hemming us in pulled forward a few yards and suddenly there was an escape route. I grabbed Norman.

'Come on. Let's run!'

And run we did. It was just lucky that Norman was as fit and as agile as he was. All his showing off and running up down escalators in airports was holding him in good stead. The woman screamed after us and the policeman waved his pen and paper but it was to no avail. We were free. Bilal and the others held off the crowd who had gathered on the pavement and we ushered Norman into the minibus, jumped in, and slammed the door. People banged on the window and waved at Norman.

'Pitkin! Pitkin! Mr Norman! Mr Norman!'

'Bloody hell, let's get out of here,' said Norman.

The driver started the van and we sped off.

'I think, after that, we need a drink,' I said, sounding considerably less like an army officer than I had done earlier.

That night we celebrated our lead singer not being crushed to death in Durres, by having dinner at the excellent restaurant where I'd met Bilal on my first ever night in Tirana. The wine flowed and morale was high.

'Hey Dad,' said Eva, pointing to the speaker on the wall above our table, 'this is one of your songs.'

Tim stopped eating and then nodded, as the voice of Madonna wafted across the room.

'Yes, it's "You Must Love Me" from the film version of *Evita*,' he said, looking rather pleased with himself.

It seems that it doesn't matter how many successful songs you've written, you still get a thrill from hearing them performed. I remembered just how excited I used to become on the few occasions when 'Stutter Rap' was played on the radio. Wherever I was, whatever I was doing, each time it was a special moment. This really did seem to be one of the underlying reasons why I'd taken on the bet in the first place. Maybe I was really longing for that feeling again – just what Tim was experiencing right now – eating a meal in some obscure part of the world, only to be delightfully interrupted by something which you'd helped to create. Yes, that would do nicely. I'd definitely settle for a moment like that.

The conversation turned to showbiz, and after Tim had related a couple of stories about working with Madonna, Norman topped things by telling us how he'd met Marilyn Monroe when they'd both been filming at Pinewood Studios. I toyed with the idea of throwing in a story of how I'd once met the bloke who used to operate Basil Brush at the Theatre Royal Brighton, but I didn't want to show off.

'What's on the agenda tomorrow, Tony?' asked Lucinda.

'Well, tomorrow is quite a big day. We're gonna try and do a PA in the park, then we'll be performing the song for Top Albania TV, before the climax of the day which will be the stadium gig.'

'Wow, is that really happening?' asked Eva.

'The stadium gig? As far as I know.'

In Albania you could be sure of nothing. Except, perhaps, that Norman would get recognised.

'So you think that the park will be a good place to do the performance?' I asked Bilal, the morning sun warming our skin as we unloaded ourselves from the minibus once again.

'Well, today is Saturday, and I think a lot of people will be gathered here,' he replied.

'So, a captive audience then?'

'Exactly.'

Norman and I rehearsed the lyrics as we began to walk through the rather pleasant park, which had a generous supply of plants and deciduous trees, and was just as busy as Bilal had promised. I did my best to concentrate on the job in hand and ignore the looks of amazement on those walkers who happened to spot my illustrious companion.

After about ten minutes of climbing up a fairly steep hill, I noticed that Norman was starting to get a little tired.

'Bilal,' I called out ahead. 'Where are we going to do this?'

'I have a place in mind that will be good,' came his reply.

'Is it far?'

'Not far. Another ten minutes.'

I was aware that we had to preserve Norman's energy for what was going to be a long day and I knew that another ten minutes on this gradient was going to take its toll, if not now, then later. I was just going to suggest a rethink when I heard the gentle hum of a car crawling up the hill behind us. Without hesitation I stepped into its path and raised my hand for it to stop. Just as the driver was ready to give me a piece of his mind for holding him up, I pointed to Norman and then watched with delight as the man's angry face morphed into that of a child who'd just been given a present. I called Bilal over and soon he and Norman had jumped into the car and were completing the journey in the company of their new, and entirely thrilled, personal chauffeur.

Ten minutes later a new problem emerged as we realised that there seemed to have been a crossing of wires about the exact spot where we would rendezvous, because when we reached our location there was no sign of Norman.

In a move that smacked of carelessness we appeared to have lost our lead singer.

'Perhaps he's been kidnapped,' joked Tim. 'I mean, I imagine he'd fetch a hefty ransom over here.'

It didn't bear thinking about.

It wasn't for a further twenty minutes, and until after we'd managed to speak to Bilal on his mobile phone, that we were able to locate our singer. The relief was palpable among our party. With each passing minute, the initial quip about kidnap had started to feel like a plausible explanation for Norman's disappearance. We'd begun to consider the possibility that the man in the car hadn't been a Pitkin fan after all, but an opportunist.

Now we were happy though, because we were all in the same place. If you don't know the rock'n'roll business as well as me, you'll be interested to learn that being in the same place as the other members of the band can definitely enhance a performance.

The spot which Bilal had chosen for our first public gig was ideal – a kind of mini-amphitheatre with a stage, both of which were located in a romantic setting before a large and splendid lake. It was absolutely perfect, or at least would have been, but for the fact that for some reason there was an audience already there – and they were made up almost exclusively of children between the ages of four and six.

'Are we going to do the song here?' asked a chirpy Norman.

'Well, it's a good location,' I replied, while surveying the scene, 'but I'm not sure whether we might get a more suitable crowd somewhere else.'

'Come on,' said Norman, 'let's do the song here. You introduce me and I'll come on from over there.'

Norman appeared keen so there seemed little point in quibbling about the demographics of the onlookers. So while the others set up the inadequate ghetto blaster and speakers, I made my announcement.

'Ladies and gentlemen, boys and girls,' I bellowed, 'please will you welcome the man who everyone loves. All the way from England, it's Pitkin! It's Mr Norman!'

The children cheered but I guess they would have done so whoever or whatever I'd introduced. No doubt I would have got a similar response if I'd said: 'Ladies and gentlemen, boys and girls, please will you welcome a bowl of pasta!'

The playback began and it soon became apparent that it was even more woefully quiet than expected. The toy brass section looked across to me and shrugged. I shrugged back. Well, what could I do? The tape had started so we had to finish. Yes, in future, we would need to find an enclosed space to perform, rather than a place where the sound just disappeared upwards into the trees and sky, almost completely missing the ears of the intended audience and indeed the very performers themselves. But for now we just had to continue.

It was a bizarre sight. Norman soldiered on like a trooper, turning in a pretty good performance on the miming front – not that anyone could hear what he was supposed to be miming to – and the rest of The Pitkins just shuffled around behind him feeling vaguely embarrassed.

'It would be good if we could sort this sound out,' said Tim, after the 'performance' had finished and the children had applauded generously, 'Somehow you feel less silly holding a toy sax if the sound around you has got some oomph to it.'

'I know,' I said, 'I'm really sorry.'

I was aware that morale would drop unless I somehow addressed this issue, but I had no idea what to do. I knew no one in Tirana who rented out PA systems, if indeed there was anyone in the entire country who did such a thing.

'At least we've got our first public performance out of the way with no real hitches,' I said, putting a brave face on things.

'Well, there is that I suppose,' said a resigned Tim, clutching his toy sax rather apologetically to his chest.

'It wasn't too disastrous.'

'No.'

But then it had hardly been a triumph either. We'd struggled through at pitiful volume performing in front of the only age group in the country who had no idea who Norman was, and who didn't know how to use a telephone. We could hardly rely on their votes to catapult us up the charts. I made a mental note not to hire Bilal as promoter for my next tour, and then I called everyone together.

'OK, that performance served as a good rehearsal,' I said. 'The next one is for TV.'

'Is this going to be "live"?' asked Norman, as we made our way into the recording studio of Top Albania Radio and TV.

'No, not at all,' I replied. 'They're just going to film us miming the song in here – and then they're going to show part of it on their news programme later.'

'You won't forget to count me in for that end bit of the song?'

'I won't forget.'

I was impressed by how much Norman *cared*. I wondered whether, if I were lucky enough to reach the grand old age of eighty-seven, I'd be that bothered about the quality of my performance on an Albanian TV network. I guess once a pro, always a pro.

We were all quite impressed by what we found inside the studio. It was well equipped with all the latest gear. I'd been told that Top Albanian Radio were a record label also, and that in this studio they produced records for Albanian acts which they then proceded to plug on their own radio station. It seemed that they had it all sewn up.

Microphones were dotted around the place in readiness, and The Pitkins began to arrange themselves ready to do their stuff.

'Tony, is there anything I can do?' asked Norman's assistant, Sylvia, as I hitched my guitar over my shoulder.

'What do you mean?'

'Well I feel a bit of a lemon standing around when you lot do the songs. Is there anything I could pretend to play?'

'I don't see why not. Have you pretended to play anything before?'

'Never.'

'Perfect. That's the only qualification you need. There are some drums over there. Why don't you sit down and pretend to play those?'

'Oh I don't know – they look a bit daunting,' said Sylvia, surveying the glistening golden cymbals and impressive spread of tom toms.

'Don't worry. Just hide behind them and then wave your sticks around if the camera points your way.'

I clapped my hands to get the attention of the others.

'Does anyone mind if Sylvia joins us?'

The question was greeted with a chorus of 'not at alls'. Sylvia looked thrilled. I wondered if this moment had meant the fulfilment of some kind of childhood dream of hers to perform – perhaps one that she may have given up on years and years ago.

I looked across the room towards the toy brass section and saw that Tim and Donald were practising a couple of little moves as they clutched their precious ersatz instruments.

'It's just like a scene from *The Blues Brothers*,' I said, giving them both a thumbs-up sign.

'At least they'll be able to blast the track out to us in here,' said Tim. 'We could hardly hear what we were playing in the park.'

'Tim, you weren't playing anything in the park.'

'Yes ... I take your point. But you know what I mean. We don't want to start pretending to play in the wrong place. Not on TV.'

Well well. Someone else who *cared*. I hadn't banked on this group being such a professional outfit.

Two cameramen arrived and began filming, while a technician moved among us fiddling with the microphones. The odd thing was that he seemed to be speaking into them so that the guy in the control room could monitor levels. Surely they weren't thinking that we were about to provide them with a *live* performance of this song? Had they not noticed that two of the band were each holding a toy sax and toy trumpet? Had it escaped their attention that my guitar wasn't plugged in, or that there was a middle-aged woman seated at a drum kit looking utterly bewildered and grasping the sticks the wrong way up?

'Excuse me,' I said, interrupting the conscientious technician, 'but do you realise that we are going to mime this song?'

'Er ... why ... what you say?' he said, ably demonstrating that English hadn't been his best subject at school.

'*Mime*,' I said slowly and at volume, which as everybody is aware, makes a word that you don't know that much easier to understand. 'We ... no ... sing. We listen to backing track and ... *mime*.'

Just as the technician was beginning to look tearful, a cameraman stepped in and offered what I hoped was a translation. For a moment, confusion reigned. The now commonplace Albanian confusion. Confusion which I'd learned to grow and love.

Well, almost.

'I think the problem,' said Donald looking around him, 'is that there are no speakers in here for playback.'

A quick shufty around the studio confirmed that he was right.

'Oh dear,' I said, the tremor in my voice not necessarily reassuring everyone of my great leadership qualities.

'What does that mean?' asked Lucinda.

'It means that we won't be able to hear what we're miming to,' I said.

'So no change there then,' quipped Tim.

'Eh? What's happening?' said Norman, who was happily positioned behind his large microphone, eager for action. 'Why don't we start?'

'We've got no speakers,' I explained.

'Speakers? What do we need speakers for?'

'To hear the track.'

'I don't understand why we can't just start. I'm ready. You're ready, why can't we just start?'

'Because the speakers are in the control room and not here,' explained Tim, 'and we have to hear the track if we're going to mime to it.'

'Well, we'll just have to go in there,' I said.

'It's tiny,' said Donald. 'It'll be a bit cramped in there with all of us and two cameramen.'

'And what about Sylvia?' said Eva.

'Oh yes. Sylvia,' I said. 'Well, I can't see how we'll be able to squeeze a drum kit into the control room too.'

Sylvia's face fell.

'I guess Sylvia will have to sit this performance out,' I said, as sympathetically as I could.

Poor old Sylvia. She'd been in and out of the band before you had time to say 'sack the drummer'. She'd just made Pete Best's time behind the kit with The Beatles seem like a very long run indeed.

'I don't see why we can't just do it here,' said a confused Norman. 'I'm ready.'

'Norman, the problem is—'

Thankfully my attempted explanation was interrupted by the appearance of the man, who up until now, had been twiddling the knobs at the recording desk which was beyond the glass that divided the rooms.

'You stay here and we will play the track in there,' he said in good English, pointing back into the control room. 'If we turn the volume up full and open the door, you should be able to hear it.'

Tim laughed.

'Will that work?' asked Donald, turning to me, wrongly assuming I'd have some kind of idea.

'I guess we'll have to give it a try,' I said.

'It's somewhat ironic, isn't it,' offered Tim, drily, 'that here we are in a recording studio, surrounded by loads of high-tech equipment, and the sound is probably going to be the quietest it's been so far.'

'Yes it is a shame, isn't it,' I replied, rather pathetically. 'Although it's good news for Sylvia. It means she's back in the band.'

I turned to her and gave her the thumbs-up. She beamed, and with both hands aloft, offered the same gesture in return.

'What's happening?' asked Norman.

'We're going to do the song in here after all,' I replied.

'Well, that's what I said, isn't it? Let's just do it here. I mean we're all ready and everything, so we should just do it here.'

'Yes, good idea Norman. We'll do it here.'

'You will count me in on the end bit, won't you?'

'Yes.'

The door was pushed ajar by a cameraman and the distant sound of the brass intro began to bleed through. It may have sounded feeble to us but to the guys in the control studio it must have been almost overpowering. I could see the technicians wince as they were deafened by the track as it belted from the powerful speakers. It can't have been doing them any good, but they wanted Norman's performance on film, and it didn't seem to matter that perforated eardrums was the price that they would have to pay.

For us, standing the other side of the frustratingly sound-proof dividing wall, the problem was altogether different.

'It's a bit quiet,' said Norman.

'Yes,' I said, starting to feel weak.

'Can't we have it a bit louder?'

'Tim will explain,' I said, cravenly moving away and pretending to busy myself with needless guitar tuning.

Fortunately for Tim, the studio engineer appeared and saved the day.

'OK guys, we know it is not perfect but we think it will work,' he said with some authority. 'Here we go – are you ready?'

We all looked at each other and shrugged, something which must be the Albanian gesture for 'Yes', because the track started and we were off again – doing what we did best – being Big in Albania. Donald and Tim, the father and son toy brass section doing their utmost to replicate the moves of Earth Wind & Fire's brass section; Eva and Lucinda swinging, swaying, clapping and jigging; me trying to look like a guitar hero; Norman waving his arms and concealing his mouth behind a large microphone; and Sylvia … well, Sylvia, bless her, looking like a staff nurse sitting behind a drum kit.

Actually, I felt it was an improvement on our previous performance, but that wasn't saying a lot. We had simply gone from being poor to not very good. Never mind though, if we carried on at this rate we could leave Albania having peaked with 'mediocre', so there was everything to play for.

After Norman had done a short TV interview with a pretty young news reporter who he'd insisted on popping on his knee, I noticed a set of bongos sitting in the corner of the studio.

'Do you mind if we borrow those?' I asked the technician, fully expecting a polite refusal.

'No problem,' he replied.

I thanked him and promised to return them safely, before handing them to Sylvia, who looked as happy as anyone can look upon being handed a percussion instrument. It meant that she'd be able to join us on all subsequent performances and her status as a Pitkin was now secure. I felt that this was good news because it further strengthened our position as a band with universal appeal. Having Sylvia on board meant that we now had a mature woman in our ranks, and we could reach out to the only section of society to which we didn't already appeal – the older gentleman.

'OK everyone,' I said, at volume, 'I'd like to announce to you that we now have a new member of The Pitkins. Sylvia is joining us full time on percussion.'

The news was greeted with a spontaneous round of applause.

'Welcome to the band, Sylvia,' said Tim.

What a happy bunch we were.

I guess that's how all bands start off. It's when they go on tours that last longer than three days that the cracks begin to show. The Pitkins had got it about right.

After the busy morning, we'd all agreed to three hours' rest time back at the hotels before meeting up for the stadium gig. I hoped that everyone would use this time to tune themselves in mentally, just like all the great rock bands do before their biggest performances. I'd read somewhere that Sting prepared for all his stadium shows by doing an hour of hard physical yoga, so I returned to my hotel room with the intention of following the example of the great man.

Having only ever been to one yoga class, during which my body had displayed an alarming unwillingness to adopt most of the required positions, I decided that the best option was to settle for a headstand over by the window. It may not have been advanced stuff, but after only a few minutes I began to realise that it was certainly having the desired effect. As the blood slowly seeped down through my body towards my head, and with each elongated breath that I took, the concerns for the forthcoming event eased away from my consciousness. It was only the knock on the door which prevented me from drifting off any further towards Nirvana.

'Tony!' I heard a woman's voice call out from the hotel corridor.

'Er … yes,' I replied, momentarily confused as to where I was, and what I was doing upside down.

'Can I have a word?'

I knew that voice. Who was it? Wait, wasn't it Sylvia's? Norman's assistant Sylvia? Yes, that was it. I was in Albania with Norman Wisdom, and I was standing on my head in preparation for a gig in the local football stadium. Suddenly everything made sense.

'Hang on, Sylvia, I'm coming,' I called, still inverse.

It was some moments before I was able to work out how to return to an upright position without injuring myself, or knocking over the two lamps which were on either side of me. However, I managed it OK, and consequently was feeling rather pleased with myself as I opened the door to Sylvia. The feeling didn't last. As soon as Sylvia saw me, she looked extremely embarrassed and immediately looked down at the floor. I suppose it was understandable. My delay in getting to the bedroom door had been exactly that length of time which can make the person waiting think that they may have just disturbed some rather grubby, untoward activity. It didn't help that my hair was all roughed up and that my cheeks were bright red.

'Hello, Sylvia, how can I help?' I asked, trying to appear unselfconscious.

'Er … Tony,' she said, still averting eye contact.

'Yes, Sylvia, what is it?' I said chirpily, thinking that robust cheerfulness somehow gave the impression of innocence. 'I hope you're about to tell me that everyone is fully rested, relaxed, and raring to go for the stadium gig.'

'Not really,' said a subdued Sylvia, before uttering the rather shocking words which served to undermine all my karmic preparation. 'Norman's lost the crown from one of his teeth.'

CHAPTER 20 UNFORGETTABLE

'What?' I said, somewhat shocked.

Only having freshly emerged from a peaceful meditative state, this sudden reference to Norman's dental condition wasn't easy to comprehend.

'Well he hasn't actually *lost* his crown,' said Sylvia. 'He's still got it, but it's fallen out.'

'Oh dear,' I said, feeling the blood drain from my cheeks. 'What does that mean? Is he in pain?'

'Not really – and he could have it put right when he gets back home but he's saying that he wants to get it sorted out right away.'

'I see.'

This was decidedly un-rock'n'roll. I was beginning to get to know what it must be like to be a holiday courier, and I didn't like it much. Besides, my forte was creating problems, not sorting them out.

'I'll ask Bilal if he knows any dentists.'

Fortunately he did, and naturally enough with the patient being who he was, it wasn't difficult to get him an appointment at the drop of a hat. Brilliant. A quick jaunt to the surgery and we would have everything sorted with no fuss.

How wrong I was.

When we arrived at the surgery, instead of being greeted by a secretary or dental nurse, two TV crews and a crowd of well-wishers awaited us in the small reception area.

'Welcome, Mr Norman,' said a man in a green smock, who

appeared from an adjoining room on hearing the commotion caused by our arrival.

Soon he was joined by other dentists in similar attire, who had presumably dropped everything to rush to see their hero. The mind boggled at what discomfort Norman's arrival might be causing some poor patient. Never mind that a jaw had just been wedged wide open and some kind of dental chisel inserted, Pitkin was only going to pop by once in their lifetime and the dentists weren't going to miss it.

By the time Sylvia had finished explaining the nature of Norman's complaint, the crowd of well-wishers had doubled in size, such was the rate that newcomers were arriving in the reception area to view the famous patient. It seemed that every friend and relative of anyone involved in the practice had been notified of Norman's imminent arrival, the moment after Bilal had made the initial booking.

The honour of administering the treatment to Norman fell to the most senior dentist, who announced with great gusto that Norman would receive his attentions free of charge.

'Thank you, you're very kind,' said Norman, as he was ushered through to the treatment room.

Sylvia looked a little concerned as the TV crews started to follow the two men in.

'They're not going to film him having his teeth done are they?' she said, shaking her head in amazement.

'It looks like it.'

It did seem extraordinary.

I wondered on what show these people were going to broadcast their footage. Did Albanian cable TV have something called 'The Dental Channel'. Was there a popular entertainment programme called 'Whose Mouth Is It Anyway'? Or 'Through The Cakehole'?

'I'm going to stop this,' said Sylvia firmly. 'There are certain things you are entitled to do or have done without a TV crew filming it.'

She was right. I could think of at least two where I wouldn't necessarily look my best, even with make-up and soft lighting.

As Sylvia ushered the TV crews back into the waiting room, I surveyed the media circus that had resulted from a simple dental appointment, and began to feel a little peeved that this had definitely generated more media interest than today's performances of 'Big In Albania'. Perhaps in this country, dentistry was the new rock'n'roll.

Emerging from the surgery Norman was cheered and applauded as he made his way down the steps towards the street. It had to be a first. Surely no one else had ever been granted such a reception after getting their teeth done.

'How do you feel, Norman?' I asked as we made the short stroll back to our minibus.

'I feel OK,' he replied, looking slightly dazed. 'They were nice people. They have invited us all to dinner tonight.'

'Who have?'

'The dentists. Sylvia has the details.'

'Wow. That sounds fun.'

A soirée with a gaggle of Albanian dentists. This trip was becoming ever more surreal.

'They didn't put you under anaesthetic, did they Norman?' I asked, opening the door to the van.

'I don't think so,' he replied, vaguely, in a manner that didn't convince me one way or the other.

'Do you think you'll be all right for the stadium gig?' I asked.

'I reckon so.'

I hoped he was right.

There was more riding on this than I'd actually let on to anybody.

The trouble was, I'd built the stadium gig up so much in my head. It meant so much more than just a wonderful opportunity to showcase the song to a big crowd, not to mention the sizeable TV audience who would also be watching in their homes. It would be the apotheosis of all my endeavours thus far, and it would mark the fulfilment of a dream. For more than six months, ever since I'd first cooked up this whole outrageous idea and then managed to get Norman and Tim on board, I'd allowed myself to visualise the scene which was now just a matter of minutes away – the moment when we stepped out on to the hallowed turf of the world-famous Qemal Stafa stadium, to be greeted by a euphoric ovation from adoring fans. It had been a noble dream, but one to which I'd begun to attach disproportionate importance.

'Do you know,' I'd said to friends, 'that I wouldn't really mind if I lost this bet, provided that we got to do the stadium gig.'

'Really?' they'd queried, incredulously.

'Yes, really,' I replied.

And I meant it.

That's why I'd made sure that I arrived at the stadium before the others. I wanted to sort out how we were going to organise the playback through the stadium speakers. Bilal had told me to 'leave it with him' but there was too much at stake to allow any delegation. Especially to a well-meaning Albanian.

'Tony, it is all organised,' he'd said. 'I spoke to my friend who works for the stadium and he has said that they are expecting you. Take it easy. Relax.'

But I hadn't relaxed, much as I'd wanted to, and I'd insisted on us getting to the ground early, just to be on the safe side.

When Bilal and I reached the iron gate which was reserved for VIP entry, the response from the policeman completely vindicated my caution.

'This guy is saying that you cannot come in,' said Bilal, after a short and brusque exchange with the uniformed officer, who looked like he might have been the type who'd have distinguished himself administering the routine beatings and torture which had taken place during the Hoxha regime.

'Why not?' I asked.

'I don't know.'

'But I thought you had arranged this with your friend at the stadium authorities.'

'I have, but I am having difficulties convincing the policeman of this. He says he will let me in, and only me, to speak to my contact.'

'Why won't he let me come with you?'

'I don't know.'

Already the reality of the 'stadium gig' was hopelessly at odds with the dream. I'd envisioned autograph hunters and Albania's prettiest women clamouring for my attention. The sour and intransigent policeman slamming an iron gate in my face had not featured in any of my previous flights of fancy. As the crowds began to gather around me in eager anticipation of the game ahead I was conscious that failure to gain entry to the ground would be a set-back of calamitous proportions. Performing the song *adjacent* to the stadium rather than inside it would certainly be less stylish.

'Leave this with me,' said Bilal, rather ominously. 'I will meet you at the café at the front of the ground.'

In contrast to a lot of football grounds, the Qemal Stafa sta-dium was a fine piece of architecture which seemed to belong in a city centre. It had clearly been built before the communist era and before functionalism had begun to take precedence over aes-thetic considerations, and so this edifice had an attractive brick facade and terraces with ornate romanesque ballustrades. The café constituted part of the original design and had a pleasant patio adorned with plants and tables with neat white parasols. It looked most out of place as the scarved and flag-waving supporters of today's teams, Partizani and Tomorit, swarmed around it before heading for the turnstiles.

Since the game was about to begin and the crowd were all now taking their seats, I was the only customer, sitting with my coffee and soaking up the last vestiges of the day's sunshine. I tried to relax, telling myself that I didn't need to worry about the fact that Norman might be comatose in his hotel room after the rigours of anaesthetic and major dental treatment. Hey, and I didn't need to bother myself about the minor detail of not being able to get into the ground either. I just had to sit back, enjoy the coffee and watch the world go by.

The Pitkins weren't difficult to spot as they made their way across the square to the stadium. Of course, they were much whiter and much taller than anyone else, but also they were the only ones wearing 'Vote Norman' T-shirts and carrying toy plas-tic instruments. When they reached my table I was shifting uncomfortably in my chair, not having fulfilled the 'sitting back and relaxing' brief very well. Tim was customarily amused when I outlined the current fiasco.

'It seems to be how things work here,' he said with a gentle chuckle.

'You mean – not at all.'

'Exactly. How about Norman?' he enquired, with a more serious expression returning to his face. 'Is he OK?'

'I hope so. He looked all right when we left the surgery, but you never know – he may have suffered some reaction to the anaesthetic.'

'Well, we'll find out in a minute,' said Donald, 'because here he is now.' Sure enough, the white minibus pulled in and out stepped a spritely Norman, looking as fit and ready for action as he had done on the whole trip.

'You've got to hand it to him,' I said to Sylvia, as Norman was immediately surrounded by gleeful football supporters, 'he's as strong as an ox that man.'

'Tony,' replied Sylvia, 'as long as he gets his little sleep in, he just keeps going.'

With still no sign of Bilal we made our way round to the VIP gate where I renewed my acquaintance with the recalcitrant policeman. This time I had the trump card up my sleeve. Norman Wisdom. I proudly paraded Norman before the man, with the look of a victor on my face. But it was premature, because for the first time on the whole trip, producing Norman made absolutely no difference. The policeman stood firm and the gates remained firmly closed.

'But this is Pitkin!' I protested. 'This is Mr Norman! You must let us in.'

There was no softening of the policeman's stubborn and forbidding expression. I began to fear that we'd been unfortunate enough to run into the Albanian superhero 'Captain Jobsworth', whose amazing powers meant that he could resist anything that got in his way, even Norman Wisdom.

Norman himself tried to help matters, but inadvertently he made them much worse. He decided that the best thing to do in this situation was to try and kiss the policeman. Unsurprisingly it didn't work terribly well. The object of his impish affections immediately withdrew and began waving his arms and railing against him, his eyes displaying a wild fury. Undaunted, Norman simply took a step back, eyed the policeman up for a moment and then moved straight back in again.

'Come on mate. Just a little peck on the cheek,' he said, with the air of innocence that he so skilfully used to camouflage his iconoclastic streak.

I leant across and pulled him away before any further damage was done.

'But I only want to give him a little kiss,' protested Norman.

'Yes, but he wants to break your neck,' I replied.

Something in the raging eyes of the policeman made Norman decide to let me pull him away without a struggle. I'd undoubtedly done both men a favour. Norman had been spared hospitalisation, and the policeman a painful conversation with his wife that evening:

'How was the game dear?'

'It was OK.'

'Any incidents?'

'Just one.'

'What happened?'

'I punched Mr Pitkin's lights out.'

'What? Mr Pitkin, the eighty-seven-year-old national hero on whom our leaders chose to bestow the freedom of Tirana in gratitude for the hours of pleasure he brought us during the insufferable regime of Enver Hoxha?'

'That's the one, yes.'

'You bastard! That's it, I'm leaving.'

Bilal's re-emergence from inside the ground did little to improve the situation. After a long and quite heated debate with our uniformed foe, Bilal took me aside, his body language suggesting the news was not going to be good.

'The man is saying,' he explained, 'that Norman can come into the ground – but not the rest of you.'

'What – no Pitkins?'

'No Pitkins.'

'But that's no use to us. We're a band. We have to perform together.'

'Yes, but he is being very difficult.'

'But Bilal, this guy is just an awkward policeman – he can't be in charge. You have to find whoever is in charge and tell them what the deal is here.'

'And the deal is?'

'No Pitkins – no Norman.'

'So that's what you want me to go back and tell the officials inside?' asked a jaded-looking Bilal.

'Absolutely. No Pitkins – no Norman.'

And on hearing those irresistibly defiant words, Bilal re-entered the ground for further mediation in what was in danger of becoming an intractable situation.

He was gone for some time. The match started and we began to hear the cheers and chants from the excited crowd. We all paced around impatiently, only able to assume that any minute Bilal would return with the requisite permissions and our transformation from unwanted outcasts to exalted idols would begin. I tried to boost spirits by discussing with Norman and the band exactly where we should perform the song once we'd gained entry, attempting to give the impression that our eventual admittance was not seriously in question. Like all good army officers I didn't want my troops to witness any sign of personal doubt.

'I suppose we could do the song in the centre circle,' I said. 'But we'd all have to turn around a lot.'

'How about doing it up one end?' suggested Donald.

'You mean in one of the goals?' I replied. 'It might look a little odd. Norman, where do you think we should do it?'

'Me? Oh I don't mind,' he replied, with the air of a man who was not entirely on top of where he was and what he was about to do.

'What about if we do it in the edge of one of the penalty areas?' suggested Tim. 'That way most of the crowd will be in front of us and we won't have to turn around so much.'

'Good idea,' I said. 'Are you happy with that, Norman?'

'I'll do whatever you say,' he said, looking more and more like a man who'd been under anaesthetic earlier in the day.

'Splendid, we'll do it on the edge of the penalty area then,' I said, clasping my hands, a little like a satisfied schoolteacher who'd just collected up the class's homework. 'Everyone happy?'

Everyone nodded, and the nods said it all. There were no rock'n'roll yelps of excitement or high fives, just nodding and pacing. That's what not being allowed into a venue can do to a group's morale.

'Hear those cheers inside the ground?' I asked buoyantly. 'Well, soon they'll be for us.'

'Do you think so?' asked Eva.

'I know so,' I said, sounding so sure that I almost convinced myself.

The first half of the football match was nearly over when 'Captain Jobsworth' finally capitulated, Bilal having produced an official at the gate who insisted that we be allowed in. The sense of relief on the faces of my colleagues was palpable, but it must have only been minuscule in comparison to mine. A disaster, albeit only a personal one, had just been averted.

'Nothing can stop us now!' I blurted out, as we made our way down the players' tunnel towards the pitch. Poor deluded fool that I was.

At the pitch-side we waited for the first half to finish and surveyed our audience with some awe. It was a long way from being a full house but the stands to the side of the pitch were pretty full, and I guess that it must have been a gate of about 5,000 or so. Waiting alongside us were a gaggle of teenage cheerleaders who were something of an untidy lot. I could only presume that being a cheerleader in Albania didn't carry the same kudos as it did for America's teenage girls, because these certainly weren't the pick of Tirana's young beauties.

'What's the plan now?' I asked Bilal, as the referee blew the whistle to curtail the opening forty-five minutes.

'Well, I understand that they have some prizes to give out at the side of the pitch and then after that will be OK for you to do your song,' he replied.

'You didn't mention anything about a prize-giving.'

'It's just that the junior sides of today's opponents have to collect prizes for different competitions that they have won.'

'How long will that take?'

'Not long.'

Quite why Bilal answered 'not long' instead of 'I've no idea', I've no idea. But 'not long' turned out to be the wrong answer. The prize-giving seemed to drag on for an age, while Norman Wisdom and The Pitkins waited like coiled springs at the pitch-side, desperate to do their turn.

'I reckon the players are going to be back out for the second half in a minute,' said Tim, almost showing a hint of uneasiness.

'I know,' I said, the despair in my voice now clearly evident.

'It's a disaster.'

But a disaster it wasn't, because seconds the later the last prize was awarded and Bilal instructed us to take up our positions. This we did, making our way across the turf towards the edge of the penalty box. Norman was like a frisky dog who'd just been let off a leash, and he took this opportunity to run around the field pretending to nearly fall over, and employing other goodies from his well-stocked slapstick comedy repertoire. The crowd, who up until this point had been largely oblivious of Norman's presence, suddenly noticed their idol and began to cheer and applaud. The rest of us took up our positions and marvelled at what we saw. This was the man who was not far off ninety years old and who'd just undergone some fairly major dental treatment a few hours earlier. None of us, if we were honest, knew Norman that well and, outside of his professional achievements, none of us was really aware of what kind of life he'd led before we met him, but we knew one thing for sure. He was living proof that age is a state of mind.

Norman did not believe he was eighty-seven.

Not right now. Not while he could hear the laughs and cheers of the crowd. The part of him that was still a child had been revived. It was almost as if the adoration he was now receiving acted like a magical tonic, an elixir which turned him into a younger man.

The noise from the crowd was building. Perhaps there was a sense of anticipation that something special was about to happen.

'OK guys, everything is ready now,' bellowed the voice of Bilal over the stadium's PA system, before uttering the immortal words, 'Is you ready?'

'Yes!' I screamed back, giving him the thumbs-up signal.

The others called to Norman and he ran back to his starting position behind the microphone, waving to the crowd as he did so.

'Hello, Norman. Hello guys – everything is set now,' called Bilal again, his voice booming around the stadium and out and beyond the apartment blocks in the ground's immediate vicinity. 'Is you ready to start?'

We all put our thumbs up and screamed that we were ready.

It couldn't have been more obvious that we were a group of individuals who were in a position of readiness.

'OK everything is set now. Shall I start to play the track?'

'*Yes!! Yes!! For God's sake yes!!*' we all cried, almost as one.

Quite how Bilal was failing to notice our desperate hand signals was a mystery. I could only assume that, quite brilliantly, he had managed to position himself in a spot where he couldn't see us.

'Oh no,' I whimpered. 'Please Bilal, just hit play!'

I could see that it was going to be a tantalisingly close-run thing as to whether we actually had time to do this performance. Every second that was ticking away brought the second half closer and increased the threat of us being called off the pitch by the ground's officials.

With seemingly nothing to do, Norman walked over towards the crowd, away from the mic. Then, as if this had been the cue that Bilal had been waiting for, the music blasted out.

'Norman! We're on!' I shouted as the opening strains of the song began to ring round the ground. 'Get over here! Quick!'

Norman obeyed, finally using his 'comic run' for a practical purpose.

It was happening. The stadium gig was under way. Well, of course it was. It had never been in doubt.

What followed in the next few minutes was remarkable. The music was loud, if a little tinny in quality, and the performance started well enough with the crowd on either side of the stadium quietly observing the happy little band of singers and musicians who had just started to jig about on the edge of one of the penalty areas. But then, suddenly all that changed. The focus of the crowd switched to something else entirely. With impeccable timing, the junior teams who had collected their prizes, now chose this moment to embark on laps of honour. Given that these lads represented the future of their clubs, the fans immediately began cheering them, or indeed booing them, depending on which particular team was passing them at the time. Since both teams were equally represented, with sets of fans on opposite sides of the ground, there was always an equal measure of booing and cheering at any one time. It made for an odd experience for us Pitkins. The feeling of being loved and hated at the same time left us feeling positively (or negatively) schizophrenic.

Then, just before I pushed Norman away from his micro-phone to begin my rap section, the junior teams left the field and once again we became the main attraction. But not for long. Even before I'd completed my eight bar section of rap, we were drowned out by a huge cheer as the two senior teams made their way back on to the field again. The Pitkins contin-ued to mime, pretending to be oblivious to the fact that our audience were ignoring our efforts. Our professionalism began to waver, however, when players started to warm up in the goal mouth behind us. We had no choice but to see the funny side, and instead of concentrating on looking like a plausible pop outfit, most of us began either to giggle, or shake our heads in amazement.

Then, just as we started into the final chorus, a ball ran through the middle of us and a player followed shortly after-wards, pursuing it exactly as if we hadn't even been there. However, the player stopped dead in his tracks when he clocked that one of these strange people on the edge of the penalty area was none other than Mr Norman himself.

Pitkin!

After performing an almost flawless double-take, the player immediately went over to Norman and planted a big wet kiss on his cheek. With the others following his lead, Norman was soon engulfed by players from both sides, who decided that they would prefer to kiss Norman than continue warming up. By the time the last strains of the song were fading from the distant speakers, Norman appeared to be buried beneath a mountain of red and white shirts.

It was surely an unprecedented, and somehow moving moment. An elderly man, who had taken no part in the game, was now mobbed by players of both sides as if he had just scored the golden goal which had brought them the trophy of their dreams. Every few seconds I could just catch a glimpse of Norman's face, and although it showed a measure of bemuse-ment, the over-riding emotion was that of joy. Was he loving this, or was he loving this? It was a tough call.

The Pitkins stood by and marvelled. From a professional point of view we may have just completed one of the least impressive performances of all our respective careers, and yet it would probably be one of the most memorable.

'How was that for you, Tony?' enquired Tim, leaning towards me and sporting a broad grin.

'Unforgettable.'

As we walked from the pitch and Norman continued his antics in the centre circle, attempting to kiss the referee, I realised that one of my little dreams had just passed. The stadium gig. Well, what had that been all about? It had happened all right, but it had borne no resemblance to the mental picture I'd carried around in my mind for so long. It had been just like the *Top of the Pops* performance all those years before. Well, almost. This time I didn't feel deflated. Perhaps that's because somewhere along the way I'd learned that life isn't actually about fulfilling your dreams. Maybe it's more to do with having a damn good shot at them and ensuring that you enjoy the process. Then, the key thing is to rejoice in the outcome, however much it may have differed from the original vision.

'I think that calls for a celebration,' I said to the Pitkins as we reached the side of the pitch.

'Yes. What shall we do?' asked Donald.

'How about dinner with some Albanian dentists?' I suggested.

'Sounds in keeping with things,' said Tim.

I got the sense that our party had now been totally seduced by the absurdity of this trip, and on the way to the restaurant everyone on the minibus had become decidedly giggly. Everything seemed silly, and potentially hilarious. If it hadn't have been such a hideous cliché, I might have suggested to everyone that we were on a 'natural high'. Only Norman failed to succumb to this immature frivolity, his exertions at the stadium having taken their toll and leaving him gently snoozing in the front seat.

When we reached the restaurant which was perched on a hillside about five kilometres outside the city, once again we didn't find what we were expecting. Instead of being greeted by a throng of partying dentists, we walked into an empty restaurant. Following what must have been a rather odd conversation between Bilal and the maître'd, we were assured that some dentists might be coming later, for the karaoke.

'Wow, they do karaoke here,' exclaimed an excited Donald. 'Great.'

'Look through there,' said Eva. 'There's a great big stage.'

It became clear that this place must have been the centre for all karaoke in Albania. Looking aound we could see that most of the tables were reserved, but we were told that they wouldn't be filled until after ten o'clock. Actually it suited us rather to have the place to ourselves for a while, giving us the opportunity to make as much noise as we liked, indulging in the pronouncements and reflections on our remarkable day.

Pamphlets on the table in front of us outlined what was available to us to sing, should the Albanian wine lure us into the humiliating world of karaoke. Like most publications or notices in Albania it came complete with a number of pleasing misspellings. If we wanted we could offer our own versions of 'Fermando' by Abba, Michael Jackson's 'Heat the World', or 'I will don anything for love' by Meatloaf.

'Anyone going to sing later?' asked Sylvia.

Everyone shook their heads, but then we hadn't even finished our first glass of wine yet.

'What are we doing tomorrow?' asked Norman, ever the professional.

'Tomorrow is our last day,' I replied, 'and it's our last shot at forcing our way into the charts. We're going to do a public appearance in Skanderbeg Square, and then we're supposed to be recorded doing the song for inclusion in their lottery TV show *Telebingo*.'

'Then we fly back?'

'Yes, then we fly back.'

'Oh that's a shame,' said Norman. 'Can't we stay on for a few more days?'

'The flights are booked, I'm afraid.'

Poor old Norman looked tired, and was it any wonder? The day's schedule had been gruelling for all of us, but Norman was the one who never got any down-time, because when he wasn't performing he was having to sign autographs or pose for photos for his adoring public.

'Norman, if you want,' I suggested, 'I'll get the minibus driver to take you and Sylvia back to the hotel after you've had your main course.'

'Yes, that would be nice,' he replied rather faintly.

In a way I was a little relieved that he wasn't there for my rendition of 'Every Breath You Take'. He might have lost respect. The problem was that the song was in exactly the same key as Sting had originally sung it, and as I found to my cost, that guy has an irritatingly high voice.

Rather predictably I'd been the first to fall victim to the wine and offer my services to the hostess who was running the karaoke. There'd been about four or five efforts from the Albanian customers who had now packed the place out, and they'd all been rather woeful. Worse still, the singers had performed their songs from their dining tables rather than getting up on to the stage. I was the first to break that trend, and was rather enjoying the attention and the applause it brought me until I realised that there were some extremely high bits coming up which I just couldn't reach. I did my best to cover the inadequacy of my vocal range with the rather cheap gag of grabbing my crotch every time I went for a high note. Norman would have been proud.

The joke had worn thin by the time I finished the song and left the stage, but nonetheless the response from the audience was enthusiastic, and I'd done enough to establish the precedent of singing on stage, something which was adhered to from hereon in.

'Hello there, that was very good,' said a drunk-looking man as I fought my way back to our table past the eager Albanian punters. 'Where's Norman?'

'I'm afraid he's gone,' I replied.

'Oh dear, that is a shame,' said the man. 'There are some fellow dentists that I wanted to introduce him to.'

Boy, Norman had missed out.

Still, that's what you get for going to bed early.

The highlight of the evening was when Donald allowed himself to be talked into doing a song. His sister Eva had just acquitted herself rather well with a rendition of Alanis Morissette's

'Ironic', and the locals were now beginning to look to our table more and more for new talent who could actually sing in something approaching intelligible English.

'What song are you going to do?' I asked Donald, as he nervously rose from his chair.

'I think it'll have to be the Meatloaf thing – but I'm going to do the Albanian version, as per the sheet,' he replied, reaching out to his sister and pulling her with him. 'Come on Eva – we'll do it as a duet.'

What followed was nothing less than heroic. Meatloaf's original track 'I Will Do Anything For Love' is seven minutes forty-eight seconds long. Neither Donald nor Eva could have been aware of this or else they surely wouldn't have taken it on. However, their performance was a triumph, causing fits of laughter from our table especially when they delivered the line, 'I will don anything for love, but I won't don that.' It just conjured up such a wonderful image – slightly pervy man holding up some outrageously kinky outfit for his lover to put on, only to find that her response is firm and unequivocal.

In the sixth minute of Donald and Eva's doughty performance, they were joined by their father, who could see they were beginning to flag and that they needed a new injection of talent. Tim stepped up onto the stage just in time to mime along with the saxophone break, producing his toy sax exactly on cue. The audience cheered and applauded wildly. Quite why Tim happened to have his toy sax with him at dinner, I don't know – perhaps he'd formed some kind of bond with it – but never mind, it made for a great end to an epic and marathon performance.

'God, I'll never pick that song again,' said an exhausted-looking Donald as he sat back down beside me, the applause still filling the room. 'It just seemed to go on and on. The trouble is, once you're up there you've got to see it through.'

He was exactly right, and it was something I knew all about. I'd been stuck on a metaphorical karaoke stage for nigh on two years now, the quest for a hit having taken me from London to Nashville, Holland, the Sudan, Romania and now Albania. Only now did it feel like my song was nearing its final chorus.

I only hoped that when I finally finished it I'd get a reception like the Albanians had just extended to the Rice family.

CHAPTER 21 THREE MINUTE HEROES

I don't know why, but sometimes the first thing I do when I wake up in the morning in a hotel room is turn on the telly. It's daft, it's unnatural, but for some reason that's what I do. Maybe it's because the TV is nearly always planted slap bang in front of the bed, and it feels like it's positively imploring you to watch it.

On this particularly morning I turned on mid-way through the news. Good, an opportunity to get a sketchy outline of world events, courtesy of the pictures. The Albanian commentary was unlikely to enlighten greatly. It looked like the usual stuff was going on – Yasser Arafat, Ariel Sharon, bombs, bloodshed and George Bush looking insidious. Hang on, that was the same news as the week before, wasn't it? Surely Albania wasn't that far behind in international current affairs. Having said that, you could imagine how it might have happened:

'Ali, here's the latest news bulletin. See that it is broadcast later today, will you?'

'Sure. Leave it with me.'

Bored with the news, I headed into the bathroom for a shave. I was just about to make the first smooth stroke with the razor blade when I thought I heard the newscaster utter the word 'Pitkin'. I cocked my head, a little like a dog who'd just heard the word 'walkies', and then I distinctly heard a 'Mr Norman' in among the incomprehensible Albanian newsspeak. I rushed back out into the room to see pictures on the TV screen which confirmed that I'd been overhearing none other than a report about Norman being in Albania, and featuring the performance we'd given the previous day in the studio of Top Albania Radio. It felt so odd to be watching Norman Wisdom and The Pitkins on the television, but it somehow served as confirmation that what we were doing here in Albania was real after all. It may have felt like a bizarre dream, but these TV pictures were proof that it was all actually happening. It was remarkable. A small part of the world was on the receiving end of our peculiarly quaint message – help make Norman 'Big In Albania'.

'How's that to kick off the morning!' I said out loud, before returning to the bathroom for what I hoped would be the only close shave of the day.

An hour later I was leafleting in Skanderbeg Square. Well, there didn't seem much point in taking a load of 'Vote Norman' leaflets back to England with me. I figured that even if Norman suddenly decided to stand for parliament, he'd probably have some new ones done which didn't bear an Albanian phone number. The square was busy. At one end some kind of illicit money changing seemed to be going on, with lots of dodgy characters wandering around in leather jackets. The central area appeared to be a meeting place where friends were gathering, possibly before moving on to the small fair which had set up shop at the end nearest our hotel.

'Vote Pitkin!' I cried as I proffered the leaflets. 'Vote Norman! With your help we can make him Number One in the chart!'

At first the locals looked at me like I was crazy, but when they saw I was giving something away then they all rushed to get a copy of the sheet of paper. Most of those around me didn't look like they'd ever even tuned into Top Albania Radio, let alone voted for a song. Still, perhaps they'd make an exception for Norman.

As arranged, The Pitkins met up near the elephants. It was difficult to tell whether they were Indian or African elephants, but they certainly differed from both in that they flew through the air on the end of big poles, wore coloured top hats, and could take two passengers in their hollowed out backs. Indeed they seemed to be the most popular fairground attraction in the square and so we had something of a ready-made audience for what was to be our last public appearance on Tirana's streets. The reason for picking this location had been simple. The guy who ran the elephant ride had a big set of speakers blasting out music, and they had agreed to let us use it for our playback.

'At last,' said a relieved Tim. 'A performance where we'll actually be able to hear ourselves.'

Tim was right, it was loud, but what was gained in volume was lost in quality. As we launched into our performance to the quite large crowd which had gathered, the bass was deafening but the brass was on a frequency which failed to make much of an impression in the mix which was belching from the huge speakers. I looked over to him and Donald and offered a sympathetic shrug. Poor old Tim. I bet things were never like this when he worked with Andrew Lloyd Webber.

Once again the crowd failed to be wowed by our song. They seemed far more excited by the actual presence of Pitkin than the fact that he was endeavouring to sing something to them. In fact for some there seemed to be no real sense that we were all actually in the midst of a performance at all, and so children were shoved next to Norman in order that their parents could take photos.

'I think these PAs don't achieve that much,' I said, after a polite round of applause had greeted the song's conclusion. 'I know that isn't necessarily a very useful observation to make when we've just completed our last one – but we know now if we ever come back.'

The silence and blank looks from my colleagues summed up the inanity of my remark.

'Aren't the people from *Telebingo* supposed to be meeting us here at eleven?' enquired Donald, breaking the silence.

'Yes. What time is it now?'

'Twenty past.'

Surprise, surprise. They hadn't turned up.

'Oh dear,' I said. 'Well, Bilal knows where the studios are, so we'll just have to turn up there and try to strongarm our way on to the show.'

It certainly wasn't the way you got yourself a TV appearance in Britain, but we were beginning to realise that in Albania, if you wanted to achieve something, then you just had to turn up and argue.

~

The studios were at the rear of the city's opera house, and entry was gained by climbing some wrought-iron stairs which were tacked on to the rear of the building, and which appeared to be the building's fire escape. If it was a rather unusual entrance then nothing could have prepared us for what lay within. It was like another world.

The huge studio was crammed full of desks which were piled high with control panels and monitors. It looked like some kind of elaborate James Bond set. I was fully expecting to be approached by some evil villain, smoking a cigar and stroking a furry cat, who would announce to me that the entire Western World would be destroyed in minutes, once he'd punched in the co-ordinates.

At the far end, there was a stage with no room for audience seating around it, just cameras and an enormous number of scantily clad girls. Strangely, I headed off in that direction, and began walking past the desks, laden with giant screens which were flashing different-coloured lights at me.

'This is where the competitors will sit when they get here later,' Bilal informed me, pointing to one of the workstations. 'They become the audience as well as players of the game.'

'Of *Telebingo*?'

'Yes.'

'Wow. It looks very complicated.'

'Not when you know how it works,' explained Bilal, helpfully.

When we reached the stage we could see that the girls were numbered. I hoped that this was because they were part of the game and that we hadn't stumbled across some sordid auction where they were being sold. After all, Albania had something of a reputation for harbouring black marketeers who specialised in the iniquitous trade of human flesh. Admittedly it was unlikely that broadcasters would view this activity as appropriate for a mainstream light entertainment show.

As we drew close to the stage, Norman was recognised, and whatever rehearsals were taking place were immediately halted. The girls launched into a spontaneous round of applause, and Norman looked delighted, as well he might. The looks of these girls suggested that being part of the *Telebingo* troupe was more of a draw than doing the cheerleading at the football stadium.

'Number fifteen is gorgeous,' I whispered to Donald, forgetting political correctness for a moment.

'Yes, she is rather nice,' replied Donald, politely.

'What do you guys want to do?' asked Bilal, who though talking to us, was also making a keen examination of number fifteen.

'Er ... yes ... er ... right,' I spluttered, trying to get my mind back on the job – or at least, the job that we'd come here to do. 'Can you ask them if we can do our song on their show?'

Bilal disappeared and two minutes later returned with the producer of the show who passed on the excellent news that they would be happy to film us miming to the song.

'Well, we're ready now – can we do it right away?' I suggested, fully expecting a rebuff. 'It's just that if we don't do it soon we might miss our flight back to London.'

'Of course,' said Bilal. 'The producer says that this is no problem.'

I liked the world of *Telebingo*. Things were so easy here.

The stage was cleared for us, apart from the girls who were instructed to stay and dance around us as we performed. Fantastic. Boy, did I like it here. We did a quick rehearsal and the sound was perfect too. For the first time in our entire stay the backing track blasted out with the ideal blend of quality and volume.

'OK guys, is you ready?' said Bilal, from his position alongside the producer.

We put our thumbs up and the track started immediately. No delay, no misunderstandings. This was the antithesis of the stadium gig. It seemed that in the world of *Telebingo* everything happens exactly how you want it.

The next three minutes were wondrous. Suddenly Norman Wisdom and The Pitkins gelled. Norman, undoubtedly lifted by the quality of the sound and the presence of beautiful dancing girls, mimed like he'd known the song for forty years. Sylvia bashed her bongos with a new zest, and Eva and Lucinda danced like angels. Tim and Donald played their toy brass like they were born to it, and as for me, well, I rapped as well as I'd rapped since *Top of the Pops* in January 1988. Fourteen years may have elapsed but I still was infused with the same levels of excitement. Right now, as the track blasted out, sounding as good as it had ever done, I suddenly felt a glow of warmth permeate my body. The supergroup Norman Wisdom and The Pitkins were looking good and sounding great on Albania's biggest rating TV show. Two knights of the realm, Sir Tim Rice and Sir Norman Wisdom, were jumping around to the music, chasing new honours. It felt wonderfully liberating because it just didn't matter what happened. We could do what we liked in the next few minutes and we weren't answerable to anyone. No one was getting rich, no records were being sold, no one had a contract to fulfil – there were no reasons other than to have a good time. Rising triumphantly above my search for a hit was the quest for fun, and we were really having it. The smiles we were sharing weren't faked for the cameras. They were unquestionably real.

'I love Albania back – ooh I dooooo...' crooned Norman, as the song finally ended.

The dancing girls cheered and hollered and everyone in the studio applauded. This had been better than *Top of the Pops*. This time I knew there was going to be no anticlimax. This time my feet were on the ground and I was liberated by the fact that it really didn't matter. This time I was living for the moment, and as moments went, this one was pretty damn good. It was about to get better too.

While Norman was still soaking up the applause he was approached by the show's presenter Ardita, who hushed everyone and began to speak into the microphone.

'First of all, we would like to welcome Mr Norman to Albania,' she said, causing more spontaneous cheering and applause. 'But we would also like to congratulate him – because "Big In Albania" by Norman Wisdom and The Pitkins has just been confirmed as being Number 18 in the Top Albania Radio chart. Congratulations Norman!'

This time the cheers, whoops and hollers were louder, because this time The Pitkins joined in. We embraced, we gave each other high fives, we shared in the moment. During one of the embraces I spun round and for a second I found myself looking straight at girl number 15. I smiled. She smiled back. This was *Telebingo* world, where everything happens how you want it. Well, *nearly* everything, because instead of number 15 moving towards me and softly kissing me on the lips, Norman tapped me on the shoulder.

'Tony,' he said. 'Does this mean we've got the hit?'

'Yes, it most certainly does,' I said, shaking his hand in a rather formal way amidst all the surrounding euphoria. 'Well done. Norman.'

'Ta,' he replied.

The bet was won. We'd done it.

At last we were Big In Albania.

By leaving for the airport almost immediately after the performance, we followed two golden rules of showbiz. Go out on a high, and leave them wanting more. Of course, how much more they actually wanted was something of a moot point. Yes, sufficient votes had come in for us to make the chart, but there was no knowing whether these were votes that had been cast out of the Albanians' love for Norman and a desire to give him what he wanted, rather than any genuine affection for the song. The extraordinary fact remained that we had made it to Number 18 in the chart without selling a single record.

'We are rich beyond our wildest dreams,' I said to Tim, as we watched Tirana disappear behind us through the minibus window. 'What are you going to spend the money on?'

'Oh I think I might have an extra sandwich at lunchtime,' he said with his now familiar chuckle.

'Careful. I wouldn't go too mad.'

'Do you know, Tony,' he said, looking reflective. 'I actually think that this is the most enjoyable overseas trip that I've ever been on. Thank you.'

'My pleasure,' I said, feeling genuinely chuffed.

'Can you see to it that you arrange something else as ludicrous as this again?'

'Leave it with me.'

FADE OUT MEANINGFUL AND MEANINGLESS

Time, few would deny, is a great healer. The problem is that it does most of its healing by helping you to forget. In overcoming painful loss or trauma this is clearly advantageous, but when you are trying to recall a PIN number, locate your car keys, or remember where you parked in a multi-storey car park, its healing qualities are less apparent.

What time had done for me was leave me unable to recall what Victoria looked like. I was trying to work out whether this was a good or a bad thing as I called her up. I decided that it was positive in the sense that it was hard to lust after someone your imagination couldn't picture – which was good news given that Victoria hadn't yet returned from New York and was therefore beyond reasonable pursuit. However, there was a strong negative in that only having a vague memory of my vanquished antagonist left the victory feeling somewhat hollow.

But hollow or not, I couldn't *not* call.

'Hello, is that Victoria?' I asked, having dialled the long number and then felt the tingle of excitement that I always feel when listening to overseas ringing tones.

'Yes,' came the reply, in an English accent. 'Who's this?'

'It's Tony.'

A pause.

'Tony *who*?'

Another pause. This one giving me enough time to register cataclysmic disappointment.

'Tony Hawks. Do you remember? We made a little bet together, two years ago?'

'Oh yes, I remember now. How are you? How did you get on?'

'Well, you won't believe it but I've just got back from Alba—'

'Tony, sorry mate,' interrupted Victoria, 'but can you call back? My cellphone's ringing and I just know that it's a really important call I'm expecting from LA.'

'Er. OK. Right.'

I heard the sound of the line going dead. She was gone. And I'd never even had chance to leave my number.

All was not lost. I still had the rewarding prospect of wiping the smug grin off Simon Cowell's face. This was going to be fun. I'd have someone make a big hat-shaped cake and I'd take it up to his office and sit and watch as he struggled to eat more than just his words.

However, before I looked in the Yellow Pages under 'Hat-shaped cakes' I made a call to his secretary, just to check on his whereabouts.

'Hello, it's Tony Hawks here,' I said.

'Tony *who*?'

'Hawks. Tony Hawks. I made a bet with Simon a year or so ago, about whether I could have a hit rec—'

'Simon's in LA right now.'

'Oh. And when will he be back?'

'We don't know. He's setting up the American version of Pop Idol. He may be gone for six months.'

'I see.'

'Do you want me to give him a message?'

'Er … no … not really.'

Oh dear.

So no 'watching of hat-shaped cake being eaten' satisfaction to be had either. I hung up the phone and looked out of the window. It was raining. A dreary rain sent by the heavens to dampen the spirits.

Well then, that was it. The bet was over. For a while at least, life would just have to return to a state of relative normality. But not before I'd gone for a good long walk.

And so I spent the afternoon back where it had all started, in the park where I had received my original inspiration for 'You

Broke My Heart Like A Bird's Egg'. I wandered rather aimlessly, feeling out of place among the young mothers who bellowed at, and fussed over, their impish offspring. I sat on a bench, scouring the clouds for signs of the next shower, and it occurred to me that I'd been here before. Not to this bench, in this particular park, but to this emotional location. This feeling was not unfamiliar. Not for the first time in my life, I'd just spent an inordinate amount of time and energy proving something which nobody really cared about, except me. What did that mean? And more importantly, what did that say about me?

Perhaps I had to accept that the completion of my betting adventures would always leave behind this odd feeling of numbness, not least because I made it my business to take on bets which turned out to be meaningful and meaningless in equal measure. It did occur to me at that moment, as I struggled hard to fight off an attack of 'maudlin', that perhaps this mirrored life itself.

When I got home, the light was flashing on my answering machine. I hit the 'play' button and was delighted to hear a familiar voice.

'Tony, it's Tim Rice here. There's something I want to ask you. Give me a call would you?'

I hadn't expected to hear from a fellow Pitkin so soon after our recent triumphs. But it felt good.

'Are you free at lunchtime next Thursday?' asked Tim, after I'd followed his instructions and called him back.

'I think so, yes,' I replied, eager to know what he wanted.

'Well, would you like to come to the Ivors?'

'The Ivors?'

'The Ivor Novello Awards for British songwriting. It's an event predominantly attended by songwriters and I think you should be there.'

'Really?'

'Well you have to face it, you're officially a songwriter now, Hawks. You've written two hits. I don't think you're a contender for the lifetime achievement award just yet, but you should definitely come and join us. It will be fun. We've got a good table. You'll be with me, Tom Robinson, David Essex and Benny and Bjorn from Abba.'

And there was me thinking it was all over. Oh me of little faith. At the very moment when I was beginning to question why I'd bothered with the whole thing in the first place, the answer had arrived in the form of an invitation.

An invitation.

Everything fell into place now. Life is an invitation, and either you accept it or you don't. It was as simple as that.

'Wow Tim, that sounds great,' I said, excitedly. 'I'll be there all right. I'm definitely up for that.'

I hung up the phone and smiled a long, broad smile. Lunch on a table full of my heroes. And the best thing was that I could share their company enjoying a newly acquired status. The official ordination had just come on the telephone from Sir Tim Rice.

I could call myself a songwriter now.

EPILOGUE

And anyway, I haven't finished living my life yet, so I could still have another hit …